ENGLISH CATHEDRALS

ENGLISH CATHEDRALS

EDWIN SMITH

AND

OLIVE COOK

THE

HERBERT PRESS

First published in Great Britain 1989 by
The Herbert Press Ltd,
46 Northchurch Road, London N1 4EJ

Edited and designed by John Hadfield

Typeset in Times New Roman

Printed and bound in Great Britain by
Butler & Tanner Ltd, Frome, Somerset

A CIP catalogue record for this book is available
from the British Library.

ISBN 0 906969 62 X

Frontispiece. CHICHESTER CATHEDRAL
Head of Christ, from 'The Raising of Lazarus'

FOREWORD

WHAT justification can there be for another book on cathedrals, apart from the impossibility of ever exhausting the richness of their visual complexity and splendour? The motive that more than any other prompted the present undertaking was that relatively few of Edwin Smith's photographs of cathedrals had ever been published or exhibited, although the subject was one to which he was always drawn.

His delight in the wonderfully articulated structures of the medieval cathedrals, and of St Paul's, which he knew intimately from his earliest youth, was that of a trained architect. But he was also deeply attuned to the other-worldly aspect of these greatest of our legacies from the past. 'I have to come to worship with the eye,' he once said as the verger's bell was ringing for Matins and he was preparing to start work in the nave of Lincoln; 'and to offer the praise of my humble craft.'

Edwin's cathedral photographs celebrate the sublime architectural forms, but they are also imbued with the spirit of praise and worship which were part of his response. So this book has been designed not only to extol the noble achievements of the cathedral builders but to relate this achievement to liturgical practice, to recall the original vision of the cathedral as the Heavenly Kingdom and to give some idea of the discharge of the functions connected with this concept.

The presence in our midst of these extraordinary buildings, rooted in the past and embodying ideals and aspirations so distant from our own, is the source of a reassuring sense of continuity. But changes, revolutionary changes since the time of the Reformation, have been taking place in the fabric and liturgical arrangement of cathedrals throughout the centuries. The story of birth, growth, change and decay naturally suggested a chronological arrangement and the inclusion of the cathedrals of parochial origin which belong to the last phase of the story. Because changes in structure and style are inextricably bound up with changes in views of life, some attempt has been made in the brief introductions to each group of photographs to take into account the shifting religious, philosophical, social and historical background.

Change continues to affect the subjects of the photographs, and as the reader turns the pages of this book he may well be confronted by an image which is not quite what he saw on his last visit to that particular cathedral. The photographs were all taken between 1949 and 1971. The picture of the chapel of Our Lady Undercroft at Canterbury (p. 135) was Edwin's last photograph. The camera was a Linhof, a very recent acquisition. For the majority of the pictures in this book the photographer worked with a half-plate bellows camera, made by Thornton Pickard in 1904 and called *The Ruby*. The focussing screen of course necessitated the use of a tripod and a black cloth over the head. The exposures varied from about ten to fifteen seconds to as many minutes, and every photograph was taken in existing lighting conditions.

CONTENTS

ACKNOWLEDGEMENTS

I WOULD like to thank all those who have helped me with this book, especially the deans and members of chapters who have responded so generously to my queries. Conversations with Dr John Boys Smith, whose intimate knowledge of Ely is unrivalled, were particularly stimulating; and I was encouraged by the warm support of the late Alec Clifton Taylor. I owe an incalculable debt of gratitude to the researches of others, most of whom are listed in the Bibliography. But specific mention must be made here of the work of John Harvey and of Gerald Cobb; and I have seldom entered a cathedral without the relevant volume of Pevsner's *Buildings of England*.

I am grateful to David Herbert for the opportunity of getting to know so great a subject a little better, and both to him and my editor, John Hadfield, for their patience in waiting so long for the material.

INTRODUCTION

'WHEN the wicked man turneth away from his wickedness....' The thinly intoned prayer echoes from the high vaults of the distant choir. And from those same far depths the unearthly sound of the surpliced choristers singing one of the Victorian anthems that still figure so predominently in the Cathedral repertory and the solemn swell of the organ spread into the crossing. It is all going on in the eastern arm of the great church; in the nave, as in a building apart, tourists talk in whispers as they look at the monuments and stained glass, sit over their coffee in the recently opened cafeteria at the west end or choose postcards at the stall near the west door. In much the same way the chant and murmur of divine worship stole upon the ears of medieval pilgrims and of medieval townsmen trafficking in the body of the cathedral. Outside a black robed cleric passes from the shadow of the immense building to cross the close, and from the venerable deanery which may once have been a Prior's lodging the Dean's wife emerges, makes her way through the cars and coaches parked in the precinct and heads for the Bishop's Palace standing in proud isolation to the south.

Such are some of the sights and sounds conjured up by the idea of the cathedral. The Barchester image persists despite the inescapable reminders of the present. And behind the Trollopean view stretches the long vista of the more remote past, periods of adversity almost as threatening as our own: the eighteenth century when enthusiasm for the classical idiom was accompanied by such disregard for Gothic that James Wyatt could recommend the destruction

of the west porch at Ely and Walpole could dismiss the interior of Peterborough as having 'no more beauty than consists of vastness'; the calamitous interval of the Civil War and the Commonwealth when for the only time in their history cathedral services were interrupted; the devastating years of the Dissolution and the whole fantastic Middle Ages when the significance and purpose of the Cathedral were realised with such architectural magnificence, such absolute conviction that, though neglect, iconoclasm, philistinism and misguided restoration have done their worst and the alarming implications of the modern hazards of pollution and inflation are all too clear, the vision embodied in the wonderful fabric, changed and dimmed though it may be, uplifts and awes us yet.

Familiarity never blunts the emotional and visual impact of the scale and splendour of the medieval cathedrals. Even in our modern age of mammoth concrete blocks the sheer bulk of these buildings is a source of wonder. The immense exotic shape of Ely seen in all the noble solitude of its former island state across the fen from Stuntney, its single tall western tower and attendant turrets heading the long glinting expanse of the nave and choir roofs with the diadem of the unique octagon lying where they meet; that other fenland church, Lincoln, floating huge on the horizon above mile upon mile of flat fields and, when we draw near, dwarfing the town with its vast screen-front and hovering pinnacles; Durham's ponderous, square-towered mass commanding the cliff above the Wear; York's gargantuan and ornate masonry bursting from a maze of narrow streets, its south transept alone filling the vista at the end of Minster Yard; the three enormous cavernous west front recesses at Peterborough yawning over the precinct with its range of irregular little stone houses – these images and their like, accustomed to them from childhood though we may be, never cease to amaze us. One reason for this is that the astonishing dimensions of medieval cathedrals are associated with a special order of perfection. Perfection on the comparatively small scale of a work such as the pure Early English interior of the parish church of Eaton Bray can give exquisite pleasure, but it is pleasure of a different and lesser degree than that inspired by the sublime experience of the giant harmony of intricate forms and multitudinous and diverse elements found in a great cathedral. A concentration of mind such as now, in a world confused by non-

Opposite. HEREFORD CATHEDRAL
The Nave from the Chancel

stop visual and oral distractions, has become wellnigh impossible, and an extraordinarily high quality of craftsmanship conspire to give a sense of unity to the work of centuries of construction, attrition and alteration. For what we think of as a medieval legacy nearly always depends for its final visual effect upon what has happened to the fabric since the Reformation. The familiar outline of Canterbury, which we accept as utterly authentic, would not exist without the north-west tower built to match the south-east one by George Austin, surveyor to the Dean and Chapter, in 1834. The fine vista facing the first page of the Introduction to this book is a typical example of the work of different periods which makes up the fabric of all the older cathedrals. The huge round pillars of Bishop Reynelm's Norman church (begun between 1107 and 1115) still dominate the interior of Hereford, but their impact is not at all what it must have been in the Middle Ages. At that time the scale of the giant columns with their characteristic west-country, narrow, multi-

scalloped capital bands, was accentuated by the low proportions of the triforium above them. But when restoration was forced on the dean and chapter by the collapse of the west tower on Easter Monday 1786, the original design was radically altered. Wyatt, who was called in to repair the damage, replaced the Norman triforium with his tall Early English gallery. He also shortened the nave and re-roofed it with an elegant but lustreless timber rib-vault. By the early nineteenth century the cathedral was again in need of renovation. Sir George Gilbert Scott and his son Oldrid carried out the restoration. Scott repaired and moved the surprisingly early fourteenth-century stalls with their animated ogee canopies from under the tower to the position they occupy in the photograph. The fronts are Victorian but so brilliantly executed that the eye accepts them as original. Scott pulled down the solid medieval choir screen and replaced it with an elaborate metal structure. This was dismantled in 1967. Another Victorian architect, Lewis Cottingham, improved Wyatt's vault by painting it and enlivening the shafts with quite vigorous corbels. Despite so much drastic alteration a sense of unity and of the medieval inspiration still pervades the whole interior; and many other examples will be found in these pages of the persistence of the original concept despite all change.

The medieval cathedrals are not only the greatest architectural inventions in our land; they are treasure houses of marvellous sculpture in stone and wood, of glass and wall painting, metalwork, textiles and manuscripts. Walking through any one of them the eye is continually excited by some unimagined delight such as the tiny but so movingly related figures of St Anne and the Virgin in the crypt at York, the naturalistic birds, especially the white falcons among sprigs of oak, which appear so unexpectedly in the great series of didactic glass paintings in the same cathedral; or the exquisitely graceful folds of the draped headless carving in the south retro-choir aisle at Winchester (*overleaf*). But the cathedral building and the superb works of art within it are all subservient to the purpose for which they were created. A cathedral is of course the 'mother church', the pivot of a diocese, a Greek word meaning *administrative area*. In Saxon England the country was divided into a number of kingdoms in each of which the Church was represented by a bishop. This accounts for the geographical distribution of cathedrals. Kent is the only county which contains two ancient cathedrals (Canterbury and Rochester) and this is due to the fact that east and west Kent were separate kingdoms in the seventh century. The seat of a bishop is called a 'cathedral' because it contains the bishop's throne (*cathedra*) although there is no bishop's throne at Ely and the bishop takes the seat of the ruler of the former monastery, the abbot. English cathedrals, like those of Germany but unlike those of the rest of Europe, are both secular and monastic in origin. Some medieval cathedrals were served by secular clergy, orders of canons who followed the *vita canonica*, a life in accordance with the rules of the Church, but were allowed to retain private property. These cathedrals, namely Lincoln, Wells, Exeter, Salisbury, Lichfield, Chichester, Hereford, London and the four Welsh cathedrals of Llandaff, Bangor, St David's and St Asaph's, were not affected by the changes made by Henry VIII. The cathedrals of Canterbury, Durham, Rochester, Winchester, Worcester, Ely, Norwich, Peterborough, Gloucester and Chester were the churches of Benedictine foundations and were served by monks, while Carlisle, Oxford and Bristol were the churches of Augustinian establishments and were served by canons regular living under the rule of St Augustine. At the Dissolution of the Monasteries all these cathedrals were converted into chapters of secular canons. The growth of population during the last two centuries and the consequent creation of new dioceses and the shifting of existing boundaries have resulted in the creation of new foundations which include the former Augustinian churches of St Albans and Southwark, both of which served as parish churches after the Reformation; the old collegiate churches of Ripon and Southwell which were already playing the part of secondary cathedrals in the huge diocese of York; the former parish churches of Newcastle, Wakefield, Manchester, Birmingham, Leicester, Chelmsford, Bradford, Derby and Sheffield and the new cathedrals of Truro, Guildford, Liverpool and Coventry, the last of which replaced the parish church of St Michael which had become a cathedral in 1918 and had been reduced to ruins in an air raid on November 14, 1940.

York, Southwell and sometimes Ripon are known as 'minsters'. The word is not synonymous with cathedral. It translates us to the early missionary days of Saxon England when the clergy whose duty it was to convert and minister to the inhabitants of a particular area lived in a community which together with their church was described as a 'minster'. The Latin for it was *monasterium*, but these clergy were not monks nor was their church necessarily the seat of a bishop. Perhaps there is some significance in the fact that the term 'minster' is associated with cathedrals which from the start were served by canons, whether regular or secular, for the canonical system was followed at both York and Southwell as early as the reign of Edward the Confessor, and at that time there was probably little difference in the ways of life of regular and secular canons. Both then lived in communities and it was only later as a result of their continued ownership of worldly possessions that secular canons tended to revert to an individual life.

As the centre of the diocese the medieval cathedral had three great functions to perform. First, the daily offering of praise and prayer to God. Second, the pursuit of sacred learning; and third, the maintenance of the highest possible

WINCHESTER: *Thirteenth-century carving in the South Retrochoir aisle*

standard of sacred music. The size and magnificence of the building were part of the daily offering, and its setting and the idiosyncrasies of its design were determined by the same high purpose. The conspicuous twin towers at the west end and the aspiring central steeple announced the presence of what was quite literally in the Middle Ages the house of God, the terrestrial counterpart of heaven, partaking of its sacred reality. The adjacent chapter house (*capitulum*), the meeting place of the clergy who served the cathedral, and the cloister, where classrooms for the choristers with a library above them might be built, were conventual in origin and perpetuated the idea of withdrawal from the world. There was never any communal life in the monastic sense at Salisbury, Wells, Hereford, Exeter, Lincoln, Chichester and Old St Pauls yet cloisters were attached to all of them. The noble structures at Wells and Salisbury rival those of any abbey.

In my opening paragraph I indicated the curious separateness of the cathedral nave and the choir and presbytery. Not all the attempts of protestant reformers to make the whole cathedral one unit for public worship have succeeded: the cathedral nave and its eastern arm might be two different churches, a distinction which becomes all the more marked when the pulpitum, the solid screen which in the Middle Ages shut off the clergy in the choir from the nave, still stands, as it does at York. The cathedral service is still confined to the eastern arm of the building: a congregation is no more necessary than it was five hundred years ago because the statutory duty of the chapter is to render daily choral prayer for the glory of God and not for the edification of mortal listeners. Mass was said not once but many times a day, a perpetual memorial to Christ's Passion. Dedicated to the constant service of God, the clergy offered prayers of intercession day-in, day-out for both the living and the dead. The principal use of the nave was for the stately processions which preceded the main service of the day, especially at the great festivals. In the later Middle Ages the nave was the scene of diverse business which had nothing to do with worship. But it has always to be remembered that when the whole of life was lived in the presence of the supernatural the line between the sacred and the profane scarcely existed. The chapter saw no impropriety in activities which were no more incongruous than the worldliness of many bishops or the sculptor's introduction of secular and ribald images into the ornamentation of capital and choir stall.

The separateness of the nave and choir in the cathedral church accounts for the accentuation of the eastern arm in the general plan. But the significance of the cruciform shape remains something of a mystery. It seems to be deliberately symbolical although the transepts may have developed from the rudimentary arms, the *bema* of Early Christian basilican churches, a raised platform between the nave and the apse which projected very slightly on either side of the building. The bema would have been lengthened and transformed into transepts to counteract the thrust of the big central tower. But there is still no structural reason for the Latin cross shape and the tropological explanation accords best with the whole concept and purpose of the cathedral.

The development of the basic plan into the richly varied, complicated outlines of cathedral structures – such extraordinary outgrowths as the incredible prolongation of the eastern arm at Canterbury with the almost circular corona at its tip and the strange constrictions where the chapels of St Andrew and St Anselm break out at odd angles from either side of the entrance to the Trinity Chapel; the narrow Lady Chapel jutting far eastwards from the sanctuary at Gloucester; or the remarkable Chapel of the Nine Altars massively set across the east end of Durham – was determined by basic liturgical needs and the convenience of the processions. The celebrant and his assistant ministers and their attendants would come down from the high altar, pass through the choir and go round the whole of the interior in a fixed order, visiting each altar. Towards the end of the ceremony those taking part would line up in the middle of the nave before the great rood which stood upon a screen one bay west of the pulpitum. The regular positions of the clergy were marked by a series of stones let into the floor in two rows. Plans of York and of Lincoln show these stones and an actual stone still indicates the place in the nave of Lincoln where Bishop Alnwick stood, for in his will of 1445 he asked to be buried beneath it. The continual additions to the cathedral fabric, undertaken because more room was needed for services as benefactors endowed more altars, were always planned to leave the way clear for the processional path. Thus in the transepts altars were usually placed against the eastern walls in order to keep the western side open as well as to enable the celebrant to face east. Sometimes to make room for yet more altars, double transepts, a specifically English feature, were constructed, as at Wells, Salisbury and Lincoln. The siting of the great series of chantry chapels at Winchester, those of Bishops Edington, Beaufort, Wykeham, Wayneflete, Fox, Gardiner and Langton, was governed by ritual needs, just as was the placing of the altars in the retrochoir at Peterborough. The design of the Galilee at Durham was also conditioned by processional requirements: the doors into it from each aisle of the nave allowed the procession to circulate freely and heightened the drama of the celebrant's utterance as he entered it: 'I will go before you into Galilee.'

The discharge of the second obligation of the medieval cathedral chapter, the encouragement of learning, was the beginning of a continuing history of development in education and also in the art of the theatre. The majestic interiors of cathedrals and their screen-like west fronts were the settings for the liturgical drama through which the story of the redemption of man from the Creation to Domesday, the theme of the painted and stained glass decoration of the great fane, was brought to vivid life for the illiterate. These cyclical enactments of the Scriptures preceded the miracle and morality plays and interludes of the fifteenth century which anticipated the astonishing flowering of the theatre in the Elizabethan period.

From the time when Theodore of Tarsus came to Canterbury with a store of Greek and Latin books, great libraries, the essential equipment of learning, have been associated with cathedrals. Cathedral libraries were of special importance during the Middle Ages when they were likely to contain a wider range of books than most monastic collections. Bishops were often men of wide learning and might, like Theodore or William of St Carilef, the first Norman bishop of Durham, make gifts of their own books to the diocese; and many ecclesiastics were ardent collectors. The Journal of William More, Prior of Worcester from 1518 to 1536 is full of references to the cathedral library. We read of yearly visits to London where More bought printed editions of books which in manuscript form were already part of the Worcester Cathedral library – Seneca, Aquinas, Cyprian, Jerome, Gregory, Ambrose, Innocent IV and Richard of St Victor – and to these were added Bishop Langland's translation of the Rule of St Benedict, copies of Bede and fine collections of statutes of England going down to 1534.

Many of the treasures of cathedral libraries were dispersed at the Dissolution. Some books went to the royal library and groups of manuscripts and books later came into the possession of antiquaries such as Sir Robert Cotton, Robert, Earl of Oxford and Edward and Robert Harley, and thence found their way into museums and university libraries. But cathedrals still house unique collections, none richer than Durham's three hundred or more medieval manuscripts. The Morley Library at Winchester, occupying the book room of the former monastery, still contains the famous Winchester Bible, written in Latin and illuminated in the twelfth century. The most perfect of the four contemporary copies of Magna Carta is kept in the library over the eastern cloister at Salisbury which boasts of nearly two hundred ancient manuscripts, including a page of the Old Testament in Latin dating from the eighth century, and two tenth-century Gallican Psalters, an illuminated Tonale of the fourteenth century with the music shown in full, and a superbly illuminated fifteenth-century Breviary.

The right of licensing schools and teachers

CHICHESTER: *The Cathedral Library*

which in *De Musica* he likened to architecture, describing both as 'children of number', equally expressive of transcendental reality, was the start of a continuous outpouring of sacred music and musical genius nourished by the cathedral. Cathedral music ranges from the development of the consecrated chant of the gradual and antiphon after it had been introduced by Theodore of Tarsus to the invention of choral harmony by John Dunstable, to the masses and motets of Tavener and Tallis; the masses of William Byrd and his glorious anthems; the great anthems of Orlando Gibbons, Purcell and Boyce, conductor of the Three Choirs Festival in 1737; the uprush of Victorian cathedral music linked with the names of Samuel Sebastian Wesley, Stainer, Stanford, Sterndale Bennett and Hubert Parry; and in our own century Elgar's moving anthems, Benjamin Britten's *Rejoice in the Lord*, which brilliantly exploits the modern idiom while preserving all the traditional character of church music; the same composer's *War Requiem* written to celebrate the opening of the new Coventry Cathedral; Holst's *Te Deum* and Vaughan Williams's *Mass in G Minor* and many fine motets. The development of organ design from a primitive instrument with a small number of notes, each controlling three or four pipes to a great instrument with a chromatic keyboard and as many as forty pipes to a note, provided with stops to shut off individual groups of pipes, was largely encouraged by cathedral patronage and enhanced the richness and splendour of the daily service.

The music and learning, the performance and elaboration of ritual, the glorious architecture and art, everything that served the cathedral purpose was the responsibility of the members of the chapter. The constitution of a chapter of canons with a dean at its head was established by either Thomas of Bayeux, who became Archbishop of York in 1070, or by St Osmund, Bishop of Salisbury (1078–99). The part played by the chapter in cathedral history and especially in its architectural history is of the utmost importance, far more so than that of the bishops. Some medieval bishops, to mention only William Edington and William of Wykeham, Bishops of Winchester, John Grandisson of Exeter, Richard Poore of Salisbury and Archbishop Thoresby of York did indeed devote themselves to great architectural enterprises. But bishops usually held high offices of state and could seldom reside for more than short periods in the palaces of their cathedral cities, and while their own contact with the

belonged to the bishop of the diocese throughout the Middle Ages and from the beginning a necessary adjunct to all cathedrals was a school where boys could be taught to sing the service. This was of course bound up with the third duty of the chapter and with the all important cathedral offering of unceasing prayer and praise. Edward the Confessor was a pupil of the choir school at Ely and the choir school at Canterbury has existed since the early seventh century. These schools offered and still do offer an education of particular value, for it combines apprenticeship to the art of music with a general curriculum. The admission of boys to the schools depended upon an examination which tested their musicality and ability to read. The number of choristers varied: at Lincoln the original number seems to have been twelve but in the fourteenth century the number was increased by a second body of choristers to serve the newly founded chantry of Bishop Burghersh. The two groups of choristers are still distinguished by their vestments: the Burghersh boys are surpliced while the others wear black choral copes. At Salisbury at the beginning of the fourteenth century there were fourteen choristers. St Augustine's love of music mother church was thus weakened, the authority and independence of the deans and chapters waxed. Prebends or 'provender', originally consisting of the daily distribution of food and money from a common source were provided for the canons by benefactors and out of the revenue from manor estates and churches which were part of the episcopal property. The incomparable collection of charters at Lincoln testifies to the gradual acquisition of lands and churches for the provision of prebends and the common fund. Prebends eventually grew into incomes, the value of which varied according to the position of each canon in the chapter. That position was also associated with the occupation of a particular stall in the cathedral church. Evidence of the connection between prebends and manors and parish churches can still be seen at Lincoln where the names of the prebends appear above the stall of each canon. Canons were thus sometimes known as 'prebendaries'.

Four of the canons held special dignities. The dean, elected by the canons from their number and confirmed by the bishop, was president of the chapter and occupied a stall at the south-west corner of the choir. The other three, the precentor, treasurer and chancellor, were appointed directly by the bishop. The precentor was concerned with the cathedral services and the music which accompanied them; he also had control of the teaching of the choristers and of song in the cathedral city. He sat in the north-west corner of the choir opposite the dean. So the two sides of the choir are known as *decani*, the dean's side, and *cantoris*, the precentor's side. The treasurer's duty was to care for the plate, vestments and relics of the church and to ensure that the altars were correctly arranged for the services; the cathedral furnishings, screens, stalls, monuments, clock and bells were also his charge. His seat was in the north-east corner of the choir. The chancellor whose stall was in the south-east corner next to the bishop's throne, acted as the chapter's secretary. He drew up all the cathedral documents and was custodian of the common seal. Usually he also held the offices of *theologus*, delivering or arranging for the delivery of theological lectures, and of *scholasticus* or master of the school for clerks attached to the cathedral and supervisor of the grammar schools in the city and to some extent throughout the diocese. Another officer who was entitled to a prebend and thus to a seat in chapter was the archdeacon upon whose shoulders fell the conduct of purely

LINCOLN: *The Song School*

diocesan work. Sometimes, as at Old St Paul's, he ranked as a dignitary. Other important members of the chapter included the subdean, who presided when the dean was unable to be present, and the sacrist who performed many of the duties of the treasurer, caring for the church and its contents with the help of lay servants. In cathedrals which were monastic the sacrist was a person of some consequence for he was involved with the care of the fabric and paid the wages of plumbers, glaziers, masons and carpenters. He might be concerned with great undertakings. When the Norman crossing tower of Ely collapsed in 1322 it was the sacrist Alan of Walsingham who organised the erection of the Octagon. At York, Wells and Exeter the fabric was the special charge of a canon other than the sacrist, called the *custos fabricae* or *custos ecclesiae*: his duty was to see that the revenues set apart for the fabric were duly collected and to organise the work of renovation within and without the cathedral.

The chantry priests who served individual chapels and altars in the cathedral were not members of the chapter: they were supported by endowments for the saying of mass for the souls of the founders. Among other officers of minor

SALISBURY: *The Close*

When the clergy of a medieval cathedral were monks they lived in buildings disposed about the cloister. The officers of secular cathedrals lived in private houses grouped about the church. Cloisters were attached to these cathedrals, as we have seen, though they were generally no more than covered walks. But the enclosures in which the great churches are set and around which stand the houses once occupied by cathedral dignitaries perpetuate the idea of the abbey precinct even though the houses are now often occupied by people who have no connections with the cathedral and are tenants of the dean and chapter. 'Close' is the usual name for this expanse though it is occasionally known as the 'Minster yard' and at Ely, where it incorporates many of the buildings of the former monastery, it has been called the 'College' ever since, at the Dissolution in 1539, the abbey was reconstituted as 'the King's New College at Ely', despite the fact that the church was converted into a secular cathedral little more than a year later.

In the Middle Ages the precincts of secular cathedrals were often as truly enclosed as those of monasteries. A wall twelve feet high shut off the close at Lincoln in the thirteenth century and at the same period the houses of the canons of Wells and Lichfield were encompassed by battlemented walls. The Exchequer Gate at Lincoln (p. 24) and the gatehouses at Salisbury and Canterbury are reminders of the close walls through which they once led. Heavy traffic and modern developments have invaded and transformed cathedral closes but in some places their separate character and their unique architectural patchwork are still sources of vivid enjoyment. The precinct of Lincoln is no longer secluded but the houses of the former inhabitants remain distinct and present a richly varied feast of domestic styles. The more romantic closes of Wells, Salisbury and Chichester afford similar visual experiences of the domestic shell in all its diverse historic guises. At Chichester the group of Bishop's Palace, a rambling flint and brick thirteenth-century and Georgian house, the Deanery and other canons' houses, divided from the cathedral by the cloister and set in landscaped gardens has all the compactness of a monastery precinct. At Salisbury the grandest and most spacious of cathedral closes is still entered by medieval gateways and still partly enclosed by the remains of its battlemented walls. In the west corner of the Close there is an extension called Choristers Green where the well-known Mompesson House

importance who were not members of the chapter were the vicars choral. They performed the work of absentee canons and were chosen for their musical ability. When cathedral chapters were first established the continual residence of canons was obligatory. But absence was sometimes unavoidable, especially when a canon had to serve the church of his prebend as well as participate in all the cathedral services; and when cathedral music became more elaborate some of the canons were not competent to take the musical part of the service, for except in the case of the precentor, canons were not chosen primarily for their musicianship. So deputies were appointed.

Cathedrals are still served by canons. Their number has been much reduced but their work as members of the chapter is still related to that of their medieval predecessors. After the Reformation the numbers of vicars choral greatly diminished and no longer corresponded to the number of canons; and in the sweeping changes of the Victorian period, when residentiaries were reduced to a minimum, it was no longer necessary for vicars choral to act as deputies and they became solely concerned with the music of the cathedral services.

stands with a steep-hipped, dormered roof above a bland ashlared front of seven bays and a noble pedimented door. On the east side of the Green and at right angles to the stables of Mompesson House is the sober, dignified Matrons' College, established by Wren's friend and fellow astronomer and mathematician, Bishop Seth Ward. Wren may well have designed the long, low brick building with the circular windows in its dormers, short, projecting wings, vigorously pedimented door and octagonal lantern. The stately mansions in West Walk are set in gardens going down to the Avon, and it was from one of them, Walton Canonry, that Constable painted the cathedral. His friend and patron Archdeacon Fisher lived in a house called Leydenhall, *Aula Plumbea*, originally built by Elias of Dereham. The Bishop's Palace from which Fisher's earliest letters to Constable were addressed, standing to the south-east of the cathedral, has become the cathedral school. It is a thirteenth- and fifteenth-century house which Bishop Seth Ward altered and enlarged in the 1670s. Malmesbury House in North Walk, just inside St Anne's Gate, set among trees, conceals enchanting Rococo and earliest Gothic Revival rooms behind its placid, seven-bayed, ashlared Georgian front. A little further along the Walk is a contrasting and picturesque cluster of cottages next to a tall Elizabethan house; then comes another house of the same period, flint-fronted and gabled with a corner turret and a thirteenth-century room inside. In the Middle Ages it was called Aula-le Stage.

At Wells architecture and setting conspire to make the long rectangular Cathedral Green one of the memorable sights of England. Dominated by the tiered and fretted Alp of the cathedral west front which fills one end of it, it is fringed by the porched, embattled, buttressed, turretted medieval and the Queen Anne and Georgian houses of the canons, one with the strange name of Erstfeld, some with their backs to the turf. To the south of the cathedral lies the cloister and beyond its high walls the Bishop's Palace can be glimpsed, moated, crenellated, tree-girt, a medieval fortress tamed and softened by the hand of the Picturesque gardener and gently touched with melancholy by the ruins of its former Great Hall.

Running at right angles to the Cathedral Green is a narrow alley of stone houses slightly and intriguingly increasing in width as one looks along it from the chapel at the north end. This is the Vicars' Close. The houses are of special interest because they are among the earliest examples

SALISBURY: *Cloisters*

of two-storeyed terrace dwellings. Although altered, the little houses, each with its walled front garden, wear much the same aspect as they assumed when they were rebuilt in the fifteenth century by Bishop Benkynton, whose heraldic device appears on the masonry. Forty-two vicars lived in the Close, each in his own small house of two rooms, one on each floor connected by a newel staircase projection. A thin chimney-breast went up between the hooded doorway and the two-light windows and ended in a delicate polygonal lantern top of trefoiled lights. A similar narrow lane of twin-ranges housed the vicars at Chichester, though here one of the terraces has virtually disappeared for it has turned its back on the Close and become shops facing onto the street behind it. The remaining terrace has suffered more drastic change than the Vicars' Close at Wells yet, ending as it does in the steep-roofed Vicars' Hall, built of flint with a twelfth-century undercroft, and fronted as it is by quiet, box-edged plots and a flag-stoned walk, its character is not quite lost.

Of all the functions of the canons it is their responsibility for building operations which has most attracted the attention of modern his-

torians. The researches of D. Knoop and G. P. Jones, of L. F. Salzman and John Harvey in particular have thrown new light on the details of medieval workshop life and the methods by which the fabric fund of a great cathedral was fed, and they have rescued from obscurity the names of many of the masons who were the creators of cathedral architecture. Later pages of this book afford glimpses of these remarkable men and some account of their conditions of work which were prescribed by the canon who was in charge of the fabric.

Cathedral fabric rolls contain much interesting information about the quarrying and carriage of stone. Because transport was so laborious and costly in the Middle Ages local stone was used whenever possible and it is this use which imparts a distinctively local character to those cathedrals which were within easy reach of quarries. It is the Purbeck marble, conveniently shipped up the Avon, polished and utilised as shafts throughout the nave and choir, which sets up the exciting rhythm of light and dark accents upon which the striking unity of the interior of Salisbury so much depends. The light stone came from the local

quarry of Chilmark and its creamy colour contrasts with the material of Salisbury's near contemporary, Lincoln, the fabric of which is partly the deep yellow ironstone of the area, partly the grey limestone of Ancaster. The quarries of Barnack were on the estate of Peterborough and stone from there was carried by fenland streams to Ely and Norwich. Local soft red sandstone is the material of Lichfield, Chester, Carlisle and Worcester and its excessive vulnerableness to weather and pollution has necessitated endless restoration. Pale magnesium limestone was brought from Tadcaster to York; and the fortress-like aspect of Durham owes much to the carboniferous limestone of which it is shaped and which came from the monastery's own quarries.

The cost of building cathedrals, of the preservation of their fabric and the discharge of their functions was always great and is now incalculable. In the Middle Ages continual and willing contributions came from every part of the diocese, for each offering gave the donor the right to be remembered in the prayers of the church and masses would be said daily for his soul. Legacies in land and money came from the rich, and

even the poor donated small sums to save their souls. Princely gifts came from the Crown, from great lords and powerful ecclesiastics desirous of raising a lasting monument to the glory of God. Rents from cathedral property and from the sale of indulgences provided a steady income; and relics and relic cults brought in vast amounts. The rebuilding of the east end of Canterbury after the catastrophic fire of 1174 could never have been carried out on such an expensive and sophisticated scale if Becket's cult had not so quickly developed. In our own days when such sources of revenue have dwindled or ceased to exist, the future of these glorious icons is in direst jeopardy. Only few are committed; and with no public subsidy cathedrals are forced increasingly to depend on the alien and wholly undesirable development of marketing skills.

There could be no more devastating indication of the fading of the vision which medieval cathedrals were designed to body forth. They are the supreme manifestations of a system as remote from our own as that of ancient Greece, an all-embracing system in which church and society were indissolubly one in a divinely ordered universe. Their modern counterparts, the pertinent expressions of our world view, are the factory and the office block. Nevertheless the vanished environment of which the vast cathedral forests of masonry are the symbols haunts us yet. The long tradition of cathedral music and cathedral architecture, even in its makeshift parish church guises, testifies to the lingering power of the transforming idea which gave them life. The Reformation brought about a profound change in the service, but the great Protestant cathedral that grew from the ashes of Old St Paul's was the equal in self-confidence, originality, power and beauty of its medieval predecessor. The more drastic changes in the service of recent years do pose a threat to the sense of continuity inspired by Wren's masterpiece. Yet the voice of intercession still goes up and the daily office hours of the medieval cathedral are still the recognisable source for the Prayer Book offices of Morning and Evening Prayer. Cathedrals are still more to us than great works of architecture and museums of fine craftsmanship. Awareness of their supernal purpose gives added lustre to their inexhaustible visual pleasures.

19

CANTERBURY: *Capital in the Crypt*

I
The Norman Impact

AT THE TIME of the Norman Conquest there were fifteen English dioceses: Canterbury, York, London, Rochester, Lichfield, Winchester, Hereford, Worcester, Wells (which had only recently been made a see), Durham, Exeter, Elmham, Dorchester, Sherborne and Selsey. Only the scanticst vestiges of these Anglo-Saxon foundations survive. The crumbled flint and puddingstone masonry of Elmham in Norfolk, curiously infiltrated by the ruins of Bishop Despencer's fourteenth-century manor house, has neither mystery nor visual interest: it wholly lacks the noble austerity of Brixworth, a Saxon minster, or the poignance of the steep and narrow nave of Benedict Biscop's monastic church at Monkwearmouth. A more expressive reminder of Elmham Cathedral, the bishop's throne, can now be seen at Norwich, where it stands in its traditional place in the apse behind the high altar. But even here it is the power of association rather than the object itself which stirs the imagination. For the original fragmented stone chair, so damaged by fire and long exposure that the carved decoration of coiling bird and animal forms is almost obliterated, has been incorporated in an unconvincing restoration. The Saxon crypt at Ripon, however, wonderfully evokes the freshness and ardour of a Church still inspired by the missionary zeal of a new religion. It was built by St Wilfrid during the short period during the late seventh century when Ripon was a cathedral. The church became collegiate in the mid tenth century, and its cathedral status was not re-established until 1836. Wilfrid had lately returned from Rome and his sojourn there may have influenced the simple plan of the crypt, for its tiny vaulted chamber is immediately reminiscent of a Roman catacomb. The steps by which pilgrims would go down to the relic chamber are much impaired and the passage and stairs by which they left have vanished. But we can still breathe the air of the quiet cell into which seventh-century wayfarers peered at holy remains, tunnel vaulted, coated with ancient cement, blotched but quite remarkably preserved, and interrupted by arched niches.

The Elmham throne found its way to the present Norfolk cathedral, a Norman foundation, from Thetford, to which the see was removed in 1075 before being transferred to Norwich in 1096. It had become apparent during the reign of Edward the Confessor that the most appropriate place for a bishop's seat was the largest town in the diocese. So some time before the Battle of Hastings, Crediton, which had become the centre of a see in the early tenth century, was moved to Exeter, and Chester-le-Street, to which the monks of Lindisfarne had migrated with the body of St Cuthbert, was abandoned for Durham. The Normans speeded the further migration of bishops from rural areas to centres of activity. The bishops of Lichfield, Selsey and Sherborne moved their seats to Chester, Chichester and Old Sarum, and the first Norman bishop of Dorchester moved the see to Lincoln.

The Conquerors, Scandinavian in origin but Latin in culture, singularly combined relentless Viking energy with a genius for organisation and assimilation. Their forceful disciplinary measures affected the Church as much as the state; and their innovations proceeded all the more smoothly because the Confessor, half French and a cousin of the future Conqueror, had prepared the way for them. He had introduced several Normans to high places in the Church more than a decade before William I was crowned, among them Robert of Jumièges who was made Primate of England. The Conqueror himself replaced Englishmen by foreign clergy in all but one of the bishoprics: St Wulfstan of Worcester, saved by his reputation for holiness, was allowed to retain his episcopal office. At Ely, not then a cathedral, the Saxon Thurston continued as abbot until his death in 1072. The abbey church of Ely became the see of a bishop in 1109 and Carlisle was similarly elevated in 1133.

Many lines of development, firm and clear, can be traced from the time of the Conquest: the introduction of canon law and a piercing interest in scholarship, philosophy and theology. Lanfranc of Pavia, who was made Archbishop of Canterbury on the death of Robert of Jumièges in 1070, and his pupil and successor Anselm of

Aosta, both powerful intellects, both former Priors of the famous Abbey of Bec, created a great centre of learning at Canterbury. Norman bishops everywhere transformed and enlarged cathedral libraries. At Durham, to give but one example, William of St Carilef found a library which already contained such precious treasures as that great work of eighth-century Northumberian art, the Lindisfarne Gospels and a gospel book believed to have been written by Bede, but the collection was small. The new bishop immediately added forty-nine volumes, among them a complete Bible, works by Augustine, Jerome, Gregory and Ambrose, missals, Bede's *Ecclesiastical History* and the poems of Apollinarius. The library went on growing and when Prior Lawrence made an inventory of the books in about 1150 there were four hundred and fifty-six, thirty of them Latin classics, while translations from the Greek included one of the only two known copies of Homer in Norman England.

The decisive part played by the Normans in the establishment of the cathedral constitution was described earlier. The organisation of a chapter of canons with a dean at its head was the system followed in Normandy and in introducing it at York Thomas of Bayeux took as his model the French cathedral where he had been both canon and chancellor. The form of worship might vary in different foundations, but it was essentially based on the popular Use of Sarum as set out by Osmund, the first Norman bishop of Old Sarum and builder of the first Norman cathedral on the site. The prefatory dialogue between the celebrant and the worshippers was that set forth in the *Apostolic Tradition* of Hippoytus dating from the third century and preserved in a recognisable form in the Anglican church until the present day, when the special language of both Bible and Prayer Book has been debased. It opened with the celebrant's words: 'The Lord be with you', followed by the response: 'And with thy spirit', and concluded with the great prayer of thanksgiving and invocation of the Spirit. The music of the services was the Gregorian chant, echoes of which can still be heard in the singing of the Psalms.

The Conqueror controlled the nomination of bishops and claimed their homage as feudal barons. They were expected to attend the high court, to advise the king and sometimes to act as ambassadors to foreign countries and to the Pope. Like lay nobles they owed knight service to William for their lands. The Bishop of Lincoln owed the king the service of sixty knights and his secular power exceeded that of many an earl. Norman bishops were great magnates and this was the source of the transference of responsibility for the organisation of the cathedral and the care of the fabric from the bishop to the dean and chapter.

The original spectacular impact of the Norman cathedrals which immediately after the Conquest began to replace their Saxon predecessors, has been tempered by alteration and rebuilding. Not one of them remains entire, yet, massive, colossal, they continue to overwhelm the eye and the mind with the power, the absolute certainty and stability of their individual forms. Only three medieval cathedrals – Salisbury, Wells and Lichfield – were built or completely rebuilt in the later Middle Ages. All the others bear the imperishable impress of the Normans, even if, as at York and Worcester, it is only in the crypt. The achievement is all the more astounding when we remember that the population of the whole country at that time amounted to no more than one and a half million. How was it practically possible to realise such stupendous imaginings? While much is known about methods of building in the Gothic period and about the master masons of that time, it is far from clear how the major Norman undertakings were organised.

The political unification of the country under the Conqueror must have facilitated the raising of funds for building, and although it did not reach its zenith until the thirteenth century the cult of relics soon became a valuable source of income. Norman churchmen were inclined to despise the native clergy and their saints. Abbot Paul of St Albans referred to his Anglo-Saxon predecessors as 'rudes et idiotas' and Lanfranc told Anselm that he doubted the sanctity of Anglo-Saxon saints. He nevertheless recognised the advantages of the devotion they inspired. Thus at Durham, for example, William of St Carilef encouraged the cult of St Cuthbert. The incorruptible body was translated to Durham in 1104, where it immediately wrought miraculous cures and brought such a flow of money from pilgrims and worshippers that the chapter was able to complete one of the greatest churches in Europe. The saint's remains lay behind the high altar, where they were undisturbed until the suppression of the monastery. The shrine itself was one of the most sumptuous monuments in all England, 'so great were the offerings and Jewells that were bestowed uppon it,' as the unknown author of the so-called *Rites of Durham* tells us. It was 'exalted with a most curious workmanshipp of fine and costly marble, all limned and guilted with gold'. The cover of the shrine was gilded and painted with sacred images; and when it was raised, by means of a pulley, to expose the vault, six silver bells 'did make such good sound that it did stir all the people's harts that was within the Church to repair unto itt and to make their prayers to God and Holy St. Cuthbert.'

The fantastic revenue accruing from the murder of Becket in 1170 has been mentioned. The monk Gervase who lived through the horrendous events of that dark winter evening of December 29 when the Archbishop was struck down at the altar, has recorded many interesting details of cathedral building under the Normans. By the time he was writing his famous account of the fire of 1174, more than a hundred years after the Conquest, most of the procedures followed in the later Middle Ages were established. The chapter, not the Archbishop (the recently appointed Richard of Dover), took the initiative after the disaster, summoned master craftsmen (artifices) from far and wide, listened to their proposals and invited estimates. Some of the masters advised the demolition of the damaged choir and a completely new building while others were for restoring the charred remains. William of Sens, a craftsman from Burgundy, who was finally chosen to take charge of the work, decided to build anew. Gervase tells us that it was he who planned and designed the construction, organised masons, sculptors and carpenters to work under him and supplied them with moulds and patterns. He also arranged for the transport of material, importing Caen stone as the Normans had done from the beginning of their rule. At Canterbury it was cut after its arrival, but often it was worked to shape before it left France. Gervase does not say how the gangs of labourers necessary for so great a project were recruited but probably the later method of impressment was used. For work which demanded more than a craftsman's skill the extent of the Norman empire enabled chapters to call upon artists from lands as remote as southern Italy and Sicily, or at least to rely on models from such places. Some of the sculpture of the Prior's Doorway at Ely is directly related to that of Trani in Apulia; the great Christ in Majesty on the wall of St Gabriel's Chapel, Canterbury wears the same magnetic and forbidding countenance as the Divinity who looks with such dazzling authority from the apse of Monreale; and the only counterpart in scale, grandeur and sureness of execution of the painted figure of St Paul in St Anselm's Chapel is to be found in the Capella Palatina in Palermo.

Technically Norman builders lacked the knowledge and experience of the great Gothic masters. They were forced to rely on a rubble core to achieve stability for their massive, heavy constructions. The fine, precisely worked ashlar which was associated with the development of the Gothic style with its thin walls and delicate shafts only began to appear towards the end of the twelfth century. Norman towers had a tendency to come tumbling down. Very soon after it was built the central tower of Gloucester 'through a defect in the foundations, suddenly crashed to the ground at the very moment when mass was completed', and the central towers of Ely, Hereford, Lincoln, Worcester and Winchester all collapsed. But the vision behind these churches triumphs still over all inadequacies of technique. Norman cathedrals reflect a view of life as compelling as that expressed by the architecture of the flying buttress, the pointed arch and the rib vault. If the one echoes the logical, ingenious blend of theology and philosophy which marked the early Gothic period, the other transports us to a more primitive world, sometimes frighteningly malign and unintelligible and above all transitory, where the cathedral symbolises the immutability of the eternal in its immense strength and evokes the mystery of Faith in its dark and numinous interior. The later creation of long vistas from the west door to the east end, destroying the original conception of the cathedral as a series of compartments, and the insertion of large windows in Norman naves and sanctuaries, in some cases, as in the choir at Gloucester, completely obliterating the eleventh-century work and letting in a great flood of light, has changed and weakened the mystic atmosphere of Norman churches. But still, confronted by the majestic naves of Ely, Norwich, Gloucester, Peterborough, St Albans and above all Durham, standing among the ranks of short columns in the subterranean and heavily vaulted crypts of Worcester or Winchester, or startled by the mysterious leaping shadows and by the alien, savage life of the carvings in the loftier, more spacious crypt of Canterbury, we cannot but be aware of our own insignificance, and for a moment we share the dependence of the builders on the awesome power of the unseen world.

Above. LINCOLN *from the Castle*   *Opposite.* DURHAM *from the River Wear*

The dramatic settings of both Durham and Lincoln, the one dominating the town and surrounding countryside, the other rising like an apparition from its rock above the Wear, are the most spectacular of the commanding sites the Normans chose for the great churches they began to build immediately after the Conquest. The actual fabric of both cathedrals has undergone much rebuilding and alteration, but each bears the ineffaceable impress of the eleventh-century Norman conception. At Lincoln two features at once stand out as unique: first the remarkable design of an excessively tall central recess flanked by two much lower side arches and then, on either side of these, hidden here behind the Exchequer Gate, yet lower recesses; secondly the strange position of the towers set back behind the front. This was the whole width of the original facade.

Early in the twelfth century, following a fire, the portals were rebuilt and enriched under Bishop Alexander (1121–45). It was he who added the frieze of popular intersecting arcading above the aisle doors and completed the Norman stages of the towers.

Three storeys of the west towers of William St Carilef's great cathedral at Durham survive with their sober patterning of tiered arcading, and the outline of the huge Norman window between the towers can still be seen. The pierced parapets and pinnacles were added in about 1801. In Carilef's time the towers may have been crowned by pyramidal roofs. They were then the decisive accents in the design. The two soaring fifteenth-century storeys add nothing to the massive impact of the west front with the Galilee spread like a suppliant at its foot.

A cathedral was rising at Rochester only seven years after St Augustine landed on the Kentish shore. Nothing of the Saxon church remains, though Gundulf, the first Norman bishop, a friend of Lanfranc and former sacrist of Bec (and therefore experienced in the organisation of architectural undertakings), was consecrated in it before embarking on the building of a new cathedral in 1077. The west front, however, belongs to the twelfth century, the original having been damaged by fire in 1137 and 1179.

The great Perpendicular window could not be anything but English, but the rest of the facade looks alien. Like the west front of St David's it has no west towers: their place is taken by turrets at the outer angles of the aisles while smaller turrets mark the angles of the nave. So nave and aisles are differentiated in a design which, despite the fact that the northern outer turret is square while its southern counterpart is octagonal in its top two stages, is French rather than English in its consistency. And French influence is strong in the composition of the west door, though that is obscured by a tree in the photograph. Yet the facade does not, as a whole, derive from any particular French example and shows typically Anglo-Norman features such as the predilection for blank arcading. The motif is used yet more abundantly at Ely (*opposite*), where it is exuber-

antly varied in form and scale and is combined with reed decoration on the angle buttresses. The viewpoint from which this photograph of Ely was taken encourages us to see the extraordinary composition of the west end as its designer intended, and to imagine a corresponding transept on the other side of the great tower. The west front was indeed symmetrical when it was built at the end of the twelfth century. The north-west transept fell in the fifteenth century. The dramatic idea of a single central west tower sets Ely apart from all other English cathedrals. It is tempting to think that this may consciously continue a Saxon tradition. The cathedral at North Elmham, the Saxon minster at Brixworth and the monastic church at Monkwearmouth were all planned with a single western tower, and Ely's Norman tower preserves and magnifies the image of its Saxon predecessor rising to confront both marauding Danes and the Normans themselves.

Instead of the fourteenth-century battlemented octagon and slender turrets which now crown the tower there was originally a short stone spire added in about 1230. The transept turrets were then capped by conical tops instead of crenellations.

The limestone from Barnack of which the cathedral is built contrasts with the local clunch of the wall in the foreground of the picture.

Above. ELY: *the West Tower and West Transept*

The photograph was taken when the cathedral still stood stemming the tide of destruction and proclaiming its original message of stability and changelessness amid the ruins left by German bombers in May 1942. The medieval symbolism is authoritatively expressed by the fortress-like towers which command attention not only by their strength but by their unusual place in the cathedral design. Instead of rising at the west end they terminate the transepts. Related arrangements occur in other regions of the Norman empire, at Cashel in Ireland and at Murbach in Alsace, but in both those cases tall, narrow towers flank very short east ends where they join the naves; so the effect is very different. The Exeter version of the idea is as unique as the single west tower concept at Ely. This distinguishing feature of the exterior of Exeter is all that survives of the great church begun under the first Norman bishop, William Warelwest, a nephew of the Conqueror. His work replaced the Saxon church which had become a cathedral in 1050 when, under Bishop Leofric, Exeter was made the see of the united dioceses of Crediton and Cornwall.

No one looking at the surprisingly extensive and expressive remains of the great monastery of Christchurch could fail to be struck by the remarkably preserved and monumental staircase leading into the North Hall. Jutting out as it does at right angles to the wall, with its elephantine entrance bay, arched on every side, with bulging zigzag ornament and scalloped capitals, with diminishing arcades keeping abreast of steep steps under a gabled roof, it has no counterpart. It was built in the mid twelfth century under a prior, Wibert, who was also responsible for the massive Court Gate adjacent to the North Hall. Thomas Becket was Archdeacon at Canterbury at the time and with the special taste for magnificence and enthusiasm for the arts which all the 'Lives' attribute to him, he may have influenced the character of the stair. The North Hall was designed for the accommodation of lay visitors to the monastery.

The original nave of Rochester (ca. 1077) was contemporary with the south transept of St Albans but the north arcade wall at which we are looking dates from the mid twelfth century, when, like the west front, it was restored after the fires already mentioned. This may account for a certain inconsistency in the design of the three-storeyed elevation, a theme which was treated with such assurance and interesting diversity in other Anglo-Norman cathedrals. Here the piers each show a different arrangement of shafts and bulky half columns, thus disturbing the rhythm of the arcade, while shafts which rise no higher than triforium level from the arcade capitals retard rather than promote an upward movement.

The transept arcade at St Albans, on the other hand, makes an impressively simple and powerful statement, further distinguished from that of Rochester by the local material of which it is made. The great church is uniquely built of flint combined with re-used Roman brick from nearby Verulameum. Although the interior presents surfaces of whitewashed plaster in contrast to the imported stone of Rochester, the harsh presence of mighty walls is nowhere more oppressively felt. The arcade piers, which are not columns and have no capitals, look like pieces of solid masonry through which openings have been laboriously cut. The effect is reinforced by the proportions of arcade, triforium and clerestory: low triforium arches (conspicuous not only for the bricks filling the tympana but for the arrangement of a pair of arches to every bay, each enclosing two openings) make a relatively narrow band between a high-arched clerestory and a tall arcade. The short colonettes of the triforium look like Saxon balusters, despite their cushion capitals. The name of the author of the whole grand and ingenious conception was recorded by Matthew Paris, the thirteenth-century chronicler. He was Robert or Rodbert. His employer, Abbot Paul, rewarded him with lands which he restored to the Abbey on his deathbed but which during his lifetime enabled him to contribute ten shillings a year towards the maintenance of the monastery.

The Abbey church, according to Matthew Paris, was founded by Offa of Mercia ca. 730 to commemorate the site of the martyrdom of Alban, a citizen of Verulameum and the first man in Britain to die for the Christian faith. In the years between the Conquest and the appointment of Abbot Paul of Caen in 1077 the Benedictine monastery suffered severely. William I laid waste its manors, houses and possessions and would have destroyed it utterly had not Lanfranc intervened. He contributed 1,000 marks towards the rebuilding of the church, and donated books, ornaments and vestments. Paul was the archbishop's nephew and may therefore, like his uncle, have come from Lombardy. So more than coincidence may underlie the suggestion of North Italian influence in the decision to use brick both inside the church and for the crossing tower (p. 245).

The Abbey church was of course not a cathedral in the Middle Ages.

31

The huge cylinder, combining immense girth and weight with a spiralling upward movement brought to an abrupt halt by the plain band of masonry beneath the capital, is the most striking object in the nave. The contrast between the form and the carved pattern is tremendously exciting and is an outstanding example of the creative use in Norman England of ideas drawn from other parts of the empire and fused with Saxon motifs. In continental versions of spiral decoration such as occur at Nôtre Dame la Grande at Poitiers or in the cloisters at Monreale the contrast which is the whole point of the Norwich column is scarcely felt, for there the pillars are relatively small in scale and the ornament is either painted or inlaid. It is the translation of the theme into sculpture which is the source of its power, and that was a Saxon invention. It can be seen in the tenth-century crypt at Repton, though there the rather loose spiral lacks force. In the hands of the Norwich mason the conceit becomes tense and dramatic.

The pier is part of the church and monastic buildings begun in 1096 by Herbert Losinga who had been Prior of Fécamp before becoming Bishop of East Anglia in 1091. It was the transference of his see from Thetford to Norwich which prompted his grandiose building programme. A thirteenth-century chronicler describes the Bishop's compulsory purchase of a large part of the town of Norwich for the cathedral church and monastery and the ruthless pulling down of houses and levelling of the ground. We do not know how the citizens reacted.

The glimpse the photograph gives of the nave arcade reveals an impressive variation on the basic arrangement of arcade, triforium and clerestory. Here the triforium and arcade are of equal height while the clerestory is diminutive. And instead of twin openings within an enclosing arch in the triforium gallery a single cavernous orifice yawns within the arch. The shafts between the bays force their way through the string course above the arcade in a determined vertical thrust, but, as with the spirals of the pier, the movement is checked, here by capitals on a level with those of the gallery piers, tiny capitals which turn the shafts into attenuated half columns.

The sculptured type of column which makes a single dramatic appearance at Norwich determines the whole visual aspect of the contemporary nave of Durham. It is the combination of the strange archaic spirit of these columns, their prodigious size and barbaric splendour, and a sophisticated, powerfully intellectual composition which makes the first sight of the Durham interior such an overwhelming experience. The camera, focussing on an individual giant column and at the same time yielding a view across the nave to another pier seen as part of the superbly proportioned and precisely articulated arcade, triforium and clerestory, emphasises the unique character of this great building. The accent is all on the rhythm and height of the colossal arcades, the incredible scale of which can be measured by a glance at the pews in the foreground of the picture. The piers, embellished with zigzags (a magnified version of the delicate zigzags on the ribs), lozenges, spirals and flutes, are of formidable girth but they are also unusually tall. They exude a sense of furious energy which is both contained and enhanced by the stately, unhurried measure of the bays. This depends on the alternation of composite piers and sculptured cylinders and upon the novel introduction of transverse and cross ribs which give each bay an individual unity and slow down the forward movement of the arcades. The whole of the interior is vaulted in stone, and the use of ribs, as has so often been said, marks the first step in the technical revolution which brought Gothic architecture into being. Ribs were soon to concentrate thrusts along chosen lines, while the masonry between them was to become no more than light infilling. But the genius who designed Durham was not Gothic in either time or spirit. The stone vaults lie heavily on their supports and the moulded ribs make a visual rather than a structural contribution to the great design.

Bishop William of St Carilef laid the foundation stone of the cathedral in 1093. The building was complete 'usque navem' by the time of his death in 1096. The nave itself was carried out to the master mason's original design under Ranulf Flambard (1099–1128). The rapid progress of the work suggests that ample funds were available and reference has been made earlier to the part played by the cult of St Cuthbert in raising them.

CARLISLE: *Looking North-East into the Nave
from the South Chancel*

GLOUCESTER: *South Nave Arcade*

Here the majestic and mystical Norman conception of the Cathedral interior can be experienced almost undisturbed. It is as though we were confronting the inexorable progress of the architecture towards the sanctuary from the stone pulpitum which, until Essex demolished it in 1770, stood between the first pair of piers of the nave, shutting it off from the chancel. Twelve of the original uniform bays of the tremendously long nave remain as they were in the early twelfth century. The height of the building is as impressive as its length, especially when contrasted with the low tunnels of the aisles, and it is exaggerated by the tall, strong shafts which run from floor to flat roof between each bay and by the proportions of arcade, gallery and clerestory. For the gallery is almost as tall as the arcade and the clerestory is only slightly less tall. Alternating pier designs, five-stepped shafts followed by fat, shafted half columns punctuate the rhythm and encourage the forward movement of the mighty composition. The severity of the forms, the plainness of the arches and of the block and cushion capitals heighten the compelling, almost hypnotic effect of the proportions, the relation of void to solid and of the solemn advance.

The nave was completed very soon after Ely became a cathedral and the Abbot, Hervé le Breton, had been appointed Bishop. But the building was planned under Simeon, a brother of Bishop Walkelin of Winchester who had been Prior of Winchester before he became Abbot of Ely in 1083. This may account for similarities between the proportions of Ely and those of the only part of the limestone fabric of Winchester to survive from the Conqueror's time, the transepts, with the building of which Walkelin had been closely associated. Simeon built on a site close to the Saxon church he was replacing; and the pre-Conquest church was pulled down. The remains of St Etheldreda, foundress and first Abbess of the double community at Ely, were however translated to the new building. They had been a source of miracles and had attracted pilgrims ever since her death in 679. The Normans found the shrine a welcome source of revenue and deliberately exploited the cult of the saint. It continued for many centuries promoted by continual reports of devils expelled from the bodies of the possessed and of instant cures, specially of diseases of the eye. The end came with the destruction of the shrine at the Reformation.

No one unfamiliar with Carlisle Cathedral would guess that the nave consists of little more than the subject of the picture (p. 36). In fact all but two of the original eight bays were destroyed during the Civil War in the seventeenth century. By concentrating on the surviving piers, so ponderous, so enormous, with such elementary capital scallops that the mighty Gloucester columns (p. 37), appear sophisticated and almost slender beside them, the photograph conjures up the formidable character of the Border church of the Augustinian priory founded by Henry I in ca. 1130. Three years later he made Carlisle the see of a diocese embracing Cumberland and north Westmorland.

Bishop Waldegrave, sculpted by John Adams-Acton in 1872, figures suitably in the foreground of the composition, for he was an enthusiastic church builder and it was during his episcopacy, under the scholarly Dean Archibald Tait, that Ewan Christian restored the truncated nave and gave it a west front.

The Benedictine monastery of St Peter, Gloucester, founded in ca. 681, was twice destroyed by the Danes, and when Serlo, the first Norman abbot was appointed in 1072 the convent consisted of but two monks and eight novices. In less than thirty years the resolute Norman had raised the number of monks to sixty, with a corresponding growth in wealth. He had started to build a new church in 1089. It was completed in about 1120 and consecrated in 1121 under Serlo's successor. The proportions of the elevation are highly individual. The triforium is no more than a narrow strip between the clerestory and the dominant arcade. The eye is riveted by the tall, awe-inspiring columns. Of creamy Painswick stone, they are perfectly plain, their minimal capital bands (seen also at Hereford, *page 8,* and perhaps a regional motif) contrasting with the piecrust zigzag ornament of the arches they so effortlessly support.

The photographs were all taken by natural light with a plate camera. In the case of Ely the exposure was 13 minutes.

Opposite. ELY: *The South Aisle of the Nave*

On the right. GLOUCESTER: *The South Choir Ambulatory*

Of all the parts of a cathedral, the ambulatory, a continuation of the choir aisles round the apse (or square east end) to form a processional path, speaks most eloquently of the time when there was hardly any difference in the round of services between a monastic and a secular church. The Sunday procession described in the introductory pages of this book would have been the same in this Benedictine abbey church (for Gloucester did not become a cathedral until the reign of Henry VIII) as at York, except that at Gloucester the perambulation would have included the monastic buildings of the cloister. The powerful, squat columns, dating from ca. 1140, preserve something of the aspect of the eastern arm of Norman Gloucester before its remarkable transformation in the fourteenth century. The fifteenth-century chapel dedicated to St Stephen, opening from the ambulatory was built in response to the demand for more altars which accelerated from the thirteenth century onwards.

At Ely we are looking in the same direction as in the photograph on page 39, but the scene has shifted to the south aisle. Once again the contrast between the low dusky aisle and the lofty, surprisingly luminous nave is brought out, but here the camera draws attention to the alternating designs and noble simplicity of the great piers. The tunnel-vaulted aisle vista is closed by a crepuscular view of the tiered arcading decorating the west wall of the west transept and corresponding to the external ornament (*see* p. 27). The light shafting into the aisle from the left comes from the open Prior's Door (inappropriately named, for it was used by both monks and prior as well as the laity). It led into the cloister on the far side of which was the Prior's Lodging. It was through this door that the feast day processions re-entered the church after having passed through the Monks' Doorway to visit the conventual buildings. The open door affords a glimpse of thirteenth-century ironwork, hinges of scroll-work foliage spreading a springy linear pattern on the timber.

The photograph records atmosphere rather than architectural detail. It was taken by natural light with a stand camera, a Sanderson, and the length of the exposure was 30 seconds. It was a grey June morning but because this crypt is, most unusually, above ground, the interior was not dark, and a sudden, unexpected shaft of sunshine streaming into the narrow passage gave the photographer a unique opportunity. The flood of light, quivering on the short pillars and patterning the heavy arches and the low vault with a flickering crisscross of brightness and shadow, recreated what must have been the effect of that burst of 'wonderful and awful' effulgence described by the monk Gervase as it flared into this very place from the fire which destroyed the choir above it in 1174. The crypt itself was not touched: it is still the crypt which was part of the rebuilding and vast enlargement of the east end of the cathedral under St Anselm (1093–1109), Lanfranc's successor after a period of five years during which the see was deliberately kept vacant, and its revenue appropriated by William Rufus. Prior Ernulf (1091–1107) supervised the work and the master mason, according to Eadmer, precentor of the monastery, writing in ca. 1100, was a Saxon, Blitherus.

The reason for the reconstruction was to accommodate seven new processional altars dedicated to early beatified archbishops. The new choir was raised up on the crypt; it was thus many steps higher than Lanfranc's nave and enhanced the drama of the great interior. The crypt itself, loftier and more spacious than any yet seen in England, was like a complete church beneath the sanctuary, with nave, aisles and processional aisles on each side.

Opposite. WORCESTER: *the Crypt looking West*   *Above.* WINCHESTER: *the Crypt looking West*

Crypts, built to enshrine sacred relics are seldom found in Norman churches on the Continent. But they were conspicuous features of Anglo-Saxon churches, and when the Conquerors embarked upon their ambitious programme of rebuilding they encouraged the retention of the crypt, possibly as a reconciliatory gesture, possibly with an eye to the revenue from the cult of relics. As building invariably started at the east end of the church, so that the parts needed for services, the choir and the sanctuary, should quickly be completed and dedicated, the crypt, situated beneath the choir, often preserves its original aspect when all else has changed.

The Winchester crypt is steeped in the atmosphere of the eleventh century. Subterranean, groin-vaulted, apsed, with short heavy plain piers and simple openings into tiny chapels and the ambulatory, it has altered little since in 1093 the remains of the sainted Saxon Bishop Swithin who had died in 862 were brought here from his first humble resting place outside the Saxon minster which the first Norman bishop, Walkelin, had demolished.

The crypts at Worcester (for there is another beneath the south chapel chancel) were built under Wulfstan, the only Saxon bishop to continue in office after the Conquest. Though he wept over the destruction of the Saxon church, he planned to rebuild on a grand scale and placed special emphasis on the crypts where the shrines of St Oswald, founder of the Saxon monastery, and other native saints and martyrs were to be set. The photograph, taken from the east end, concentrates on the most remarkable detail of Wulfstan's design: we are looking straight into the semicircle of apse columns which is the imaginative climax of the seven-bay-long crypt.

The impression of exotic richness made by this interior derives wholly from the exuberant use of the chevron ornament, a particularly popular motif in twelfth-century England. Placed at the west end of the cathedral the building was both a Galilee or entrance vestibule and a Lady Chapel, an early example, for the cult of the Virgin was a Gothic speciality. Lady Chapels were invariably added to the *east* end of the cathedral church and the position of the Durham version of the theme is unique. According to legend repeated attempts to build the chapel behind the high altar were frustrated by St Cuthbert who, because of his loathing of women, caused the foundations to collapse. But it is a fact that Bishop Pudsey or de Puiset (1151–95), under whom the Galilee was built in ca. 1170–5, wished to keep women away from the east end of the church. He let a grey marble line into the floor of the nave, roughly level with the north doorway, beyond which women were not permitted to go. The chapel, divided into a nave with double aisles, is only four bays long and very broad. With its tall, light, coupled shafts of Purbeck marble and delicate, waterleaf capitals, this room is quite different in character from the nave (p. 35). While entirely Norman in its detail the building is a harbinger of Gothic in its lightness and elegance, and it is perhaps significant that at the end of his life Bishop Pudsey showed much appreciation of new architectural developments. Of course the windows which admit so much light to the chapel, are later in date. When it was built the Galilee was lit by smaller openings, later filled in, in the upper part of the inner aisles.

Paintings of St Oswald and St Cuthbert dating from Bishop Pudsey's time decorate an arched niche, though they cannot be seen in this photograph; and the big plain tomb-chest of the Venerable Bede, to whom Durham owes the preservation of the Cuthbert legend, stands in the Galilee. It dates from 1542, but the remains have been in the chapel since 1370.

On the left. ELY: *the Prior's Door, corbel and detail of the Tympanum*

Opposite. ELY: *the four Orders on the left side of the Monks' door*

The three superb carved doors at Ely all appear to be by the same hand and to date from ca. 1140. The tympanum, which was probably carved in the sculptor's workshop, is made from three courses of Barnack stone, the joins of which are visible in the photograph. The deep undercutting suggests that the artist used a chisel, a new tool at the time. The expressionist approach both of the tympanum relief and the alert corbel head recalls the Anglo-Saxon 'Winchester' style, and if he did not have access to illuminations of that period the sculptor could well have seen a manuscript of his own time in which the style persisted, the *Historia Eliensis*, now in the library of Corpus Christi College, Cambridge. But whatever the source of his inspiration his idiosyncratic interpretation, vigour and emotional intensity were his own. His conception of the angels is breath-taking. With beating wings and on enormous feet going right through the tympanum down onto the lintel, they stride unexpectedly away from the central Christ, though their heads are turned towards him; and their fantastically elongated arms are contorted so they can grasp the rim of the mandorla with their huge hands.

If the style of the Prior's Door tympanum has affinities with Anglo-Saxon illumination, the treatment of the splendidly enriched shafts and capitals of the Monks' Door points to possible acquaintance with carved ornament in foreign lands. The artist may have seen S. Michele, Pavia, for instance, as Arthur Kingsley Porter suggested as long ago as 1917. His knowledge could also have been acquired by looking at drawings brought back by travelled monks. And there is again an echo of the *Historia Eliensis* in the foliage decoration. But if the Ely sculptor did use such models he transformed them. His design is distinguished by the alternating of square jambs with round shafts, by the different treatment of each order and the sudden concentrated profusion of foliage scrolls on the inner jamb.

The Monks' Door served as a ceremonial entrance for the monks.

WINCHESTER: *Detail from the font*

The font is of black marble from Tournai in Belgium and is the most interesting of ten such examples in this country. One of them, carved with giant leaves and monsters, is part of the furniture of Lincoln Cathedral. The fonts were imported ready carved and the style, harsh and resolute, and, in the beaded ornament, the decoration of the building and the treatment of garments, more like the work of a goldsmith than a stone carver, presents a great contrast to that of such Anglo-Norman sculpture as the impassioned Lazarus panels or the expressionist creatures in the library at Chichester (pp. 52 and 53). An extraordinary sense of power emanates from these stocky figures with their heavy-lidded eyes. St Nicholas of Bari is standing outside the church of Myra of which he was bishop, and is baptising converts.

The frieze of sculptured scenes above the lowest recesses in the cathedral facade were, like the encrustations of Norman zigzags and blank arcading, added to the composition under Bishop Alexander. The panels at which we are looking show Noah building the Ark, Daniel in the lions' Den and The Departure from the Ark. It seems likely that the Daniel panel is out of order. The first thing that strikes one, however, is the strong classical influence in the carving of these figures. They could derive from late-eleventh-century sculpture on the west front of the Duomo at Modena, and perhaps Bishop Alexander, with his lively interest in contemporary art, invited a North Italian artist to do the work.

CHICHESTER: *The Library, corbel heads*

These sculptures were part of the corbel table of the original Norman cathedral built under Bishop Ralph de Luffa who succeeded to the see in 1091, some fifteen years after it had been moved to Chichester from Selsey. Norman cathedrals are architecturally the monumentally integrated expressions of a new order and the lordship of a confident society, but so often the ornamental details challenge the certainty of the buildings.

There is an interesting correspondence between these stone images and those on the opposite page which is reinforced by the similarity in the treatment of the leaf-like hands. More crudely carved, these big heads and dwarf, crouched bodies powerfully convey a feeling of nightmare as well as of overwhelming fear and grief. The very sight of them prompts the cry: 'Angels and ministers of grace defend us.'

CHICHESTER: *South Choir aisle, detail from 'The Raising of Lazarus'*

The relief of which this detail showing the heads of Mary and Martha is part, and its pair representing Christ entering their house, were discovered behind the choir stalls in 1829 and it was then thought they had come from Selsey and were Saxon. But they are carved in stone from Caen and Dr Zarnecki's date of ca. 1125–50, based on resemblances to German ivories of the period, has now been accepted. Nevertheless the style relates the sculptor's work to that of the Winchester School and the large hollow eyes (once set with enamel), so different from the bugle eyeballs of the corbel heads in the library (*opposite*) are those of Saxon imagery. But it is the artist's unique, unforgettable interpretation of this moment of awe and unspeakable grief which is important: his strong, simple lines, his extraordinary sense of drama and psychology, the gravity and intensity with which he invests the subject. In their deep humanity these great masterpieces foreshadow the remarkable developments of the thirteenth century.

II
A Transforming Vision

THE GREAT north transept of York Minster shown on the opposite page epitomises the extraordinary change in outlook which in little more than a century after the Norman invasion had begun to transform church architecture. By the time the transept was built in ca. 1253 the new view of life and the new forms were fully established. The ponderous mass and mysterious penumbra of Norman cathedrals had given way to an exhilarating sense of weightlessness and transparency conveyed by huge windows, high narrow-pointed arches and vaults which instead of resting inertly on solid walls seem to rise organically from their slender supporting shafts. The essence of this new conception is expressed by the windowed wall at which we are looking. The immensely tall lancets, each 5 ft wide and 55 ft high (and there is another which we cannot see in the photograph), the seven graduated lancets filling the gable above them, the first and last blank, and the unbroken blind arcade, trefoil-headed and with capitals of tightly folded, stalked leaves, together constitute a design of impressive formal simplicity and precision, the proportions of which concentrate the eye on the enormous central lancets and their wonderful translucency. The composition is a visual counterpart of the exaltation by thirteenth-century theologians of geometry and light as attributes of the Divine. For the logic and ingenuity of Gothic invention, the technical discoveries, were all part of the intellectual and philosophical tenor of the age.

The preoccupation with geometry and light derived from St Augustine's interpretations of passages such as that from the Wisdom of

Solomon: 'Thou hast ordered all things in measure and number and weight' and the description in *Revelation* of the Celestial City. Augustine related proportion to music and to architecture, the audible and visual harmonies of which prefigured the order and perfection of the world to come. During the second half of the twelfth century Augustine's theology was expanded by the group of eminent Platonists at the Cathedral School of Chartres, who, curiously merging Christian doctrine with a Platonic fragment, the *Timaeus*, emphasised the importance of geometry and proportion, which they thought could unlock the secret of creation and the mystery of the Trinity. One consequence of these ideas was that the Bible account of the building of Solomon's temple, with its recital of dimensions, became part of the medieval liturgy for the dedication of a new church. Furthermore it was the Platonic School that conceived of God as a master builder and thus inspired the many medieval representations of the Almighty holding a pair of dividers. The image occurs conspicuously on a boss in the nave of Norwich Cathedral and in a window in the south transept of York Minster where the Creator holds an orb in one hand and a large pair of dividers in the other. The dividers are those used by medieval masons and an actual pair is still preserved in the cathedral. In submitting to the laws of geometry the cathedral builder was emulating the work of the Creator, erecting a model of the cosmos and a replica of heaven. So when a Gothic illuminator wished to depict the dwelling place of God it inevitably took the form of a cathedral. And in responding to the visual harmony of the cathedral men were experiencing an ultimate reality for which there could be no rational explanation. St Augustine and his pupil Boethius had described moments of intense perception as the result of the illumination of the human mind by the Divine, and one of the most influential writings of the twelfth century was Erigena's translation of the *Celestial Hierarchy* which drew upon the sublime conceit in St John's Gospel of the divine Word as the 'Light that shineth in darkness,' and which 'lighteneth every man that cometh into the world'. The author was the mysterious Denis the Pseudo-Areopagite, believed in the Middle Ages to have known St John the Evangelist and to have witnessed the eclipse of the sun at the hour of Christ's death. The Platonists, echoing St Augustine, revered light as the transcendental reality which illumined men's minds for the understanding of

Opposite. YORK MINSTER: *the North Transept*

truth and was the source of all visual beauty. Thomas Aquinas defined beauty as the fusion of proportion and luminosity, and Robert Grosseteste, Bishop of Lincoln (1235–54) and before that a great teacher at Oxford, designated light as the mediator between the spiritual and the material, the creative principle in all things. The Gothic architect's special awareness of light and his dramatic transformation of stone walls into frames for stained glass are the outward expression of such notions.

The most influential early embodiments of the metaphysics of geometry and light were the austere Cistercian churches designed according to the precepts of St Bernard and Suger's reconstruction of the abbey church of Saint-Denis dedicated to the saint who had converted France to Christianity but who was also thought to be identical with St Denis the Pseudo-Areopagite. St Bernard's harsh condemnation of ornament concentrated attention on structure and proportion, the perfection of which distinguishes such severe architecture of his Order in this country as the ruined naves of Rievaulx and Fountains. Suger, on the other hand, pressed every enrichment into the service of devotion, and light, radiating from huge windows and reflecting the lustre of precious gems and of gold and silver was the quality which for him most determined the revolutionary style of his splendid new church. He spoke of replacing a dark church by a bright one:

Et l'œuvre magnifique qu'inonde une lumière nouvelle resplendit

The peculiarly English architectural interpretation of the theology of geometry and light from the time of its first inspiriting stage in the development from Romanesque to Gothic in the choir of Canterbury to the full expression of its early morning freshness, energy, nobility and exquisite lucidity, its humanity and awakening delight in nature at Lincoln, Wells and Salisbury cannot be divorced from the strange chances which guided history at that time as at all others. King John's unsuccessful attempts to defend his Angevin inheritance had ended the intimate character of the connection with Normandy which is so clearly reflected in the mighty cathedrals of the Conquerors. A bastard French was still spoken by the King, nobles, knights and bishops but they were becoming insular, interesting themselves in questions relating specifically to England and establishing a Common Law and a Parliament which

were to set England apart not only from the political life but from the cultural development of Latin civilisation.

The revolution in style which began to emerge at Canterbury had no counterpart in the organisation of ecclesiastical affairs. The Norman settlement had produced an order so stable that four hundred years were to pass before there was any addition to the number of dioceses. However, it was during the thirteenth century that the custom was introduced of appointing vicars or deputies to take the place in choir of absent canons. The conditions relating to the appointment of vicars choral are first set out in a statute of Salisbury of 1222. Each canon, on the death of his vicar, was to present another, who had to undergo a year of probation. During that time it behoved him to learn his psalter and antiphoner by heart and to give proof of his piety and good character. He was required to swear an oath of obedience to the dean; and he was asked to act as his canon's personal agent in communications between him and the chapter. A further statute of 1268 reveals that a vicar was in priest's, deacon's or subdeacon's orders according to the gradation of his canon's prebend. He received payment from the common fund of the cathedral and from his canon. A vicar's presence at matins had always been obligatory; it was now enacted that he must be present at the other canonical hours: absence meant loss of commons for the day. No vicar could accept a secular appointment which might interfere with his duties in church. Sometimes, as at Lincoln under Bishop Hugh of Wells, vicars were compelled to attend the schools and the necessity for them to study singing and music is specially stressed.

There was one important change of location during this period: the removal of the bishop and his clergy from Old Sarum to the new town of Salisbury in 1219. Old Sarum, now a bleak eminence with remains of earthworks, was then a little walled hill town with a castle built by Bishop Roger (1107–39), who also enlarged the cathedral church founded by St Osmund (1078–99). King Stephen deprived the bishop of his castle and from that time the clergy and the garrison were at odds. The hilltop was always short of water and was so exposed that the howl of the wind drowned the recitation of the divine office in

Opposite. SALISBURY *from the Avon*

choir, the *opus Dei*. When therefore, by the beginning of the thirteenth century, the clergy needed more space the bishop and chapter resolved to move to nearby Salisbury. The present cathedral, begun in 1220 and completed within sixty years, was built on ground belonging to Bishop Richard Poore.

The inconvenience of an unfriendly site was a unique reason for rebuilding. Catastrophe was a less unusual one. A few months before St Hugh of Avalon was called in 1186 from the Carthusian monastery of Witham, where he was Prior, to become Bishop of Lincoln, an earthquake had shattered the Norman cathedral. So the new bishop was immediately confronted by the task of rebuilding the entire church except for the west front. It was catastrophe in the form of fire which urged on the reconstruction of the eastern arm of Canterbury (pp. 60 and 61). But the commonest motives behind the many important building projects of the thirteenth century were the desire of prelates to enhance the splendour of their churches with additions and alterations in the new style, both for the glory of God and as lasting monuments to their own endeavours, and the need for space for more altars, chapels and elaborate processions and hence for increasing numbers of clergy. Growth in the numbers of canons was a particular reason for the extension and rebuilding of secular cathedrals. When, during the century after the Conquest, monastic influence was paramount, secular chapters consisted of but a few canons, perhaps not more than five or six, and the churches themselves could not compare in size and grandeur with such monastic cathedrals as Ely, Durham, Norwich or Peterborough. During the late twelfth and thirteenth centuries the secular cathedrals added to their estates, grew immensely more wealthy and much enlarged their chapters. The magnificent new churches at Lincoln, Salisbury and Wells were rising just at the time when their chapters reached their full quotas of fifty or more canons. These three secular cathedrals are the most glorious expressions of the Early Gothic style. At York Minster, also a secular cathedral, a grandiose rebuilding programme was initiated by Walter de Grey (1215–55). His transepts, at one of which we have just been looking, set an example of vast scale to the builders of a later time and made York the largest and most majestic English cathedral.

Rebuilding in all cathedrals, whether secular or monastic, was encouraged by the need for more chapels dedicated to the saints and martyrs whose profit-raising relics cathedral chapters were acquiring in ever greater abundance. Although Becket was the principal attraction at Canterbury the cathedral also enshrined the bodies of St Dunstan, St Odo, St Anselm, St Wilfrid and St Alphege, as well as miscellaneous skulls, teeth, fingers and hands and 'some of the clay out of which God fashioned Adam' (J. Wickham Legg and W. H. St John Hope: *Inventories of Christchurch, Canterbury*, 1902). The trend, set by Canterbury, of removing the remains of a cathedral's most revered saint from the crypt to a shrine behind the high altar, and a growing devotion to the Blessed Virgin and the fashion for building special chapels in her honour were further incentives to embark on new architectural enterprises.

In general it was the eastern arm of the cathedral that was transformed by rebuilding. Because of the various needs just outlined the eastern arm was extended until it was often almost as long as the nave, and it then assumed the square end which is such a distinctive feature of most English cathedrals. In contemporary France, where a similar need arose for more altars, it was met by building many chapels to encircle the short existing apse. The English solution is perhaps most strikingly manifest at Durham in the famous Chapel of the Nine Altars, built in 1242 in emulation of the Nine Altars eastern chapel at Fountains to a T-shaped design. In the middle, behind the high altar, stood the shrine of St Cuthbert, while against the eastern wall were nine altars, each dedicated to two saints. At Worcester where the object of veneration was the shrine of St Wulfstan the whole of the eastern arm was similarly reconstructed to include an eastern transept projecting beyond the aisles; and the builder of the presbytery of Rochester adopted the same plan when the shrine of William of Perth was erected. The sumptuous new eastern arm of Ely, completed in 1252, rehoused the shrine of St Etheldreda; and the east end of Winchester was altered by Bishop Godfrey de Lucy when St Swithin's shrine was moved from the crypt. A Lady Chapel was also built at the east end of Winchester at this time; and chapels dedicated to the Virgin rose at the east ends of Norwich, Chester, St Albans and Hereford. The square-ended Angel choir at Lincoln which absorbed the apse of St Hugh's church, housed the shrine of the saint and was also dedicated to Our Lady.

All these and other ambitious cathedral projects of this time were paid for by offerings at the new shrines and altars, by substantial individual benefactions such as that of Bishop Jocelin, who continued the rebuilding of Wells begun under Bishop Reginal de Bohun in 1188, and by contributions from all over the dioceses. Indulgences were granted to all who gave to the cathedral works; and every gift or bequest entitled the donor to a mention in the prayers of the church. Without the sale of indulgences at Salisbury under Bishop Bingham in 1244 it might have been impossible to complete the building.

Too little is still known of the identity of the men who created the masterpieces of Early Gothic architecture. The rebuilding of Salisbury was supervised by one of the canons, Elias de Dereham, whose name is so closely connected with a number of important undertakings that it has also been associated with the actual designs. He was in charge of the king's works at Winchester and at Clarendon and one writer, W. D. Bushell, author of the monograph *Elias de Dereham*, 1906, believes him to have been the *Ingeniator* working for Henry III in London. Matthew Paris named Elias together with Walter of Colchester, sacrist of St Albans, as the designer of the shrine of St Thomas Becket and calls him *artifex*. Elias of Dereham has also been mentioned in connection with the Chapel of the Nine Altars at Durham and it is worth noting that when it was going up Richard Poore of Salisbury had been transferred to Durham. Yet while it seems probable that Elias of Dereham was more than an able administrator, nothing is certain beyond his keen interest in the arts. The principal designer of the Durham chapel was Richard of Farnham, described as 'architector novae fabricae'; and the master mason who was responsible for carrying out the work at Salisbury was Nicholas of Ely. Bishop Poore rewarded him with a dwelling house with land and outbuildings immediately outside the cloister. Meanwhile Gervase of Canterbury's famous account of the rebuilding of the choir reveals not only the name but significant events in the life of the man whose work pioneered the new architecture. William of Sens was a man 'active and ready, and as a workman skilful in both wood and stone' and 'of lively genius'. Having procured stone from Caen, for the transport of which he devised 'ingenious machines', he started to build on September 5, 1175. Four years later he had reached the crossing and was supervising the necessary preliminaries for the construction of the vault when the scaffolding gave way beneath him and he fell some fifty feet to the ground. Though permanently injured he continued for some time to direct operations from his sick bed, deputing as his overseer a monk who had 'skill and industry', more indeed than the masons liked. Eventually, however, William had to retire. He returned to his native Burgundy and another William took his place. William the Englishman brought the work to completion.

The name of the great master Geoffrey de Noiers to whose brilliantly individual style and sense of mystery the whole romantic character of Lincoln is due, was recorded by St Hugh of Avalon, the first bishop to keep a record of his doings. More of Geoffrey will be told and seen in the following pages.

Documents, including wills, become more plentiful as we advance into the later Middle Ages and it will be possible to ascribe many of the fourteenth- and fifteenth-century masterpieces of cathedral architecture and craftsmanship shown in subsequent pages to artists of whom not only the names but many details of the careers are known.

CANTERBURY *from the East, and city wall*

The splendid vista (*right*) shows the first integrated architectural expression in England of the Gothic spirit manifest some years earlier at St-Denis. A new vision materialises in the tall piers, round or octagonal and shafted, to mark the entrance to the transepts, in the leaf-frond capitals, the pointed arches and bossed rib vaults and in the invigorating use of Purbeck marble to create a shifting pattern of light and dark. A sudden unexpected narrowing of the composition and rise in floor level at the entrance to the Trinity Chapel concentrates attention on the chapel which housed the shrine of St Thomas and on the Corona beyond it where the saint's head was once preserved in a silver reliquary. The curves in the design were dictated by the need to incorporate the Norman side chapels of St Anselm and St Ambrose in the new building which took the place of the Norman choir, destroyed, as has already been related, in the fire of 1174. But the great architect, William of Sens, has exploited that necessity to intensify the dramatic flow of movement towards the Trinity Chapel and the Corona. He did not live to see the finished elevation. William the Englishman who took his place completed the Trinity Chapel and the Corona in the spirit of the Frenchman.

The photograph of the exterior, taken just before the outbreak of a storm, draws attention to the unique circular termination of the great church and to the buttresses and large windows of the emerging wall-reducing Gothic style. The battlements and tall buttress finials were eighteenth-century additions, carried out at the expense of a retired naval officer, Captain Humphrey Pudnor.

The flint wall with its projecting bastions, which survives in long stretches to mark the boundaries of medieval Canterbury, dates from the fourteenth and fifteenth centuries.

CANTERBURY: *view from the Choir to the Trinity Chapel and the Corona*

CANTERBURY: *the Trinity Chapel and the Corona*

The Canterbury detail shows the persistence of Norman influence in the zigzag ornament round arches and window openings, but this consorts with the new-fashioned, beautiful and boldly carved acanthus leaves of the capitals curling to form volutes under the abaci and so deeply cut that the serrations become separate leaves. Related to contemporary French versions of Corinthian capitals like those at Sens, they foreshadow the stiff leaf foliage of the fully developed Early English style. At Sens too, coupled columns like the one in the foreground of the photograph figure conspicuously in the design. William the Englishman who built the Trinity Chapel may

well have relied on drawings left by his predecessor, William of Sens. The shafts of the piers are of Purbeck marble, echoing the colour and texture of the marble shafts in the Corona.

The photograph of the exterior of the Corona illustrates the novel relation of wall to window. Here we see the proportions from within and the strong pattern made by the armatures of the late twelfth-century glass, the dazzling array of which in the eastern arm of the cathedral culminates in the Corona with representations of the Death, Resurrection and Glorification of Christ. The shield-bearing angel leaning over the scene belongs to the tomb of Henry IV.

CHICHESTER: *detail from the East wall of the Retrochoir*

Again, as in the Trinity Chapel at Canterbury, angels preside over the composition, and here too they are of later date than the architecture. The spirited being shown in the photograph leaning out from a trefoil opening in the spandrel above a winged lion, symbol of St Mark, is, like the exuberant foliage and inner trefoil arches, a later addition to a building which immortalises the moment when Romanesque was giving way to Gothic. The round arches of the Norman style consort with pointed two-light openings and capitals with rounded abaci and stiffly formal foliage. The perfection with which these diverse elements have been brought into harmony is a source of perpetual delight.

Opposite. CANTERBURY: *the Trinity Chapel, roof boss*

The boss and the crescent look down on the very spot where the shrine of St Thomas Becket once stood. Stephen Langton, one of the truly great Archbishops of Canterbury, organised the removal of St Thomas's remains from the crypt to the Trinity Chapel and the translation took place on July 7, 1220, the anniversary of the martyrdom. The faultlessly staged ceremony was the most splendid event ever to have taken place in the cathedral up to that time. The procession from the crypt to the chapel was led by the young King Henry III, followed by the four bearers of the shrine, the Archbishop himself, the Archbishop of Rheims, Hubert de Burgh the Justiciar and Randulph, the Papal Legate, all the bishops and abbots of the realm and a great train of nobles and notables. After the ceremony the Archbishop entertained all the distinguished visitors in the Palace beside the west front. He did not neglect the multitudes of pilgrims who had come to Canterbury for this tremendous occasion: fodder had been provided for their horses along the route from London; on arrival they were invited to drink their fill at the Archbishop's expense.

The shrine rested on an arched stone base and the Martyr's remains reposed in an iron chest within a wooden coffin all plated with gold and set with countless gems which had been donated by kings, princes and pilgrims from all over Europe. Among the precious stones was the Regae of France presented by Louis VII. The whole shrine was covered with a canopy painted with sacred images and on important occasions a monk stood by to raise it by means of pulleys with a fine dramatic effect. Elias of Dereham, a canon of Salisbury and Walter of Colchester, sacrist of St Albans have been credited with the design of the shrine (*see* p. 59). It was utterly destroyed in 1538 at the order of Cranmer who had presided over the trial in which St Thomas had been declared a traitor.

The foliage of the huge boss is still based on the acanthus leaves of the capitals in the Chapel but the breaking up of the fronds into little individual leaves springing from the central vein, is much more intricate and the windblown arrangements presages the later development of carved foliage. The crescent, made of gilded wood, was brought back from the Crusades as an offering to St Thomas, the patron saint of many crusaders.

The new ideas which inspired the masonry of the Canterbury choir are fully realised in the noble display of lancets on the front of Ripon, a composition as serene and restrained as that of a classical temple. At the time when it was built (ca. 1230) Ripon was the church of a college of secular canons and part of the manor of the Archbishop of York, Walter de Grey (1216–55), who granted indulgences to all who contributed to the building fund. Surprisingly the effect for

which he was responsible and in which we delight, owes its preservation to Victorian restoration. Flowing tracery was inserted in the tier of lancets above the portal in the later Middle Ages. Sir George Gilbert Scott, with true feeling for the perfection of the original design, removed it.

The towers were crowned by timber spires in the Middle Ages. These were taken down in the seventeenth century to save the cost of repairs.

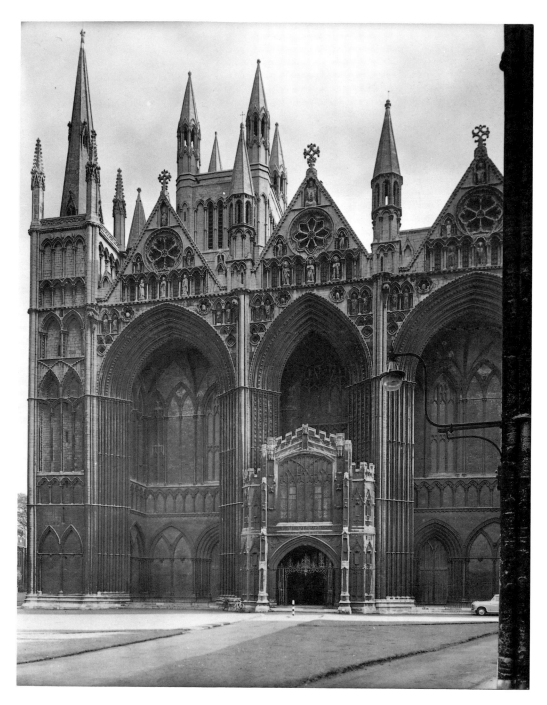

After the calm of Ripon, the drama of Peterborough. This eccentric composition never fails to excite, however familiar it becomes. The magnificent Norman monastic church was completed by the end of the twelfth century but the west front, a screen front like that of Lincoln, only assumed its present form at the time of the consecration in 1238. The three giant cavernous recesses, the scale of which contrasts so forcibly with the fine detail of the sculpture, wheel windows and arcading of the surmounting gables and with the proportions of the flanking turrets, make an impact which triumphs over the assymetrical presence of a single west tower behind the front and the disturbing incongruity of the central porch added in the late fourteenth century. The splendour of this front reflects the great wealth of the abbey in the thirteenth century, the result of a campaign of forest clearance and the reclamation of the fens it adjoined. The work was carried out with the help of the abbey's own knights and freeholders.

WELLS: *detail of the West Front*

WELLS: *the West Front*

There it stands across the Green like some strange gigantic totem. It must have looked even more fantastic just after its completion in about 1240, for the whole elevation was then richly coloured. Essentially English in its proportions, its great width increased by the placing of the towers outside the aisles, this Wells facade is, like those of Lincoln and Peterborough, conceived as a screen, but of a very different kind. The front is all of a piece except for the towers, and the comparative insignificance of portals and windows in the composition is immediately apparent. The horizontals of mouldings and arcading and the powerful verticals of shafts, gables and mighty buttresses form a highly organised grid which, together with quatrefoils and niches, provides the framework for a great *Te Deum* of sculptured praise. This extraordinary

work is indeed a stupendous reredos in which architecture and imagery conspire to expound the systematic theology of the early Gothic period. There were originally more than 400 figures showing forth the whole vast theme of the Old and New Testaments, from the Creation and the Fall to the Redemption together with images of the Prophets, the Apostles and Martyrs, saints, bishops and doctors of the Church. The figures in the outer niches of the buttresses in the photograph on the opposite page are kings, nobles and bishops. The lower tier of this vast assemblage suffered in the wholesale destruction of the Reformation and the Commonwealth, and all the sculpture has been ravaged by pollution. Recent cleaning and conservation have restored this unique masterpiece to something of its former splendour.

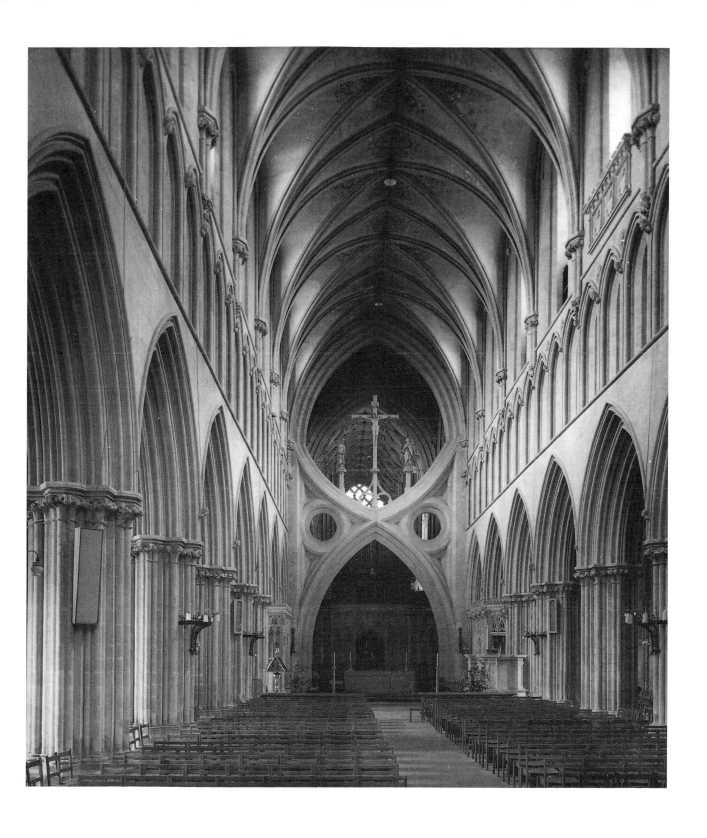

Opposite. LINCOLN: *the Nave*

Above. WELLS: *the Nave*

These pure and lovely interiors, although only fifteen or twenty years later than the Canterbury choir, are both wholly Gothic and wholly English. The Englishness of Wells is at once proclaimed by the designer's avoidance of the fierce upward thrust of French Gothic and his predilection for a firmly horizontal articulation in the lower stages of the elevation to balance the vertical movement of the high oblong vaults. The marvellous serenity of the conception for which the grey Doulting limestone in which it is executed is the perfect medium, is accentuated by the dramatic contrast of the huge strainer arches. But they are of later date and for the moment must be disregarded. They are the only intrusion into the work of Bishop Jocelin's time (1206–42).

The horizontal effect depends chiefly on the architect's most original invention – his treatment of the triforium as a continuous band, not divided into bays. The massive, many-shafted piers reinforce the eastward sweep and, so that nothing below clerestory level shall impede it, the most effective vertical elements in a Gothic elevation, the vaulting shafts, are restricted to the topmost stage instead of soaring from the pier capitals. They do this at Lincoln; and here the tall arcade arches, the less heavy piers and the branching ribs of the vault all lead the eye upwards to the longitudinal ridge rib and the symbolic imagery of the bosses which adorn it at every junction. The roof is thought to have been started in 1233 when Bishop Hugh of Wells (1209–35), brother of Bishop Jocelin, gave a hundred marks to the fabric fund and all the felled timber on his estate. The vault, finer and more elaborate than that of Wells, consists not only of the essential diagonal and transverse ribs but of eight additional ribs, four on each side, meeting at the ridge rib. Despite their name, tiercerons, both they and the continuous ridge rib are peculiar to England. Although in Bishop Hugh of Wells's rolls a certain Michael is named as *magister operis* the ridge rib was the invention of St Hugh of Avalon's architect, Geoffrey of Noiers, and had already appeared in St Hugh's choir.

English too is the profuse and brilliant use of Purbeck marble for the shafts of the piers, for the colonettes of the triforium and clerestory and of the enchanting blank arcading in the aisles. Everywhere its dark colour contrasts with the pallor of the local limestone.

One of the delights of both Wells and Lincoln is the beauty and variety of the stiff leaf foliage, again an English speciality. The view of the bell ringers' vestry at Wells, at the west end of the Cathedral, under the north tower brings the eye closer to some of these capitals than the pictures of the naves. They are of two kinds here, tightly coiled in double rows and bursting open in the fullness of maturity. In the photograph one type of foliage is brightly illumined, the other is in shadow. It was this which attracted the photographer. The pattern of light and dark, the arching forms framed by the crepuscular oval opening and the surprising effect of the different levels of the capitals seen from this angle had to be recorded. The strange relative positions of the capitals of the vaulting shaft and the window shafts could well go unnoticed if seen from another viewpoint and in an altered light.

We are looking up across the south wall of the south-east chapel. The photograph enables us to see a most charming detail of the original Norman cathedral; the gable of the aisle recess with its unusual decoration, a chain mesh motif made up of alternating large and small links. But it is the turret on the left which at the moment is the principal object of interest. It is one of the pair of turrets which enclose the front and was the work of the thirteenth-century designer who turned the Norman facade into a huge screen (p. 24). The turret presents the liveliest contrast to the austere and static Norman stages of the south-west tower. The strongly moulded blank arcading of varying proportions, the shafted colonettes with their emphatic abaci and animated stiff-stalked foliage, the frieze of dog-tooth ornament, the gablets and almost three-dimensional geometric ornament and the little heads emerging from the spandrels of the lowest arcade, all convey that sense of movement and harmony, that spring-like freshness and reassuring humanity which we always associate with Early Gothic design.

The eastern parts of the cathedral were rebuilt and enlarged in the thirteenth century, largely with money offered at the shrine of St William of Perth. He was a baker who had been murdered at Rochester in 1201 when on a pilgrimage to the Holy Land. His tomb in the cathedral soon became the scene of miracles and the source of the revenue which enabled the sacrist, William of Hoo, to embark on the reconstruction of the choir and presbytery. The vaulting shafts are of Purbeck marble, the one shown in the photograph rising from a marble corbel at the level of the lowest string course and boldly carved with heads peering from coiling foliage which is a free, impressionist version of that of the Canterbury choir (p. 61).

Above. SALISBURY: *The Nave from the Triforium*

Opposite. LINCOLN: *West wall of the North Transept*

The startling photograph above, taken with a large plate camera, brilliantly captures the lucidity and linear elegance of the Salisbury nave; and in making the black Purbeck marble column the pivot of the composition the photographer underlines the importance of the contrast between this darkest marble and the Chilmark stone of the fabric, for it is this which brings the flawless logic of the elevations to life.

Salisbury is the only medieval English cathedral to present a completely unified image. Except for the tower and spire it was built to the original design in the short space of about sixty years. The circumstances of its building and the possible designer have already been discussed (pp. 58–9). The heavy, uninterrupted string course, the broad proportions of the triforium openings and the band effect of the marble colonnettes impart a strong horizontal emphasis to the composition, all the more marked when compared with the contemporary aspiring lancet pattern of the transept at Lincoln. Low twinned blank arches, two pairs to a bay, articulate the first stage of the elevation and they, together with the lofty gallery are embraced by immensely tall outer arches, two to a bay like the gallery openings. Above that is yet another gallery, a high-raised repetition in design of the lowest stage. Between each bay, springing up from the capitals of the elongated columns of the tall arches, vaulting shafts soar up to clerestory level. The overlaying of one form by another which is such a striking and eloquent feature of the Angel Choir is already adumbrated here.

When the present cathedral building was begun in 1220 two of the foundations stones were laid by William Longespée, Earl of Sarum, and his wife, Countess Ela. He was the son of Henry II and Fair Rosamond and half-brother to King John; Ela founded Lacock Abbey after her husband's death. That took place in 1226 and already work on the cathedral was sufficiently advanced for the Earl to be buried there. The pose resembles that of the Purbeck marble figure of William Marshall, Earl of Pembroke (d. 1219) in the Temple Church, London, which is perhaps the first representation of relaxed recumbency in knightly effigies. Earlier knights (again to be seen in the Temple Church) lay stiffly with straight legs, staring upwards, without a pillow. William Longespée's legs, slightly apart, are still straight, but his head turns gently to the right and is supported by a flat cushion. The Earl wears a hauberk or long hooded shirt of flexible chain mail composed of small steel rings and a surcoat to protect it from moisture. Upon his long isosceles shield are rampant royal lions, originally gold on a blue ground.

It is not the eroded stone which makes his noble head that of a type rather than an individual. All effigies of this period were stylised and though some carving was done on the spot, the work was usually carried out in London or some other big town. William Longespée's tomb is of Doulting stone and so was probably made locally. The name of Canon Elias of Dereham, a friend of the Earl, is associated with the design. Elias of Dereham's connection with great architectural and artistic enterprises has been mentioned earlier.

Opposite. LINCOLN: *double arcading in the South Choir aisle*

On the right. WORCESTER: *arcading in the South-East Transept*

One of the most arresting features of Lincoln is the syncopated arcading in those parts of the cathedral rebuilt under St Hugh of Avalon after the disastrous earthquake of 1185. The inventor of this delightful motif was Geoffrey of Noiers, St Hugh's 'constructor'. Although his name sounds French, his work owes nothing to French example and his name probably indicates nothing more than French ancestry. His double arcading is as innovatory and as peculiarly English as his use of the ridge rib in the choir. He clearly loved ornament for its own sake but he must too have been attracted by the suggestion of transparency in the concept of forms overlaying each other, a concept to be so brilliantly refined and developed in the Angel Choir. The free-standing Purbeck marble columns on which the trefoiled arches are set rise directly in front of the apexes of the pointed arches of the blind wall arcading behind them, thus creating a feeling of movement as well as of luminous depth. The precisely sculpted stylised capital leaves, entwined or breeze-blown and unfolding above their clustered stalks, reinforce the splendid vitality of the arcading.

The wall arcades of the eastern transepts of Worcester Cathedral were reconstructed after the fall of the tower in 1175 and a fire of 1203. Though they move to a simpler rhythm, the rich mouldings of the trefoil arches, the tightly furled early stiff-leaf foliage and the wiry figures in the spandrels convey as strong and irresistible a sense of life as Geoffrey of Noiers's syncopation. Of the spandrel sculpture the subjects we can see in the photograph are the Resurrection (the dead pushing up their coffin lids) and a sprightly angel joyfully escorting two of the redeemed to Heaven. Below these agile figures lies the still Purbeck marble form of a nameless knight, in the cross-legged pose which became popular for knightly effigies after about 1240 and remained fashionable for the next hundred years.

The photographs were, of course, taken before the fire of 1984 when lightning struck the transept destroying the roof and the vaulting timbers (for the medieval vaults of York were of wood), blackening the stonework and fracturing the glass of the rose window into minute fragments. The cross on the charred gable was untouched. Seen from the low, dark street the great pale, soaring transept, towering so far above the tiny figure silhouetted against its brightness, still evokes that vision of supernatural reality it was intended to represent. The effect and the whole drama of the contrast between the enormous bulk of the Minster and the domestic proportions of the brick-built alley are encouraged by the silvery Magnesian limestone of the cathedral fabric. The stone was brought by water from Tadcaster in the West Riding when Archbishop Walter de Grey (1215–55) began to rebuild the church. The composition of the transept facade is dominated by the immense and splendid rose window, a design of two circles of pointed arches on columns wheeling about a sexfoiled roundel. It hovers like the sun, for which it was indeed a symbol, above the street opening, balancing the upward movement of the gable in which it is set. The three needle-pointed gablets over the door strike a discordant note; they were part of Street's restoration in 1871.

Because it concentrates upon effects of light rather than on architectural detail the photograph of the interior conveys something of the supreme importance of light in the new vision which transformed cathedral building during the thirteenth century. Light flows through the rose window and the tall lancets, permeating the whole wall. These windows are not so much structural openings as transparent walls. To its builders the transept was a representation of Divine light transfiguring the darkness of matter.

82

The smith was one of the most important of medieval craftsmen. It is the ironwork, not the carpentry, on which the strength and beauty of Norman and early Gothic doors depend. The Prior's Doorway at Ely shows the simple bold style of the twelfth century: the hinges arc like great swords with crescent-shaped guards and from them coil one or two primitive scrolls. Throughout the thirteenth century ironwork became more and more elaborate. This ravishing pattern of wiry tendrils, quickened by slight irregularities, conveys the same heightened sense of organic life as the Wells capitals. The design is similar to the wonderful displays on the doors of the parish churches of Eaton Bray and Leighton Buzzard and to that of the grille of Queen Eleanor's tomb in Westminster Abbey, for which Thomas of Leighton was paid £12 in 1294.

Shortly after St Hugh of Avalon, Bishop of Lincoln, was canonised in 1220 the event was celebrated by a work known as *The Metrical Life of St Hugh*. The author mentions the transept and the rose window, referring to it as *orbiculare*, so its date must be rather earlier than the *Life*. The arching ribs of the sexpartite vault seem to have been set deliberately low to frame the glorious roundel and to concentrate attention on the way it rests on the string course immediately above the seven narrow lancets. The simplest shapes – circles, trefoils and a quatrefoil – make up the flower-like design, yet it is a strikingly original composition, unlike any other rose. The glowing thirteenth-century glass survives, rich in symbolism, the various scenes with their layers of meaning radiating from the figure of God in the centre.

Special chapels built in honour of the Blessed Virgin were a thirteenth-century innovation and were often placed, as here at Hereford, at the east end of the church. After the grandeur of great naves and vast facades this exquisite chapel of ca. 1220 seems almost domestic. It is agreeably broad and low and the simple quadripartite vault contrasts with the rich shafting of the windows and the decorative roundels and almond shapes enclosing quatrefoils. The glass in the five lancets, said to have been designed by Cottingham, is an instance of Victorian sensibility, for even a black-and-white photograph shows how well the shapes accord with the thirteenth-century architecture.

It has only been a cathedral since 1905. In the period to which the retrochoir belongs it was the Priory of St Mary Overie (over the walls). Again, as in the Lady Chapel at Hereford, one is instantly captivated by the calm and comfort of the proportions. All else, except for the quadripartite vault, is different. Piers divide the space and apart from the delightful large scale blank cusped tracery in the heads of the wall arches, the design is conspicuous for its lack of ornament. The shafted piers and moulded capitals are of the plainest. The retrochoir was built after a fire of 1207. It was restored in 1822 after a period of neglect lasting from the time of the Civil War. The doorways seen through the piers must date from the restoration.

On the left. LINCOLN: *East end of the Angel Choir*

Opposite. LINCOLN: *Interior of the Angel Choir*

The rich ornamentation – crockets, gablets, blank arcading, niches (once filled with statues), the echo of the central window design in the patterning of the aisle gables – is an immediate source of visual pleasure. The gables are themselves decorations for they hide lean-to roofs and are as unfunctional as classical pediments. They differ in height and this is a blemish not just aesthetically but in view of the metaphysical significance of geometry and proportion to the medieval builder. However, the huge central window, 59 ft high, which is the focus of the composition is not only a source of light but an eminently logical geometric conceit. The great outer arch encloses two sharply separate arches within each of which are two further arches, each of two lights, while the tympana above them hold foiled circles, parabolic suns transmitting the light of sunrise to the interior.

It has already been related that the purpose of the Angel Choir was to accommodate the shrine of St Hugh and the pilgrims flocking to it. In 1255 the chapter successfully petitioned Henry III for permission to take down part of the old town wall in order to extend the cathedral eastwards. Work started in 1256 and the saint's remains were enshrined behind the high altar in 1280. The photograph, taken from the triforium, directs the eye to the proportions of the elevation and the conspicuous size of the clerestory. The system follows that devised by Geoffrey of Noiers for St Hugh's choir and for his most remarkable effect the designer of the Angel Choir has developed Geoffrey's ingenious and telling use of layered open forms. The tracery of the generous four-light clerestory windows is repeated on the inner side of the wall passage, so that one diaphanous, fretted layer is mysteriously seen through another.

The triforium pier in the foreground of the photograph shows the extreme richness of the design: between the dark, shining Purbeck marble shafts are strips of pale stone leaf forms and the stalked foliage of the capitals sprouts luxuriantly. Looking across to the north side of the Choir we can see that similar ornate and exuberant leaf clusters completely cover the long, tapering corbels which support the vaulting shafts. The juxtaposition of such intricacy with the simplicity of the huge trefoils in the arcade spandrels is one of the many marks in this superb bourgeoning of the Gothic style of the genius who planned it.

The Choir takes its name from the angels filling the spandrels and half spandrels of the triforium openings. The part they play in the design can be seen in the previous photograph. The idea of carving angels in this position may have come from Westminster, but the treatment is quite different: crisp, precise and decorative at Westminster; softer, more dramatic and more varied in composition at Lincoln. The sculptures seem to be the work of two masters. One of them was responsible for the enchanting series of heavenly musicians, each playing a particular instrument, and for the scroll-bearing angels, all in the more easterly spandrels. But as work went on towards the west an artist with a very different conception took over. He is one of the great sculptors of a period when the art had reached a pinnacle of achievement. Noble, monumental, stern and awesome, these angels are going about divinely appointed and often terrible tasks. Of them all the Angel of the Expulsion is the most powerful and most brilliantly original. The image of the archangel's expelling gesture, so implacable in its intentional awkwardness, his great sword and his giant proportions beside the figures of the mortals, the artist's mastery of emotional expression, the way in which the composition has been so perfectly and inevitably adapted to the spandrel shape, all alike make an indelible impression.

The relief of the standing Virgin and Child with a censing angel in the most westerly bay on the south side of the Choir shows another aspect of the master's genius: here the forms are slighter and deliberate distortion and simplification conspire to express ineffable tenderness and a strange intensity.

The carvings were done before erection, for there are certain misfits here and there; and in one case the wings of the angel, the one grasping a hawk, are too long for the space enclosing them. The stone is local limestone of a pale brownish colour, though of course the sculpture was originally painted and gilded. A few stars survive on the background of an angel holding up crowns, faint reminders of former splendour.

The photograph conveys the elegance and lightness which distinguish the whole harmonious interior of Salisbury. No other cathedral so vividly illustrates the contrast between early Gothic architecture and the habit of mind which inspired it and the dark, heavy and portentous churches of the Romanesque. The consistency of style, however, which is the special feature of Salisbury is accidental rather than actual in the east transepts. The beautiful strainer arches, arches of many mouldings with inverted arches on their apexes, which separate the transepts from the chancel, were inserted later to shore up the piers of the crossing. Yet they are in absolute accord with the atmosphere and architectural detail of the earlier work. The use of Chilmark stone for the shafted piers of the strainer arches instead of the Purbeck marble of the crossing piers which might have been the choice of a mere imitator, reveals the designer's appreciation of the effects of light and dark in the original conception of the interior.

The paintings in the choir vault are mentioned by Celia Fiennes, who remarked that they looked 'as fresh as if new done, though of 300 years' standing'. (300 years was the age she ascribed to anything medieval.) So they seem to have been part of the thirteenth-century choir. William Dodsworth, author of *A Guide to the Cathedral Church of Salisbury with a Particular Account of the late great Improvements made therein under the Direction of James Wyatt*, 1792, and of *An Historical Account of the Cathedral Church of Sarum or Salisbury*, 1814, refers to the paintings as 'the efforts of a wretched taste', and describes how Wyatt, whom he greatly admired 'buff-washed them'. When Sir George Gilbert Scott attempted to remove Wyatt's coating in 1863 he found it was impossible to do so without destroying the paintings underneath it. But drawings of all but two of them had been made by Jacob Schebberlie before they were covered, and were preserved in the Bodleian Library. These, together with surviving traces of the paintings revealed by damping, enabled Clayton and Bell to reconstruct them as we now see them.

SALISBURY: *Central pier of the Chapter House*

The octagonal Chapter House dates from after 1279 for according to Gleeson White's *Salisbury, the Cathedral and See*, 1896, pennies of Edward I's reign were discovered below its foundations. The fashion for polygonal chapter houses with vaulting ribs radiating from a central column was peculiarly English and was particularly associated with secular cathedrals. Damaged though it was by Puritan iconoclasts and extensively restored in the last century, the Salisbury Chapter House remains one of the most thrilling of architectural conceits. The huge four-light windows between the angles of the octagon, the slender, high-shafted pier and branching ribs; the fine detail of the leafy bosses and the charming idea of setting light leaf-shaped frond-clusters about

the bosses and between the ribs to define the circular centre of the vault, create an image of ethereal delicacy all the more compelling because it is carried out in stone.

Lincoln, the earliest of the polygonal chapter houses, is ten-sided. A reference to the building operations in *The Metrical Life of St Hugh* written between 1220 and 1230 gives some idea of its date. The atmosphere is quite different from that of the Salisbury Chapter House. The feeling here is of an immensely exhilarating confined movement, a fountain of ribs bursting thickly and forcefully from the central pier to merge with the stone jets of the vaulting shafts shooting up between the pairs of lancets.

The unevenness of the shadowy mounting steps, worn by the tread of six centuries of canons going up to their appointed seats under the blank arcading below the Chapter House windows, the turn of the stairway towards the doorway, the unexpected branching of the steps to continue straight ahead, all make this one of the most romantic and evocative of cathedral vistas. The double-branching which is so effective was not planned. In the mid fifteenth century, long after the octagonal Chapter House was completed, a bridge known as the Chain Gate was built to connect the cathedral with the Hall at the southern end of the Vicars' Close. In the photograph we are looking towards the bridge. The gate beneath it has a carriage way and two pedestrian passages. With the Chapter House doorway a new phase of Gothic begins to emerge. It is heralded by the large-scale cusping of the arches, undulating rather than crisp, by the curved triangles above them, by the rich and curious pattern of the tracery, foiled circles and almond shapes, spread above the blank arcading in the little vestibule and by the multi-branching ribs in the Chapter House itself. We cannot see the extraordinary central pier of this splendid room in the photograph, but we look towards one of the wall shafts from which clusters of ribs are breaking out to meet the rayed ribs of the great central stalk-like column. There are thirty-two of them, closely set, whereas at Lincoln, which is already ornate, there are twenty. And wherever the ribs meet there is a sumptuous leaf boss.

The doorway leads from the main south transept into the choir aisle and is matched by another opening from the north transept into the north choir aisle, an unusual feature. These doors are among the great beauties of the cathedral. The detail alone exhibits the contrasts of light and dark and of plain and ornamented surfaces upon which the character of these remarkable doors so largely depends and it most eloquently conveys the invention and sheer delight of the figurative sculpture. The high-spirited juxtaposition of the dragon slayer and a leaf spray bigger than himself is irresistible. Every shaft of the doorway is surmounted by a similar capital design showing, like a strip cartoon, a different stage in the killing of the fairly harmless-looking monster. The free informal treatment of the leaf forms suggests that the sculptor is already drawing inspiration from the hedgerow.

SALISBURY: *spandrel*
of the arcading
in the Chapter House

Thirteenth-century arcade spandrels provide a comprehensive survey of the remarkable development of relief sculpture during this period and are of absorbing iconographical interest. This example from Salisbury (ca. 1275) is later than the Worcester reliefs we have already seen (p. 81) and shows greater command of composition and three-dimensional form. It is one of three reliefs telling the story of Jacob. Here he wrestles with the angel (Genesis 32) while on the right two lesser angels ascend the ladder of Jacob's dream to a heaven of sculptured cloud. The reliefs were restored and repainted in the 1860s (though the paint was later scraped off) but the work was skilfully done and the charm and the liveliness of the interpretation have survived the ordeal. The hood-mould stop is one of an outstanding series of firmly and sensitively carved freestone heads of every type and expression – male and female, young and old, humorous and tragic, smiling and scowling, gap-toothed or with protruding tongue or twisted mouth, turning sideways, looking up, looking down or staring ahead.

III
Enrichment and Invention

SEVERAL of the photographs which have already been seen – those of the Angel Choir at Lincoln and of the entrance to the Chapter House at Wells, for instance – show the direction in which cathedral architecture was moving towards the end of the thirteenth century. The springtime purity of the earliest Gothic was yielding to the heat and profusion of summer. Elaboration, spectacular invention and enchanting decorative detail were the special delight of patrons and the fields in which masons and sculptors excelled during the reigns of Edward II and Edward III. It was a period of economic prosperity and the great wealth of their cathedrals encouraged prelates to rebuild and enrich them. The west front of York, ornate yet strong and deeply modelled, the design of Ivo of Raghton; the central towers of Hereford and Lincoln, the former encrusted with ball flower and supported by exquisitely detailed twin angle buttresses; William Eyton's lofty eastern Lady Chapel at Lichfield, which heralds such high aisleless churches of the later Middle Ages as King's College Chapel, Cambridge; the brilliant work done at Bristol under Abbot Edmund Knowle (p. 128); the unique Octagon at Ely (p. 123); the imaginative retrochoir and Lady Chapel at Wells (p. 126) and the form, unparalleled in the Middle Ages, of that Lady Chapel vault, a lierne structure taking the shape of a single huge star within and a dome without – all illustrate the ingenuity and originality of fourteenth-century architects and their mastery of visual complexity. The extraordinary skill of sculptors at this time is celebrated in the Southwell Chapter House capitals (pp. 112 and 113), while the increasing exuberance and sophistication of carved ornament is reflected in the tropical growth of the stone vegetation in the Ely Lady Chapel (p. 125) where the nodding ogee arches over which it flows set up the rippling rhythms which, encountered again and again in fourteenth-century work, were replacing the clear and simple lines of the Early English style.

The patterns of multi-ribbed and lierned vaults and above all the intricate window tracery, so different from the plain circles with the inscribed trefoils or quatrefoils of the previous century, testify as eloquently to the predilection for ornament and luxuriance. The great east window at Carlisle by Ivo of Raghton which has nine lights surmounted by a huge and bulbous central leaf shape flanked by smaller leaves and all filled with elongated quatrefoil and mouchette motifs; the Bishop's Eye at Lincoln displaying two giant, eccentrically veined leaf forms, the butterfly shapes in the south aisle windows at Gloucester (p. 127); the west window at York with its curving ogees and central sacred heart flanked by mouchettes and surmounted by a leaf like the one at Carlisle and so probably designed by Ivo of Raghton, these are but a few examples of the linear fantasies of the period.

The splendour, the undulations, the ogival, spherical, triangular and mouchette shapes and the luxuriant foliage ornament were part of every form of ecclesiastical art. Woodwork, in which English craftsmen of the fourteenth and fifteenth centuries had no equal, and which, despite destruction and alteration, has survived in such abundance, suddenly achieved a pinnacle of accomplishment and sparkling inspiration. The possibilities of the light, fibrous material as distinct from stone were expressed in such astonishing towering pinnacled and canopied conceits as the choir stalls of Lincoln, Winchester (p. 138), Ely (p. 123) and Chester. The bishop's throne at Exeter (1313–17), probably designed by Thomas of Winton and made by Robert of Galmpton (Collumpton) for Bishop Walter Stapledon (1308–26), is a unique three-tiered structure sixty feet high with nodding ogee arches, sprouting foliage and bedizened pinnacles in receding stages, all crowned by a tall, finely fretted, extravagant spirelet. The undersides of the hinged stall seats gave carvers the opportunity to indulge their own fancies and to create numberless little masterpieces of incredible variety. Sometimes the subjects are scriptural and saintly but more often they illustrate fables and folk tales or record dom-

Opposite. EXETER: *a corbel in the Nave*

estic, rural and urban events from everyday life and usually the scenes are accompanied by supporters taking many forms, animal, human and vegetable. These vigorous and often humorous images are the most intensely living memorials of that distant Gothic world and the most poignant, for they speak directly of the strong and simple influences that made it, the faith, the sense of wonder, the closeness to nature, influences which have now been overmastered by others, ugly, mechanical and materialistic.

The opulent furnishings of fourteenth-century cathedrals encouraged a more elaborate liturgy. Ecclesiastical dress was enriched: the mitre which, first adopted in the eleventh century, had previously been no more than a low cap with a right-angled point, began to grow steadily taller and more curved; vestments were more intricately embroidered, often with architectural arcades and canopies of the same wavy form as the stone arcades amid which their wearers moved. The English craft of embroidery, *opus anglicanum*, had originated in the cloister and was already famous in France and Italy, but now professional workshops were supplying chasubles and copes. The names of some of the designers and embroiderers are recorded, among them Alexander le Settere, Thomas Carleton, Stephen Vyne and Robert Ashcombe, all working in London. The Archdeacon of Lichfield ordered a choir cope from Alexander le Settere in 1307 and the Bishop of Worcester was presented with a cope made in London in 1308. New and sumptuous pulpitums like those at Lincoln, Southwark and Exeter enhanced the spectacle of the liturgy. Under Bishop John Grandisson the Epistle was read and the Gradual and Alleluia, the latter rendered by older choristers wearing silk copes, were sung from the loft of the magnificent verandah-type pulpitum at Exeter. The Deacon, after humbly receiving the blessing of the celebrant, passed from the choir to the pulpitum preceded by the thurifer and accompanied by cross, candles and incense-bearers and by the Archdeacon reverently clasping the book of the Gospels in his left hand. They ascended to the loft where the Subdeacon took the book in his right hand and offered it to the Deacon to be kissed. A further musical and theatrical flourish enriched the ritual when a number of choir boys went up into one of the galleries which are such a conspicuous feature of the cathedral to sing to the accompaniment of instrumentalists. The introduction of these balconies was just what one would expect of a

man like Grandisson, a great patron of the arts as well as a prominent churchman. He had studied civil law at Oxford and theology in Paris and before coming to Exeter in 1329 he had held canonries at York, Wells and Lincoln. He had also made a name for himself as an international diplomat and was the author of a life of St Thomas Becket, now in the library of Exeter Cathedral. He refounded and built at his own expense the splendid collegiate church of Ottery St Mary, commissioned fine ivories of Italianate character, some of which now belong to the British Museum, and was the owner of a superb collection of textiles, manuscripts, jewels and goldsmiths' work. It is largely to Grandisson that the cathedral nave at Exeter, with its arching roof, great bosses and galleries, owes its opulent and romantic aspect. The delightful balconies are wonderfully decorative and offered exciting possibilities in the fourteenth century, when new musical techniques were being developed and plainsong was varied by polyphony, counterpoint and harmonisation.

Exeter is the one cathedral church which was entirely rebuilt during the fourteenth century. And it is significant that the rebuilding was occasioned neither by disaster nor, as at Salisbury, by the inconvenience of an ill chosen site, but solely by the desire of a succession of bishops to make their church fashionable and beautiful. It is also significant because characteristic of an age remarkable for the transformation of existing buildings: the original Norman cathedral was not replanned but given a new guise ingeniously fitted to the lines of the original structure and incorporating the lower part of the Norman walls and some of the buttresses. While the work was going on John Grandisson wrote to his friend Pope John XXII, then established at Avignon telling him that 'the Cathedral of Exeter, now finished up to the nave, is marvellous in beauty and when completed will surpass every church of its kind in England and France.' It does indeed surpass others of its period in the fullness of its expression of the temper of the age. The nave corbel with which this section opens instantly conjures up the rich, chivalric atmosphere of this cathedral and of the relaxed character of art and society after the second Edward came to the throne. The sculptor of the tumbler performing to the music of a viol player with a dog at his feet may have had in mind the jongleur of the French legend, who praised Our Lady by practising his art before her altar. But the images are also, like that of another acrobat, the unchallenged choice of subject for the underside of the seat of the Dean's stall at Lincoln, the blithe response to a general easing of former austerity. The same mood dominates the gorgeous pulpitum and the minstrels' gallery on the front of which sturdy mortals posing as angels play fashionable instruments: the trumpet, the gittern, the new portable organ, the shawm, timbrel and cymbals; bagpipes, recorder, citole, viol and jew's harp. There is an air of romance about all these things which accords with the contemporary vogue for tournaments and the emphasis on the tiltyard as a make-believe counterpart of the battlefield and which echoes the spirit of the Round Tables at which knights played the parts of King Arthur and his legendary peers and which led to Edward III's creation of a new order of chivalry, the Garter, the most prestigious of the European confraternities of knights in the Middle Ages.

Records of the building carried out at cathedrals during this period are plentiful, especially at York and at Exeter. The fabric rolls show that the organisation and execution of structural work continued in much the same way as that described by Gervase of Canterbury. At York, when the choir was rebuilt, the archbishop, at that time John Thoresby, contributed substantially to the expense, describing the church as his spouse whom he must clothe in fine raiment. The dean and chapter were the employers of labour but their duties were delegated to clerks of the fabric, vicars choral or chantry priests. They paid the masons, heard disputes between workmen and punished infringements of the rules, prescribing hours of work and standards of conduct. At Exeter one of the vicars choral was clerk of the works in association with the master mason, Thomas Witney, while at Lincoln the custom was to select two canons annually as masters of the fabric. At York the payments made to various types of workmen – masons, carvers, carpenters, 'wallers and setters', 'rough masons' as distinct from freemasons (workers in freestone), and labourers, who fetched and carried materials – are recorded in lump sums. At Exeter masons were hired by individual agreement and weekly paysheets show the name of each man and the sum due to him at the rate of sixpence or fourpence a day according to his status. In winter the less skilled masons' wages were reduced. The master mason was given a house in the close and an annuity. In 1352 William de Hoton, who then held that office, was to get half his stipend of £10 per annum should he become blind or incurably ill. At Hereford John of Evesham, designer of the Chapter House in 1359–70, had a house let to him at 10s. a year and received a white loaf daily and 3s. a week for life.

The York and Exeter records reveal that masons, even the most skilled of them, were subject to arrest and imprisonment if they attempted to break an engagement before the completion of a project. Master masons might often come from distant places, but the majority of the men employed on a cathedral building remained in their native districts, handling the local stone with which they had long been familiar. And even though master masons might be engaged from another region they invariably came from places where good stone was available. Thus William of Shockerwick, master mason of Worcester in ca. 1316–24, had acquired his skill in the Somerset quarries and Thomas Witney who is immortalised at Exeter had first worked with Cotswold stone.

A close watch was kept on the quantities of material received and used as well as on the quality of the work accomplished and on the number of hours devoted to it. The York rolls for 1345 contain the following interesting reports of negligence of these duties (we are not told who *he* is):

Item; be it noted that as regards the church fabric, he says that alienation of timber, stone and lime has often occurred and he does not know where.... Item, he says that wood, stone, lime, mortar and so on are often alienated; and he says that, as regards alienation of stone, more evils arise from the quarry, and that at home nothing suitable for the fabric is carried away.

Item, concerning the paying of wages: whereas payment is accustomed to be made fortnightly, it is sometimes put off to the month, and even further on occasion....

Item, he says that he once paid Roger de Hirton, mason of the same fabric, his wages for nearly a whole fortnight, though he was absent all the time and did not work.

The fabric accounts curiously make no definite mention of payments for plans and drawings showing elevations and church furniture such as occur in the famous notebook of Villard de Honnecourt. There is just one entry in the Exeter rolls recording a payment for parchment on which the mason was to show 'the form of the work', and as for working drawings, it has been suggested that lines incised on the floor of the Chapter House at Wells bear some relation to the work going on in the cathedral in the fourteenth century. But the present writer fails to see anything resembling architectural forms in the maze of scratches.

Perhaps the highest delight of worship that can be kindled through the eye is to be found in the magnificence of fourteenth-century English cathedral building, so full of humanity, so richly proclaiming and combining the fleeting pleasures of earthly life and the immutability and splendour of the kingdom of heaven and still as overwhelmingly manifest after century upon century of despoilation and decay. It represents a climax and the background already holds elements of threat and disruption. The reported bad conduct of fourteenth-century vicars choral is probably not of much significance. At Wells they would walk about the nave while services were going on, chatting to lay folk and bargaining with others for goods on sale; at Salisbury they carried arms, and the Close and common hall were often the scenes of quarrelling and bloodshed; at Ripon they attended dances, were suspected of housebreaking, and played a game called ding-thrift. But they were young and had too much time on their hands. Outbreaks of lawlessness during the reign and after the murder of Edward II were more serious, for the cathedral precincts were sometimes invaded. In February 1322 citizens of Lichfield were seeking shelter in the Close because of the unsettled state of the country, and William Eyton, master mason, his seven assistant masons and four labourers under one Walter took an oath to warn the chapter should they hear of impending danger and to help in the defence of the Close.

The great natural disaster of the Black Death which burst upon the land for the first time in 1349 was a long-term dislocating force. The plague swept away some distinguished churchmen including two Archbishops of Canterbury, John Ufford and Thomas Bradwardine, and some eminent masons, among them John of Wisbech, perhaps the designer of the Ely Lady Chapel. Labour shortages resulted in legislation compelling stonemasons and skilled craftsmen to work at rates current before the plague; and it was probably owing to the more stringent conditions of employment that masons began to organise themselves into gilds, though there is no suggestion in the rules that individuals should conspire together for their own interest and protection: the gild's chief concern was for standards of workmanship. It is in the next century that we first hear of strikes. Meanwhile grandiose architectural enterprises such as the building of the nave of Exeter went on with scarcely an interruption, and at centres like Gloucester creative work continued with undiminished vigour and inspiration. The plague actually encouraged a particular form of structure – the chantry chapel. An already lively apprehension of the sufferings of the soul in purgatory was quickened by the accelerating occurrence of sudden and untimely death. Priests had been saying masses for the repose of souls for many generations, and it had become the custom for a wealthy man to endow a chantry, which meant ensuring regular payments to a priest to say the required daily soul mass. Now, in reaction to the horrors of the pestilence, chantries grew in importance. Instead of endowing an altar, small chapels were built within the church enclosing the tomb and often an effigy of the person for whom masses were to be said. Sometimes the chantry was founded and the chapel built in the lifetime of the donor. Thus the Black Prince founded two chantries at Canterbury more than ten years before his death. But this was only the first stage in a development which was to reach its bizarre zenith in the ferment of the last decades of the Middle Ages.

A more explicit portent of change was the Hundred Years War, supposed to be justified by the genealogical claims of Edward III to the throne of France. Despite all the inspiriting victories and the triumphs of English archers going forth 'with grace and might of chivalry' the war marked the beginning of the rise of materialism: it enriched individuals with plunder and ransom and grotesquely augmented the power and encouraged the greed of the fighting nobles while bankrupting the government. It marked a stage in the passing of the Middle Ages.

But of all the shadows that were falling athwart the marvellous cathedral creations of the age none was heavier than that cast by Wyclif and his denial of transubstantiation. The background for his heresy had been prepared by the emergence before the end of the thirteenth century of the itinerant friars. Their influence, brought to bear through impassioned popular sermons and religious instruction, had steadily increased. By enhancing the importance of the pulpit the friars were preparing the way for the Lollards, Protestants and Puritans who were eventually to destroy both them and the medieval cathedral ritual. Wyclif's denunciation of those who 'drawen ye peple by coryosite of gaye windowes..., peyntings and babwynerie', his total

rejection of art and architecture, his attacks on bishops and prelates, his egalitarianism, had their effect in his own lifetime. Some of his Lollard preachers who were undermining respect for churchmen encouraged the rebellious mob led by Wat Tyler. During that fatal rising the Prior of Bury St Edmunds was murdered and the gentle Archbishop Simon of Sudbury, who was in London at the time, was seized as he was saying mass in the Tower. The rebels dragged him out and butchered him with repellant savagery. The militant Bishop of Norwich, Henry le Spencer, avenged the outrage by marching at the head of an army he had personally assembled against Wat Tyler's Norfolk followers and defeating them.

The rising was suppressed, Lollardry was persecuted, but the forces they represented were to undermine the authority and disrupt the daily life of the church, profoundly affecting the great buildings which enshrined that ritual and which were the focus of that authority.

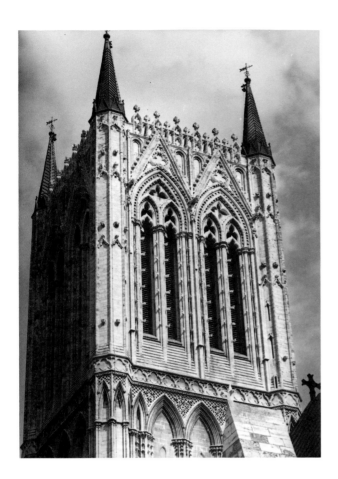

The contrast between this sumptuous belfry and the earlier work, the narrow Early English arcading with its chaste and delicate stiff leaf capitals and its backgrounds of flat lattice patterning, explains instantly and more vividly than words could ever do how this fourteenth-century architecture come to be called 'Decorated'. Shafts, gables, arch mouldings, all are adorned with crockets larger than any seen before, and with ball flowers, that typical ornament of the period which resembles both the globe flower of the north and the little bells on a jester's tunic, while the lights of the tall windows introduce the ogee curve, perhaps the most characteristic shape of mature Gothic art.

When it was first built the tower was surmounted by a lead-covered timber spire, blown down in 1548. The lead angle pinnacles and the pierced parapet, which so perfectly accord with the spirit of the whole design, date surprisingly from the mid eighteenth century. Like the exterior, the interior vault beneath the tower presents an illuminating contrast to the earlier work. From the photographer's chosen point of view we can see three stages in the elaboration of vault design at Lincoln. The comparatively simple sexpartite vault of the transept with transverse and longitudinal ridge ribs, the work of 1236, yields to the branching vault of the nave, begun in ca. 1237, and both contrast with the intricate, web-like tower vault which belongs to the later fourteenth century. Here pattern has become more important than structure. Star shapes merge with a central square set in a diagonal square, all enclosed by the square walls of the tower. The effect is achieved by the use of liernes which bridge the light arches of the network of ridge and diagonal ribs and tiercerons. The lierne rib is as characteristic of later Gothic construction as the ogee. Every junction is marked by an ornamental boss.

The original tower, built in the time of St Hugh, collapsed in 1237 or 1239. It was then rebuilt and crowned with a wooden spire sheathed in lead. Only a little more than fifty years later, soon after the completion of the Angel Choir, the chapter decided to heighten and enrich the tower. In 1307 indulgences were offered to all who would contribute to the undertaking, and the tower must have been finished by 1311 for there is a mention in the episcopal registers of that year of the bell ropes. The architect was Richard Stow, a mason who had recently been working on the Lincoln Eleanor Cross. He brought his tower design into harmony with the top stage of the thirteenth-century structure by continuing the polygonal angle buttresses.

This photograph, with the feathery branch in the foreground, though taken from the cloister, recalls Constable's description of the view from his friend's, Archdeacon Fisher's garden, the spire 'shooting up like a needle' and 'framed by the leaves of an unusually high alder tree'. The picture isolates the tower and spire from the rest of the church and enables us to concentrate on the masterpiece which completed the cathedral fifty years after the building of the cloisters and Chapter House in 1284 had brought the great thirteenth-century creation to its conclusion.

Of all the many features of the Gothic church which expressed the strength and aspiration of the design and the reality of the spiritual world, none was more eloquent than the spire. And this spire is the supreme emotive evocation of a power beyond the material and the earthly, not just because of its dizzy height, 404 ft, but because of its wonderful grace, brilliance and delicacy. It renders the sublime with something of the sparkle, purity and delightful ornamentation which transport us in the highest flights of Mozart's genius.

The spire rises from a cluster of filigree pinnacles and little gabled openings which bridge the transition from the square to the octagonal structure in a unique way: the tower buttresses terminate in short crocketted pinnacles, and behind these rise taller, more ornate pinnacles. In the middle of each of the four sides of the tapering octagon which are not hedged in by pinnacles are the lucarnes beneath their richly crocketted gables. The spire itself is adorned with three bands of carved, crisscross motifs faultlessly spaced. These bands are related to the sumptuous friezes of the two upper storeys of the tower and emphasise the unity of the whole composition, and this is strengthened by the ball flowers bursting from the angles of the octagon among their entire length and thickly encrusting the mould-

ings of the tower. The close similarity of the two storeys of the fourteenth-century tower has sometimes been condemned as a defect, but repetition is the source of the rhythmic perfection of the tower and spire, and there are minute differences in the organisation of the buttresses which subtly animate the twin features.

As with the central tower of Lincoln the fourteenth-century work at Salisbury contrasts with the restrained Early English substructure which, rising only a little above the nave, comprised the whole of the thirteenth-century tower. It was a bold venture to set so much more weight on such a base. The load on the piers of the crossing was tremendous. Some of the ways in which the strain was met were described earlier (p. 93). The spire was built about interior wood scaffolding like the ribs of an umbrella. It survives and can be seen at the cost of a nerve-racking climb. Cecil Hewitt, the authority on medieval carpentry, has made a fine detailed drawing of this timber skeleton, showing its central post, arches and bracing. The wooden windlass which the medieval builders used to hoist material to the base of the spire still exists and is still used. The spire was strengthened by tie-rods by Wren when he surveyed the cathedral and by Scott in the nineteenth century. Bronze ties were inserted in 1939 and further strengthening due to rust was necessary some ten years later. The spire is now threatened by pollution which has damaged the beautiful decorative bands.

The designer of the tower and spire was Richard of Farleigh. He began his career at Bath Abbey where he was granted a corrody in 1325 and he probably designed the tower of Pershore Abbey and the lierne vault of the choir there, one of the earliest of its kind.

With its three spires, the central one paler than the others, its bedizened front like a fabulous piece of embroidery, the unexpected colour of its sandstone fabric, a dusky ochre-pink, and its relation to the intimate little Close at its feet, Lichfield is one of the strangest and most romantic of cathedral images. It has been a place of worship for almost three thousand years. Before ever Saxons built a church here to house the remains of St Chad, seventh-century Bishop of Mercia, there was a pagan temple on the site. Its stone altar was discovered at the east end of the present cathedral. The west front is again, like that of Wells, of the English screen type. The tiers of arcading and statuary and the ornamental trefoils, quatrefoils and cinquefoils are spread across the whole facade, so that the lower stages of the rich and heavy towers seem to be hidden behind it instead of part of it. Yet although the inspiration of the building at which we are looking is wholly medieval and although the actual design of the west front, which dates from ca. 1280 – ca. 1327, is still basically that of the masons Thomas Wallis and William Eyton, the detail of the structure is nearly all Victorian.

Lichfield suffered more than any other cathedral under Cromwell. He seized the cathedral lands and revenue and reduced the building almost to ruin by bombardment. The Restoration brought a restored cathedral. The work, which will be described later (p. 187) was carried out under the famous Bishop John Hacket, largely at his own expense. It was rededicated to St Mary and St Chad in 1665. Very substantial repairs were necessary towards the end of the eighteenth century, when Wyatt was called in. His work was mostly in the interior though he replaced the tiers of shattered statues on the front with cement and stucco images by Robert Armstrong. Three of the original figures survived and these served as models for Sir George Gilbert Scott when he purged the front of Wyatt's work and began his extensive restoration from 1856 onwards. His statues are recognisably Victorian, but at least they are of local stone. Scott was also responsible for the big west window which had been given a huge rose window in the seventeenth-century restoration quite unlike the original medieval opening. The original window was recorded by Hollar before the Civil War and reproduced in Dugdale's *Monasticon*.

Despite the stormy history of the cathedral and the ordeals of restoration it has undergone, the nave, one of the most beautifully organised designs in the early Decorated style, still retains much of its original character. The photograph, taken on a sunny morning in early October, focuses on the features which distinguish it: the imaginative play on foiled circles – three trefoiled circles in the clerestory, the circles themselves making a single large trefoil; encircled quatrefoils in the heads of the triforium openings; and – a most unusual motif – huge cinquefoils within circles in the arcade spandrels with the vaulting shafts bisecting them; the bold dog-tooth enrichment and the capitals, where completely naturalistic foliage makes its first appearance.

Above, left. LICHFIELD *from the West*

Opposite. LICHFIELD: *detail of the Nave*

On the left. SOUTHWELL MINSTER
*Capital on North wall arcading of
the Chapter House*

Opposite. SOUTHWELL MINSTER
Arcading above the Chapter seats

The philosophical trend of the early Gothic period, roughly represented by the rediscovery of Aristotle's *Metaphysics* and St Thomas Aquinas's *Summa Theologicae*, celebrating the beauty and unity of all creation, resulted in an ever-increasing delight in natural forms and their inexhaustible variety. Among the countless visual expressions of this delight, in wood and stone carving, in metalwork and textiles, the famous leaves of Southwell are among the most memorable. The foliage capitals adorn the passage leading from the choir to the Chapter House, the vestibule and the Chapter House itself. The latter is of the English polygonal type, but unlike Salisbury and Lincoln it has no central pier and is rather a plain room. This concentrates the eye on the thrilling impact of the carving.

The first impression of the stalls running around the walls is of incredibly abundant foliage, overwhelmingly vibrant and varied, and of the strong chiaroscuro of the deep, crisp cutting. Leaves like flickering flames undulate along the mouldings of the stall heads, fill the tympana and cluster about the capitals. The sculptured leaves of vine and ivy and of oak, buttercup and hop convey the essence of their hedgerow counterparts in their extraordinary freshness and realism. The artist's enthusiasm so overbrimmed that he could not resist overlaying the mouldings of the springing arches with further leaves. Yet this is not the naturalism of the botanical draughtsman, content with fidelity to nature: it is the sculptor's sense of wonder which so deeply moves us, it is the synthesis of naturalism with superb mastery of design which so ravishes the eye. Though the forms are true to nature, the scale is not, and the arrangement of the leaves in two tiers on the capitals, like much stiff-leaf foliage, is such that the forms of the capitals round which they grow and of the mouldings up which they climb, are never obscured.

The head looking out above the buttercup capital is overshadowed by the vitality of the leaves, but the features and expression show it to be a portrait carved with the same power of observation as the foliage and with the same humanity which moved the sculptor to depict the supernatural not as his predecessors had done in the shape of a fearful monster but as the mild and harmless little dragon seen to the left of the head. The Southwell carvings show three different styles and are related to work at both York and Lincoln, but we know nothing of the masters who responded with such zest to the shape and texture of growing leaves. The capitals shown here are all by the same hand.

The York Chapter House, like that of Southwell, is polygonal and without a central pier. Southwell was in the diocese of York and the collegiate church, as it then was, was closely associated with the cathedral. Several Archbishops of York resided at Southwell. So it is probable that the architect and sculptor of the York Chapter House, which is a little later in date, took Southwell as their model. But there is greater enrichment at York: the canons' seats are set in niches with elaborate canopies above them, supported at the sides by Purbeck shafts and with leaf pendants carrying the front trefoiled arch. The canopies set up a lively undulating movement round the walls. The capitals show the same eager observation of nature as those of Southwell, though the treatment at York is less precise. It is the artist's eye for the human head which leaves such an indelible impression after a visit to the York Chapter House. The elderly woman looking out expectantly from the front of the canopy on the left of the photograph, the contrasting types of wimpled, kerchiefed heads and above all the leaf-framed face staring impudently from the fore-most column are informed with such super-abundant vitality that a first encounter with them is electrifying. The head adorned with foliage represents Jack in the Green, the chief actor in the May Day ceremonials in which pagan spring rites were remembered. The smiling oak-crowned woman beside him is his queen. Accompanied by her he would ride through the town, a custom which was still kept up in some northern villages until the Second World War. The presence of this image in the Minster is proof not only of the persistence of pagan traditions in a Christian society but of the close relationship between man and nature at this high point of the Middle Ages.

Opposite. YORK MINSTER: *Capitals of the Chapter House stalls*

Above. YORK MINSTER: *East End, South Arcade*

The square headdress of the figure on the left gives the date of the building, ca. 1370. The east end of the Norman church remained unaltered until 1360, but the need for a Lady Chapel and space for more altars and clergy then prompted an ambitious rebuilding enterprise, the cost of which was largely defrayed by Archbishop John Thoresby (1352–73). The architect deliberately followed the design of the nave, and this imbues the whole interior with a sense of harmony surpassed only at Salisbury, Lincoln and Exeter. The arcades are very tall, 51 ft high, so that it is only with the help of the camera that we can appreciate the life-like figures which seem to be breaking out of the vaulting shafts at arch level. The charming portrait of the smiling youth, which captures a fleeting expression with all the directness of a photograph, is informed with as keen an awareness of everyday life as the Chapter House sculptures, but here the interpretation is more worldly, and at the same time the former intense delight in natural forms has yielded to a more conventional approach: the capital leaves can no longer be identified but, wavy and agitated, begin to resemble seaweed. Whereas the tightly furled, stylised leaves of Early English capitals impart an overwhelming sense of new-springing life, these leaves are autumnal and on the verge of disintegration.

Begun in 1291, the nave took almost fifty years to build. The scale was determined by that of the transepts which had already been rebuilt. At first sight this vast interior, as revealed by a black-and-white photograph, inspires admiration rather than enthusiasm. Yet the camera's recording of the sunrays shafting through the high clerestory windows does convey something of the warmth and brightness with which the fourteenth-century glass, only some of which has survived, once animated the august building. Great breadth is combined with a markedly vertical and linear design, the forerunner of the more earthbound art of the fifteenth century. The vaulting shafts, set in front of the piers, run straight from ground to roof, and the piers themselves are very tall. The vertical, linear effect is heightened by the flatness of the novel upper stages of the elevation: there is no triforium passage to give recession and chiaroscuro, for triforium and clerestory are conceived as a single unit, and the mullions of the huge windows run right down to arcade level. The vault, originally designed and built by Philip of Lincoln in 1354, a carpenter who first worked at York in 1346, is of wood. It was badly damaged by a fire in 1841, and restored by Sidney Smirke.

York is one of the few cathedrals where the natural division between the distinct parts of the church still partially survives, for the stone pulpitum set at the west end of the choir, still separates the nave from the eastern arm. The organ originally set upon it was not the instrument seen in the photograph, but would have been the primitive organ of the Middle Ages with a small range of notes, each controlling a number of pipes and manipulated by a blow of the fist, just capable of accompanying the plain-song chant. The fabric rolls mention the existence of such an organ in 1375. A new organ was ordered from John Dallam of London in 1632 at the desire of Charles I, who also stipulated that the new organ should not stand on the screen. It cost £1,000, a sum raised by levying tax on a local squire for incest. Later in the seventeenth century Archbishop Lamplugh (1688–91) directed that the organ was to be put back onto the pulpitum. That instrument was destroyed by fire in 1829, and the one we now see was built in 1837.

116

Opposite. EXETER: *the Nave*

See also on the following two pages: the Pulpitum, and the Nave Arcade and Musicians' Balcony in the North Transept

Standing in the sumptuous nave of Exeter, with its thick and vigorously branching vaults, huge figured bosses, sculptured corbels, exotic pulpitum, musicians' galleries and intricate tracery, we are more acutely aware than in any other English cathedral of how much the medieval vision of the church as the Kingdom of Heaven had come to depend on rich decoration. That vision is here most captivatingly expressed by eminently approachable imagery borne of the newfound feeling for man and beast and leaf. Visually as unified within as Salisbury, Exeter was rebuilt in a period of about ninety years, from about 1279 when work was begun under Bishop Bronescombe (d. 1280). He had been present at the consecration of Salisbury, and what he saw there may have prompted him to renovate his own old-fashioned Norman church. But the opulent interior which eventually took shape owed nothing to Salisbury's restrained elegance.

The survival of an unusual number of fabric rolls establishes dates for the various parts of the cathedral. Under Bishops Quiril (1280–91), Bytton (1291–1308) and Stapledon (1308–26) work advanced steadily from the east end to the first bay of the nave. The bosses in that bay had been painted by 1309. The basic design of the nave accords with that of the eastern arm, but its strikingly individual character is a reflection of the personality of the man under whom and through whose munificence it was built, Bishop John Grandisson (1329–69) (*see also* p. 102). The master mason was Thomas of Witney who had been working at Exeter since 1313. The unbroken stretch of the powerful tierceron vault with as many as eleven stout ribs bursting and arching from each vaulting shaft dominates the interior. The multiplicity of the ribs is matched by that of the arcade mouldings and by that of the curiously striated, Italian-looking Purbeck marble shafts of the great diamond-shaped piers. And the continuing theme of rich profusion is emphasised by the extreme narrowness of the triforium which is in effect no more than a dividing band of luxuriant ornament.

The pulpitum was erected under Bishop Stapledon and the fabric rolls, recording payment for materials and the work of various craftsmen, show that work went on from 1317 to 1326. The prices paid for some of the materials include £4. 10s. 3d. for two hundred and forty-three feet of Purbeck marble for steps for the pulpitum and £1. 16s. 8d. for two altars with marble fronts and fittings and 15s. 5d paid to a smith called Crockernwell for 50 lbs of iron. Of the three bays only the central one was open towards the choir. The two side bays were closed at the back and formed little chapels. That on the north was dedicated to St Nicholas while the one on the south contained the altar of Our Lady at which the morrow-mass priest said the first mass of the day. In the fourteenth century both altars were screened, and behind each altar enclosed stairs mounted to the loft. Where the large and handsome organ case (made by John Loosemore in 1665) now stands a great rood rose above the pulpitum. The organ used in Bishop Grandisson's time was small and portable, like that held by one of the musician angels on the front of the nave balcony. At the solemn celebration of mass in the pre-Reformation cathedral the epistle and gospel were read from the loft of the pulpitum. Under Bishop Grandisson the rubrical order at Exeter directed that surpliced choristers should sing the Gradual in the pulpitum.

The paintings which can be seen at the back of the loft showing the great cycle of events from the Creation to the Descent of the Holy Ghost at Pentecost date from the seventeenth century. Originally sculptured reliefs filled these spaces. It was in 1878 that the eastern walls of the pulpitum were torn down to expose the choir to full view from the nave. The whole wonderful structure was then in danger of demolition; even the Exeter Diocesan Architectural Association supported this appalling sacrifice to community worship. We owe the survival of the pulpitum, like so much else in our cathedrals, to Sir George Gilbert Scott.

The photograph of the transept gallery with the lively, angular carving of a strong man in the foreground, supported in his mammoth task of holding up the vault by two sturdy attendants, isolates the deeply romantic effect of these balconies. This one is upheld by miniature spreading half-vaults which echo the grand design of the nave roof.

EXETER: *the Pulpitum*

120

EXETER: *the Nave Arcade and Musicians' Balcony
in the North Transept*

Opposite. ELY: *Nave and Crossing from the Choir*

The photograph records one of the most exciting of all cathedral architectural experiences, and it is worth remembering that it is one that could not have been enjoyed when the famous Octagon was built, for a solid stone pulpitum then closed the view to the west. The vista, though aesthetically satisfying, has been achieved at the cost of a great work of art and through the disorganisation of the medieval cathedral plan. James Essex wantonly destroyed the great Norman pulpitum in the eighteenth century and replaced it with a Gothic organ screen. The present open screen to which we owe the view was the work of Scott who also removed the organ to its unusual position on the north side of the choir triforium. The length, the solemn, relentless rhythm and calm light of the Norman nave seen through the screen, and the high western arch of the crossing contrast with the unexpected shape, the upward movement and the sudden brilliance of the hovering Octagon and with the liveliness of the ornate stalls in the foreground of the picture.

The Norman tower collapsed in February 1322, and the task of replacing it fell to the sacrist, Alan of Walsingham. According to the *Liber Eliensis* he was so overcome by the disaster that at first he 'knew not whither to turn himself or what to do'. But then, so the same source informs us, after he had cleared the space where the new tower was to be constructed, he measured it out 'with architectural skill' into eight parts. This indicates that the daring and experimental idea of an octagonal crossing, which had no predecessors and no progeny until Wren built St Paul's, did indeed come from Alan of Walsingham whose name has always been traditionally associated with the structure. The resident master masons at the time, under whom the work was carried out, were John of Ramsey and later John Attegrene. The octagonal design may have been suggested by the polygonal chapter houses which had become popular towards the end of the thirteenth century. For the octagon is strangely like one of those buildings raised on high.

The full effect of this wonderful invention is only felt when one is standing directly under it, but the photograph reveals its unique relationship to the rest of the interior and draws attention to the remarkable way, readily grasped by the eye, but baffling to the intelligence, in which eleven ribs spring up like the jets of a fountain from the capitals of the shafted piers, five of them seeming to support one of the eight sides of the lantern while the remaining six, three on each side, contribute to the design of the gigantic three-dimensional, eight-pointed star of which the lantern is the dazzling centre. In fact the lantern is not upheld by the ribs at all, but by a timber frame concealed by the vault, and the lantern itself is constructed of wood to lessen its weight. The vast span of the Octagon – 70 ft – posed an enormous structural problem. The ingenious carpenter who solved it was William Hurle or Hurley who was working at Ely in 1334–5 and again in 1336–7. He had previously been employed at the Palace of Westminster and at the Guildhall Chapel and was chief carpenter to Edward III from 1336 until his death in 1354. His salary at Ely was £8 a year plus board and lodging. Trees of sufficient size for so great an undertaking were becoming scarce even at this date. They were eventually found at Chicksands in Bedfordshire and were brought by water to Ely. Hurle's imaginative powers matched those of the originator of the design, for he adapted a hammerbeam roof composition to the polygonal plan, using the great upright posts of the lantern as the hammer posts and making a pattern which from the ground echoes the star-shaped vault of the lower stage of the Octagon.

The splendid stalls in the foreground of the photograph are also ascribed to Hurle, although the reliefs in the upper canopies, as a close inspection (not possible in the picture) at once reveals, are not medieval. They were inserted by Scott and are (according to Bernard E. Dorman's *Ely and its Cathedral*, 1945) the work of W. Abloo, a sculptor from Louvain. The medieval place for the stalls was under the crossing to the east of the pulpitum. James Essex shifted them to the presbytery in 1770 and Scott moved them to the threshold of the eastern arch in 1851.

NORWICH: *detail of the arch of the Prior's Door*

Like the Ely Lady Chapel (*opposite*) the Prior's Door at Norwich is a striking example of the tendency for fourteenth-century decorative sculpture to dominate the architectural forms it embellishes. The original feature of this delightful door is that instead of filling a tympanum the figures stand in richly crocketted ogee gables which follow the shape of the arch, and this gives the whole eccentric structure a feeling of airy movement which is strengthened by the graceful, swaying attitudes of the figures. Those seen in the photograph are Christ seated between ecstatic angels. The master mason at the time was John of Ramsey.

The Octagon was not the only great architectural project carried out at Ely during the fourteenth century. The Lady Chapel (1321–49) was one of the most sumptuous monuments of the period. The basic form of the building, a simple rectangle, is unadventurous by comparison with the Octagon; but the ornament crowding the walls and vault is spectacular. When the whole room was radiant with colour and gilding the effect must have been staggering. Yet though the stained glass has gone from the great windows, except for a few fragments, and though the local clunch, the material of the carvings, is reduced to its original chalky pallor, this blanched and evenly lit interior is profoundly moving, its present luminosity pitilessly revealing the horrible mutilation of the sculpture. Of more than a hundred images illustrating the life and miracles of the Virgin the larger figures have all vanished and the rest are headless victims of the Reformation. But this has not diminished the effect of the complicated forward and backward movement of the canopied niched stalls running along the walls with their densely crocketted nodding ogee arches and gablets, nor does it check the extraordinary animation of the parsley-like foliage rampaging over the capitals of the shafts which merge into the apexes of the arches and frame the reliefs on the walls behind them. A man's head, another Jack in the Green, has become one with the foliage. It is a translation into concrete form of that sensation of dissolving identity which is expressed in every mythology. The author of this work is not known for certain, but the mason in charge was an Ely monk, John of Wisbech, who, as has been mentioned, died of the plague in 1344.

Opposite. WELLS: *Choir, Retrochoir and Lady Chapel*

GLOUCESTER: *South Wall of Nave Aisle*

The photograph confronts us with a spatial conceit as extraordinary and as exciting as one of Borromini's or Balthasar Neumann's fantasies and reminds us, despite the difference of idiom, of the affinity between the two great architectural expressions of the same faith, the Gothic and the Baroque. The external aspect of the Wells Lady Chapel vault, which assumes the shape of a small dome, underlines the parallel. We are looking from the choir and are sufficiently distanced from the great east window (with the row of feeble twentieth-century figures beneath it) and from the high altar to appreciate the sudden change from the right-angled discipline of the choir to the shifting diagonals of the multi-shafted vista of the eastern projection beyond the arches. Retrochoir, side chapels and Lady Chapel, each differently planned, merge in a design charged with mystery. The Lady Chapel is octagonal but by a subtle play upon axial views it becomes part of the elongated hexagon of the retrochoir, the angles of which are marked by clustered shafts. The architect who, according to John Harvey, may have been William Joy in ca. 1320–40, has drawn the choir into the composition by using the two piers of the central arch as a steadying element in the composition.

At the period to which this wall belongs, Gloucester had not become a cathedral and it was under Abbot Thoky (1318–29) that the south aisle, which had begun to lean outwards, was rebuilt. This wall offers a most attractive display of Decorated art – buttresses (shoring up the defective structure) square on plan, niched and pinnacled and with sculpture in the niches, ball-flower thickly outlining every shape, and the nervous, linear pattern of the tracery, which, entirely different in feeling and rhythm from the flowing repeat patterns of the Wells Lady Chapel windows, takes the unusual form of a butterfly.

127

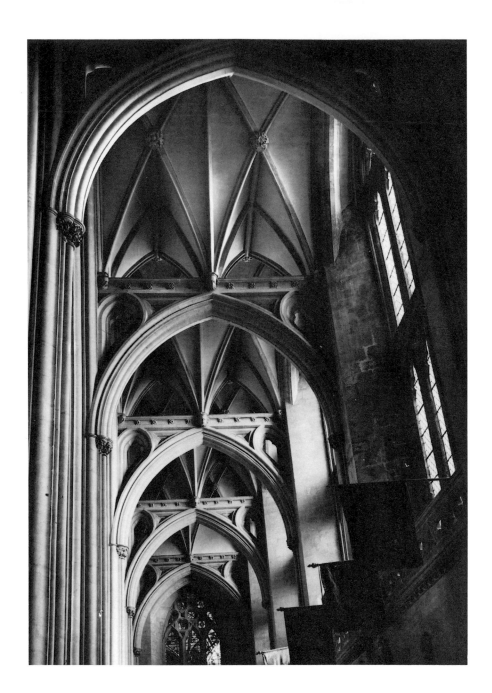

We have already seen one of the most original creations of a period of remarkable fertility of invention, at Wells (p. 126). The imaginative freedom of the architecture of this time is equally manifest in the contemporary chancel of Bristol, then an Augustinian monastery. The aisle is part of a rare design in which, as in German hall churches, nave and aisles are of the same height, so there is no clerestory and the aisle vaults are splendidly lit by lofty traceried windows. The ingenious horizontal struts resting on transverse arches take the thrust and transfer it to external buttresses. The struts accentuate the division into bays, and call attention to the artist's most arresting idea: to roof each bay, with its own energetic and acuminated ribbed vault shooting up from the centre and sides of each strut. The amazing concentration of pointed shapes is balanced by the scale and form of the mouchette motif filling each spandrel.

This unique building owed its existence to the determination and generosity of Abbot Knowle, for the monastery was so impoverished that the canons were begging for food from the citizens.

WELLS: *The Crossing from the South Transept*

The important part played by the spandrel mouchettes in the Bristol aisle (*opposite*) is paralleled by that of the giant roundels in the astonishing strainer arches which were an unknown master mason's response in 1338 to the threat that the crossing tower, only completed in 1322, might collapse. The aisle vaults at Bristol and these giant arches have more in common, for both designs rely for their impact on the idea of a pointed shape standing in its head on a pointed arch. The strainer arches can also be seen as two intersecting ogee curves. We have seen the effect of one of these audacious gargantuan structures in the nave (p. 71). But there support on the east side of the crossing comes from the pulpitum. Here we look through two of these yawning scissor-arches to a vista which, meshed by their monster curves, become surreal.

Abbot Thoky, a close friend of Edward II, received the king's corpse at Gloucester three months after the brutal murder on September 21, 1327, at Berkeley Castle. Modern scholarship repudiates the hitherto accepted story that the Abbots of Malmesbury, Kingswood and Bristol had refused to bury the king out of fear of Queen Isabella and her lover Mortimer. The funeral at which the far from disconsolate Isabella, the 'she-wolf' was present, was of great magnificence: the hearse was painted with golden leopards, the heraldic beasts of England, and upon it stood figures of the four evangelists with gilded censing angels.

Popular revulsion against the horrifying crime soon made a martyr of the king and his monument became a source of vast income. It was erected between 1327 and 1331 by the dead man's young son Edward III; so the genius who designed it was probably one of the royal masons employed by Edward at Westminster. The inspired architecture of the fantastically pinnacled and diagonally buttressed canopy is not the subject of the photograph, which concentrates on the striking, unforgettable beauty of the idealised head and the tenderness and finely realised pose of the angelic supporter. Like Marlowe's masterpiece it invests the tragic tale of the king's incompetence, weakness and dreadful death with universal significance.

The image is one of the earliest to be carved in alabaster, a stone which had only just come into use for funeral effigies. The chief centre of the alabaster trade was Nottingham, and there are records of works at York and Lincoln, but for sculptures as important as royal monuments the material would have been sent to a London mason. The texture of the alabaster, almost translucent, is most effectively contrasted here with the Cotswold stone of the canopy and the dark Purbeck marble of the tomb chest.

On the left. CANTERBURY: *Heraldic Beast on the tomb of Edward the Black Prince in the Trinity Chapel*

Opposite. CANTERBURY: *Effigy of Edward the Black Prince in the Trinity Chapel*

Edward, the eldest son of Edward III and Philippa of Hainault, has only been known as the Black Prince since the sixteenth century. The name was probably suggested by his black armour. He excelled both on the battlefield and the jousting ground and fought at Crécy when he was only sixteen. He played an essential part with his father in the founding of the Order of the Garter in 1348. His romantic marriage on 1361 to his cousin Countess Joan, the Fair Maid of Kent (p. 134) enhanced his reputation in chivalric society and endeared him to the populace. When to this is added his magnanimous treatment of King John of France, who became his prisoner at Poitiers, it is not surprising that Froissart called him 'the flower of chivalry of all the world'. The Prince was also a patron of the arts: he recognised the talent of such masons as William Helpston,

Robert and Thomas of Gloucester and John Tyryngton, whom he took into his service; and Henry Yeveley, who was to be the designer of the glorious nave of Canterbury (p. 140), was described as early as 1359 as the Prince's mason. His bequests to Canterbury, which included manuscripts, vestments, ivories and church plate, testify to his discriminating eye. He was associated with Canterbury from his childhood when Prior Hathbrand was his tutor; and his instructions for his funeral procession and burial there were precisely stated in his will written in French and dated June 7, 1376, the day before his death, aged forty six. He had asked to be buried in his chantry in the crypt but the chapter decided that so illustrious a prince should lie close to the shrine of St Thomas Becket. The funeral procession, however, which took place on September 5, 1376,

was carried out according to his will, the bier preceded by 'two destriers covered with our arms and two armed men in our arms and in our helm', one for war and one 'for peace with our badges of ostrich plumes'. Archbishop Simon of Sudbury (1375–81) conducted the funeral service.

The effigy, which is not a portrait, is cast in gilt-latten, and though the pose is stiff, for the figure is 'all armed in steel for battle' in accordance with the Prince's will, it is charged with energy: the detail is as vivid and as incredibly meticulous as that of the Southwell leaves (p. 112), while the alert watchful animal supporting the feet (a cat but for the paws) has greater haunting intensity of life than many of the visitors who press about the tomb. The sculptor must have calculated the effect of the long pointed sollerets shooting up like horns behind the devilish feline face. The

Prince's armour is that of the time of his death. He wears a steel bassinet (the point of which is hidden in the photograph) from which the head mail or camail depends, and the gauntlets are of the type which are embossed at the knuckles, contract at the wrist and bell out in a cuff. The rivets round the edge of the cuff held the cuff of the leather lining-glove in place. These gauntlets are exact replicas of those actually worn by the Prince and which, with his helm, shield and jupon, originally hung above his tomb. All the achievements have now been replaced by copies, while the originals are presented in a show case.

The sculptor of the effigy may have been John Orchard who made six angels for the tomb of the Black Prince's mother (d. 1369) and to whom the bronze-gilt effigy of Edward III (d. 1377) in Westminster Abbey is attributed.

On the left. CANTERBURY: *Boss in the Black Prince's Chantry.*

The rich chiaroscuro of the photograph revives the former splendour of the chapel, described by Erasmus just before the Reformation as more beautiful than the famed shrine of Our Lady of Walsingham. When he saw it the suns and stars painted on the vault were still bright, and the centre of every sun was a convex silver mirror reflecting the light of countless candles. They were soon to be destroyed, together with the silver statue of the Virgin, now replaced by a seventeenth-century Portuguese sculpture. We look at it across the alabaster effigy of the fashionably dressed Lady de Mohun, for whom masses were being said in 1370 although she did not die until 1404. The Romanesque spiralling columns survive from the Norman crypt, this eastern part of which was transformed in the second half of the fourteenth century by the stone screens which now completely fill the arched openings. The design, slender verticals terminating in elongated trefoils and quatrefoils and overlaid by a lavishly decorated and unusually steeply gabled arcade, is an enchanting example of the inventiveness of the period.

The south side of this part of the crypt was enriched at the same time. In 1362 the Black Prince endowed two altars in gratitude for the papal dispensation which enabled him to marry his cousin. They were dedicated to Our Lady and the Holy Trinity, and were maintained by two chantry priests. The Chantry Chapel was given an elaborate lierne vault with vigorous bosses so deeply carved they are almost in the round. They are also remarkable for their precise detail. The boss shown here is thought to be a portrait of Joan, Princess of Wales, and, unlike her husband's effigy, it is almost certainly a portrait. The extraordinary square headdress, the 'nebuly', composed of closely placed frills and with a hood behind it, was fashionable from ca. 1350.

LINCOLN: *a stall misericord*

The stalls of monastic and cathedral churches, and sometimes those of parish churches, have tip-up seats called misericords, a concession to human frailty, for the clergy, forced to stand for long hours of devotion, could sit on the tipped-up ledges of the hinged seats. The undersides are usually carved, and for a number of reasons they are sources of special pleasure and interest: many of them are perfectly preserved because of their protected position. The sculptors rarely chose religious subjects and so present us with a vast range of scenes from everyday life, folklore, fables and proverbs, the style and execution of which vary as much as the themes.

The author of this finely carved and composed relief of a knight falling from his horse pierced by an arrow may, in the view of Dr Harvey, have been the great carpenter Hugh Herland. The knight's armour, rendered with remarkable fidelity of detail, closely resembles that of the Black Prince, and so suggests a date of ca. 1370. The carving has a near counterpart in Cologne Cathedral. There was a good deal of interchange between the two cathedrals during the reigns of Edward II and Edward III, so the resemblance may be more than a coincidence.

CHICHESTER: *a stall misericord*

The stall whose seat is enlivened on its underside by this relief of a dancer and musician is on the north side of the choir and the canon who occupied it was a prebendary of Somerley. Whereas the knight on the opposite page is the sophisticated work of a highly accomplished artist, this wonderfully spontaneous expression of vivid life and movement is an engaging piece of folk art. It immortalises a moment of ecstasy when the viol player, dancing as he plays, is about to kiss his nimble, curvetting partner.

The central image of the misericord is usually balanced by two supporters or ears which here take the form of pigs' heads. The Lincoln knight is flanked by wyverns.

The elaborate Winchester stalls, which are among the earliest and finest of the considerable number of ecclesiastical wood furnishings surviving from the fourteenth century, are imaginatively conceived, as the photograph shows, in the form of a double screen. Steep, crocketted gables rise in front of arched and intricate back panels supported by attenuated shafts. The spandrels of the back panels are closely carved with vines and foliage, already beginning to resemble the knobbly leaves of the Ely Lady Chapel (p. 125), with animals and with this figure of a smiling falconer. The gifted artist was William Lyngwode, a carpenter from the Bishop of Norwich's manor at Blofield in Norfolk. In a letter dated 1308 (quoted in the *Archaeological Journal* of 1927) Bishop Woodlock of Winchester writes to the Bishop of Norwich asking if Lyngwode might be allowed to go on staying at Winchester until his work was completed.

ELY: *detail of choir stalls on the North side*

We have already glimpsed the cusped and ogee detail of the high-niched Ely stalls, as well as the Belgian reliefs added by Scott when he tidied up and moved the furniture (p. 123). The stalls date from ca. 1341–2 and, as has been mentioned, are ascribed to William Hurle. Instead of showing the canopies or one of the numerous popular misericords the photograph reveals a less obvious detail, the beautiful curving movement and carving of the arm rests. The figure of the zestful woman with the legs of a lioness is typical of the human abnormalities derived from bestiaries in which medieval artists delighted.

139

IV
Changing
Horizons

AT THE TIME when the great nave shown on the opposite page was built (1379–1405) the unified and intricate structure of medieval society and its identification with the Church were still, it seemed, secure. Profoundly disturbing events had threatened that structure during the very years when Henry Yeveley was working at Canterbury. The Archbishop who had donated 3,000 marks towards the cost of rebuilding the Norman nave, and who longed to see it completed, was murdered by Wat Tyler's men and, as was briefly mentioned, elements of social and religious revolt had been inflamed by anarchical preachers like Wyclif and by the sermons of itinerant friars disseminating ideas of apostolic poverty and evangelism. A sense of impending disaster was intensified by recurrent plague and the sight of decaying towns – the population of Lincoln sank at one point to 200 and at Winchester in 1430 there were 997 empty houses. Yet for a short period at the opening of the fifteenth century radical movements, political, social and religious, were successfully countered by increased solidarity between the ecclesiastical and secular hierarchies. The ordered picture of the universe created by centuries of synthesising thought and faith was still intact. So there is no hint of unrest or catastrophic change in Henry Yeveley's splendidly confident design. Indeed it is possible to see it as the glorious culmination of the whole progress of cathedral architecture and the most successful expression in stone of medieval theology and philosophy. The formidable, heavy Norman cathedral churches rigidly divided into parts had advanced towards ever lighter, more airy, more aspiring and above all more highly organised harmonies. Finally, at Canterbury the nave pre-

CANTERBURY: *The Nave*

sents a completely unified design which the eye accepts as one great whole. No longer are arcade, triforium and clerestory seen as separate stages in the elevation: the composition moves directly upwards, its verticality stressed rather than impeded by the delicate annulets encircling the vaulting shafts. Together with William of Wynford's brilliant conversion of the Norman nave at Winchester, Yeveley's creation is one of the last as it is one of the most flawless materialisations in cathedral form of the Heavenly Kingdom.

But for all the exquisite logic of its parts, for all its originality and majesty, the Canterbury nave is less exciting and expresses less intensity of feeling than the interiors of Wells, Lincoln or Exeter. The ineffable grace, the youth and vigour of the two former, the mellow beauty of the last, are wanting. The subtle balance between the material and the spiritual in cathedral architecture of the thirteenth and fourteenth centuries could not endure any more than the burning faith and intellectual enthusiasm upon which it depended. The vision was beginning to fade. Change could not be stayed. Between 1450 and 1550 its pace accelerated until it ended in what amounted to a revolution overwhelming both the theology and the art of the Gothic world. Though the actual collapse did not come immediately there were many indications of its approach. No more than a few inadequate generalisations and meagre descriptions can be attempted here, but they may suffice to recall the climate of the age in which the subjects of the next twenty or so photographs were created.

The apparent strength of the ecclesiastical body and the relative ease with which it had seemed to quell opposition in the form of Lollardry were illusory. The passing of a statute, *de Heretico Comburendo*, under Henry IV to revive the power of the Church to burn and to persecute heretics was surely a symptom of insecurity. One of the martyrs was Archbishop Scrope of York, executed by the king for his unorthodox views, and it may have been on account of this that such resentment was felt at York when, two years after the Archbishop's death, Henry IV sent his own mason, William of Colchester, to take charge of the rebuilding after the central tower fell, that the local workmen made an attempt on the master's life. These events took place against a background of dramatic and disquieting change. The narrow limits of the medieval world which made its thoroughly integrated faith entirely acceptable were breaking down. The developments which preceded and made possible the spectacular happenings of the reign of Henry VIII are familiar to everyone. The whole medieval cosmos together with institutions which seemed unalterable though sometimes questioned, and beliefs which despite learned controversy were held to be unchallengeable, was dissolving. As the vision of classical antiquity became clearer and more detailed, it illumined horizons beyond the confines of the Gothic heaven and hell; and with every voyage of Columbus and Cabot, of Diaz and Vasco the material universe was expanding. Printing, invented by Kloster of Haarlem in 1438 and introduced to England by Caxton in 1477, and copperplate engraving, which became popular a little later in the century, replaced the monastic scribe and illuminator. The stream of books pouring from the presses of every European country encouraged mental contacts and possibilities of learning hitherto unimaginable. And of course the press was henceforth to be the weapon of religious dissent. Caxton printed and published more than one hundred books, among them Chaucer, Malory's *Morte d'Arthur*, Gower, Lydgate and his own translations of Cicero and of Aesop's fables.

The decades preceding the Reformation were marked by other less obviously threatening changes which were just as influential in bringing it about. Fine houses such as that of Grevel in Chipping Campden, and brasses like that of John Browne and his wife in All Saints, Stamford, announce the rise of a new merchant middle class as wealthy as the nobility, many of whom had disappeared on the battlefields of the Wars of the Roses. They supported a new money economy inimical to the old order of a feudal society dominated by the Church. The secular interests and pronounced worldliness of prelates were of particular significance in a grasping and acquisitive society. Although they were assured of an income from episcopal revenues most bishops held high secular office and often played a prominent part in politics. The trend was well established by the close of the fourteenth century when as many as thirteen bishops were preoccupied with secular matters; the Bishop of Salisbury was Chancellor of Lancaster and both Archbishop Sudbury and William of Wykeham were Chancellor of the Realm. The grand finale of the practice of appointing bishops to an office of such great authority was the career of Wolsey, a magnification on a colossal scale of the pride, greed and luxury of bishops which inevitably encouraged the anti-clerical revolution.

Whether or not they were actively engaged in affairs of state outside the Church, fifteenth-century bishops were obsessed by legal and constitutional questions. The period was characterised by a striking shift of interest from theology to law as an intellectual discipline. The Inns of Court became the chief centres of training for the sons of landowners – Thomas More, Sir Thomas Eliot, Audley, Rich and Cromwell were all lawyers – and the majority of deans, among them the reforming Colet of St Paul's, and residential canons at the time of Henry VII were lawyers. Their overriding concern is reflected in the additions made at this time to cathedral libraries. The great collections of the works of St Augustine, Jerome, Gregory and Bede, of the Latin classics, of psalters, missals and breviaries were joined by source books on civil law and by the voluminous, often querulous, commentaries of jurists who set more store on pecuniary than on moral and aesthetic values. Prolonged disputes and litigations are part of the history of every cathedral at this time.

Sometimes dissension led to actual violence within the sanctuary itself. Dean John Macworth's quarrel with his chapter at Lincoln is a celebrated example. His aim was to magnify the authority and the material benefits of his position at the expense of the chapter. The struggle ended only with his death, and on one occasion Macworth's servants, acting on his orders, set upon the chancellor during the recitation of the divine office, pulled him from his stall and beat him. This scandalous incident took place in the choir built by the saintly Hugh of Avalon. Such direction of energy to purely personal ends was one expression of the increasing assertion of individuality. This is perhaps most clearly manifested in the ostentation and fantasy of fifteenth-century chantry chapels (pp. 174, 175 and 177). It is interesting that at the Dissolution, which was in part a great affirmation of individuality, chantry chapels were not at once suppressed but outlived the monasteries for almost a decade.

The sepulchral effigy within the chantry chapel or resting on a richly carved tomb chest in the cathedral aisles, often beneath a sumptuous canopy, assumed a new importance. The head was no longer idealised like that of Edward II, but, when the subject was a monarch or a great ecclesiastic, a portrait, immortalising the deceased. The tomb of Henry IV (p. 171) confronts us with a troubled, heavy face, frowning, bearded but shaven-cheeked, with very short hair worn in a roll beneath the royal crown. We cannot doubt that we are looking at the treacherous Henry Bolingbroke. The sympathetic head of Abbot Newbery at Bristol (p. 172) is equally and instantly recognised as a likeness. At the same time the fashionable details of dress are rendered more meticulously than at any other time in the Middle Ages and there is usually a flourish of heraldic shields proclaiming the subject's ancestry and connections. The tomb of Archbishop Warham at Canterbury, made on the eve of the Reformation, but still fully Gothic, with a huge triple canopy above a comfortably reclining figure, is one of the most resplendent of all. There are few if any representatives in cathedral churches of the new professional and merchant classes, who were making sure of their memorials in parish churches, but tombs of the nobility are conspicuous even when the effigies are standardised designs made in the workshops. At Ripon, on entering the north transept, the eye is at once drawn to the tall, shield-adorned tomb chest of Sir Thomas Markenfeld and his wife despite the arresting character of some of the later monuments in that arm of the cathedral.

Cathedrals had always played a major role in education. A. F. Leach, writing in the early years of the present century, traced the whole of the English school system back to the grammar school of Canterbury Cathedral, first mentioned in 631. Fifteenth-century bishops were often more interested in the building of schools and colleges than in their cathedrals, and while no cathedral was founded, new schools and colleges with their fine chapels and quadrangular plans abounded. Among those closely associated with cathedrals were William of Wykeham's two great institutions at Winchester and Oxford, Bishop Alcock's Jesus College, Cambridge, Wolsey's Cardinal College (Christ Church, Oxford), Rotherham founded by Archbishop Rotherham of York, and All Souls, Oxford, founded by Archbishop Chicheley. At least two of these colleges were built with proceeds from the early suppression of religious houses; and even if, as in the case of Wykeham's and Chicheley's foundations, students were required to attend a daily mass, it was a soul mass for the founder. The emphasis in every case was on academic rather than religious education, and in every case the teaching of Latin was the basis of the curriculum. It was then, of course, a real medium of speech and an essential

CANTERBURY: *Entrance to the Pulpitum, North side*

requirement in any professional career.

Amid the gloomier aspects of the pre-Reformation decades the establishment of England's unique system of education, springing though it partly did from the prevailing desire for self-aggrandisement, stands out as a noble endeavour. It held out a promise of continuity and revival even while the schools themselves were training scholarly laymen who would be active in the great upheaval shortly to take place.

Another and brilliant manifestation of the continuing vitality of the cathedral as an institution is the great flowering of liturgical music at the very moment when the liturgical tradition of the past was threatened. Elaborate choral compositions were written for masses of all kinds and for all the occasions of the liturgical year by a galaxy of composers as diverse as the eminent and mysterious John Dunstable, who opened this golden age of English music, Richard Hygens, master of the choristers at Wells in 1479, Robert Fayrfax (b. 1465), organist at St Albans and author of *O Quam glorifica*, a five-part Mass of the purest linear pattern, his associates William

Cornish and the famous John Taverner, Christopher Tye, organist at Ely, and Thomas Tallis who began as a choir boy at St Paul's and who is linked to the post-Reformation period not only because he adapted to the needs of the changed ritual but because he was the master of William Byrd.

The concern of the age with personalities and the consequent stimulation of self-regard were not without effect on cathedral architects and designers. Names multiply in the late fourteenth and fifteenth centuries, some of them associated with great masterpieces. Dr John Harvey unearthed enough information about Henry Yeveley to write a full-length biography, we know something of the lives of William Wynford, Stephen Lote, John Wastell, Reginald Ely, Robert Everard and William Orchard, and many of the fifteenth-century works shown here can be attributed to particular artists. Sometimes an artist could not resist leaving a memorial of himself in the form of a carved likeness in the building on which he had been working. Henry Yeveley's portrait appears on a boss in the Canterbury cloisters, and the alert person fixing us with his keen watchful eye as we prepare to mount the northern stair in the hollow of the pulpitum may well be Stephen Lote who designed the elaborate westward facing elevation for Prior Thomas Chillenden (d. 1411) to encase the earlier pulpitum built under Prior Eastry. Perhaps the sculptor was John Massingham, a Canterbury man who carved the figures on the screen. However, much less is known of these important artists than of the bishops, priors and deans who employed them. It is possible that even as late as the fifteenth century cathedral architects and craftsmen were conscious of working for a cause infinitely more significant than their own reputations. Nevertheless, changes were taking place in the building trade which point to the emergence of a different spirit. Conditions were beginning to approximate to those of modern times. Shortages of labour caused by the plague led to a more rigorous organisation of masons and craftsmen and also necessitated greater mobility on the part of masons. Altered social conditions were encouraging a switch from church to lay patronage and the commercial development of the trade. Overtime and piece-work had been introduced before the end of the fifteenth century and firms of mason-contractors were specialising in the production of details and ornaments ready cut and of sculpture carved from stock patterns. These businessmen-contractors, however, might still, unlike their later equivalents, be distinguished artists. William Orchard at Headington Quarry near Oxford was an architect of genius. Thomas Drawswerd of York, on the other hand, head of a large firm of carvers who were asked to estimate for the tomb of Henry VII, was mayor of York and a member of Parliament, and the actual carving was probably carried out by his shopmen.

What is abundantly clear is that there was no decline in skill. The small selection of work shown in the following pages, the roofs of Norwich and of Christchurch, Oxford, the wonderful choir of Gloucester, the amazing stalls at Manchester, the tomb of Henry IV and Queen Joan, the cloisters of Gloucester, Canterbury and Worcester, the finely carved ornament of the chantries of Bishops Fox and Alcock and of Cardinal Beaufort, the exquisite interior of Bell Harry, all bear witness to the astonishing dexterity of the artists. But the chantries with their rich vaults and stone panelling are more like ornately-appointed rooms than chapels, and breathe an air of aristocratic luxury. Here, as sometimes in the work of sculptors in wood, the medium of some of the most startlingly original creations of the period, skill and ingenuity are used, as at Manchester, in the service of complexity for its own sake. Occasionally a slackening of inspiration and a loss of vigour is revealed by monotonous repetition, as in the central tower of Gloucester where the upper stage exactly matches the lower. This tower, like most others in this age of tower building, including the tower of Bell Harry at Canterbury and the central tower of York, was never intended to carry a spire. The omission of this feature, which never fulfilled a structural requirement but was of profound symbolic importance, is particularly revealing of the tenor of the age. The one fifteenth-century cathedral spire, that of Norwich, is equally revealing for, built in an earlier style, it was prompted by an understanding of the past which was a new phenomenon. The happiest example of this interest occurs at Wells in the west towers William Wynford built to complete the facade (p. 69). His design shows not a trace of incongruity: the towers merge unobtrusively with what was there already.

The new trends in both thought and architecture set in very early owing to the emergence of brilliant masons responding intuitively to worldly attitudes and owing to the existence, through the former generosity of Edward III, of the resources needed for extravagant projects. The first manifestation of changing habits of mind is seen at Gloucester. The choir with its enormous canted window has the atmosphere of a stately secular mansion. The window, like the west window at Winchester, is so great in scale that glass entirely takes the place of wall; and yet neither of these giant compositions arouses that irrefutable, utterly convincing sense of a spiritual dimension experienced when standing in the shafts of light streaming through the north transept lancets at York. At both Gloucester and Winchester the principal mullions rise straight to the containing arch without a break, but the vast breadth of the window so diminishes the effect of the strong vertical accent that there is no upward rush. The light of those huge windows is terrestrial, and at Gloucester, for all its opulence, the choir is earthbound, the temper cool.

It was in the cloisters at Gloucester that the purely English device of fan vaulting made its first appearance. It was as though the branching, aspiring ribs of a vault like that of the Exeter nave had been subjected to pressure causing the roof to flatten and the ribs to expand yet further to form inverted semi-cones or fans. The panelled decoration of the great fans varies from the wiry precision of the ceiling of the retrochoir at Peterborough to the laciness of the Bell Harry interior. The cathedral examples of the device are the work of masters, among whom John Wastell, the probable author of both the vaults just mentioned, was outstanding. But because it was standardised in all its parts, the fan vault could be mass produced, and because the rib and panel design was illusory, the complete work being cut from the solid block, it threatened the whole Gothic concept of the rib vault. All the same, nothing can dim the spectacular beauty and ingenuity of the original conceit or lessen the impact of that related and equally astonishing structure, the pendant vault, of which the only cathedral example is the marvellous roof of the choir at Oxford where fans merge into lierne star patterns and rise from lanterns of stone suspended in the air.

The fan vault is not known on the Continent, but the same urge towards elaboration and opulence was at work, and it may be rewarding to glance for a moment at one or two of the late Gothic works in other countries. The undulating octopus-like forms rippling over the vault of the Annenkirche at Annaberg; the singular net vaulting in the monastery church of Belem, Portugal; the strange tree forms in the Chapel of Ladislas II in Prague Cathedral, where the ribs resemble branches from which a tracery of twigs overspreads mighty pendants as they do also in the Lady Chapel of Caudebec, Normandy, they all seem grotesque and tortuous beside the clearly articulated and formalised fan. And by comparison with such exotic and extravagant buildings as the excessively intricate front of Rouen Cathedral, the spire of Freiburg composed entirely of tracery, or the gargantuan, half hexagonal and fantastically tricked-out porch of Nôtre Dame, Alençon, the whole Perpendicular style seems to stand apart from that of the rest of Europe in its controlled serenity. Instead of the frenzy of the late Flamboyant style there is a stiffness and an angularity in the design of window, arch and panelled wall; and the lavish ornament of chantry chapel, pulpitum and stall is subdued by severity of line. While a loss of mystery and spirituality and an undertone of materialism is common to both the extraordinary developments on the Continent and to Perpendicular architecture, the uniqueness of the English forms remains and seems to body forth the uniqueness of the Church which was to be established in consequence of the Reformation.

Opposite. GLOUCESTER: *The Choir, looking East*

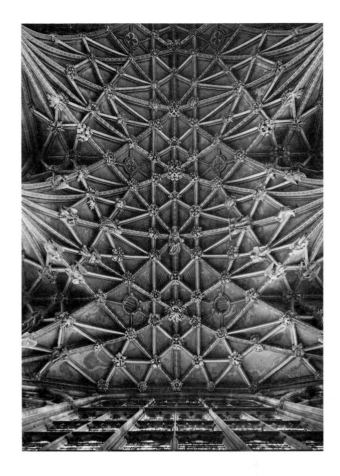

On the right. GLOUCESTER: *The Choir Vault*

The choir of the Abbey Church of St Peter, as it then was, is very roughly contemporary with the rebuilding of Exeter. The interior into which we are looking was begun in 1337 under Abbot Staunton, and completed between 1351 and 1367 under Abbot Horton. It is an incredibly skilful conversion, for the structure is a mask sheathing the original Norman wall surfaces. It was financed by offerings at the tomb of Edward II. It is as sumptuous as the nave of the Devon cathedral, but it is expressive of an altogether changed way of thinking. The atmosphere and visual character of the stately building are not determined by the richness of the ogee-arched stall canopies, bowed down with the heaviness and abundance of their crowded, metal-like detailing, nor by the complexity and charm of the amazing tierceron and lierned web of the vault, but by the stern rejection of the flowing curve, and the rigid verticality of the panelled walls and the enormous east window, the largest in the country. The thin vaulting shafts soar aloft in an unbroken sweep, the mullions of the windows continuing the lines of the stone panels. The walls are seen not as masonry pierced by openings, but as a uniform system of panels, no matter whether of stone or of glass. Thus the east window, which completely fills the wall, is conceived as a series of panels, divided vertically into three parts by emphatic mullions. The design gives it something of the look of a giant transparent triptych and this impression is strengthened by the fact that the window is canted to withstand wind pressure.

This is the earliest window to show a tiered arrangement of full-length figures. The theme is the Coronation of the Virgin, but the panels present historical personages, including Edward II, and the lights under the lowest tier display roundels and heraldic shields which, popular throughout the Middle Ages, had passed into ecclesiastical use as decorations for tombs and memorials and as the mark of donors. The glass is white, blue, yellow and red, but the general effect is cool and silvery and without mystery. The high altar and reredos were designed in 1873 by Sir George Gilbert Scott, who was careful to base the details of his little turrets and canopies on those of the setting.

This part of the Minster was an extension, financed by Archbishop Thoresby and carried out in 1361–70, of the Norman choir, which was itself replaced in 1380–1400. The architect planned it to harmonise with the nave, but its general character – the rectilinear emphasis, the panelling above the arcade arches – is Perpendicular. The huge east window, donated by Walter Skirland, Bishop of Durham, a composition of three major lights, each divided into three, is, however, filled with motifs such as leaf and heart shapes and mouchettes which are still Decorated in feeling.

Eighty-one of the dramatic and superbly drawn stained-glass panels, the work of John Thornton of Coventry, illustrate the Revelation of St John, a unique representation of the theme in stained glass. The artist's monogram and the date, 1408, appear in the tracery. Thornton was paid 4s. a week, £5 extra for each year's work, and an extra £10 for completing the window in three years.

The wooden vault and the imitation Perpendicular screen behind the altar were designed by Robert Smirke in the 1830s.

Perpendicular elements are as much in evidence in the exterior of the York east end as they are within – in the dominance of panelling and severe linear verticality – but echoes of the Decorated style survive in the crocketted ogival gable and the dazzling array of sharp little gables and spirelets, the outer pair crowning pretty octagonal turrets. The row of closely set heads beneath the big east window is a novel and charming variation on the Norman theme of corbel table heads.

The photograph brings out the lively contrast between the east end and the strange shape of the octo-pyramidal Chapter House in the background, both towering over the town houses. The important-looking building in the foreground on the right, with a half-timber oversail above a stone ground floor (restored by Temple Moore), is St William's College. Originally a prebendal house it became a chantry college for twenty-four priests in 1461, by which time the altars in the cathedral had much increased in number. The College was founded by Bishop Neville of Exeter and his brother Richard, Earl of Warwick.

149

The massively proportioned, lantern-like central tower of York was begun early in the fifteenth century after the collapse of the original tower in 1407. Work continued until 1472. The designer was William of Colchester, who was Henry IV's master mason at Westminster Abbey. York had been hard hit by recurrent outbreaks of the plague, and the dean and chapter were forced to look outside the region for architects and craftsmen. John Thornton, the glass painter from Coventry has already been cited. The York craftsmen and labourers strongly resented the appointment of master masons from the south, especially if they were king's men, for it was only two years since Henry IV had executed Archbishop Scrope who was revered as a martyr in Yorkshire. William of Colchester and his assistant William Waddeswyk were brutally assaulted and injured, Waddeswyk seriously. But both survived and remained in office.

Like so much cathedral rebuilding, Colchester's central tower enormously enhances the character and atmosphere of the building. The light flowing down into the crossing transforms the temperate majesty of the interior. The lierne vault at which we are looking is, surprisingly, of timber, and the fabric accounts show that it was painted blue, vermilion, white and ochre and gilded. The carver of the bosses was James Dam, who Dr Harvey suggests may have been a Flemish immigrant from Damme, near Bruges. The figures in the foreground of the photograph are those of Kings Stephen, Henry II and Richard I, three of the fifteen statues of kings adorning the west front of the pulpitum. This splendid screen was the work between 1475 and 1505 of William Hyndeley, another master mason from the south. He was persuaded to move from Norwich and settle in York with his family and household goods. James Dam was carving 175 crockets for the pulpitum in 1479 and a few years later David Dam, John Hintley and William Bushel were making crockets at sixteen pence per score and gargoyles at 1s. a piece. In 1498 and 1499 nine masons were employed on the pulpitum together with a sculptor, John Fodergall. With their seaweed-like hair and individual lineaments and poses the statues make a lively impression, and the boldness with which they are executed contrasts with the fine detail and proliferating motifs of the high canopies above them. The tiny angels leaning forward under the parapet above the canopies are plaster intruders inserted by Bernasconi at the beginning of the nineteenth century. A few years later in 1830 Canon W. V. Vernon urged the removal of the pulpitum as 'an excrescence of late origin and in an incongruous style'. Robert Smirke, the official architect, did not support the Canon but proposed moving and re-erecting the pulpitum to the east of the crossing. Fortunately both suggestions came to nothing.

Opposite. YORK MINSTER
Screen and interior of central tower

The eastern and southern walls of the central tower of the collegiate church, as it then was, collapsed during a violent thunderstorm in the summer of 1458 and wrecked part of the choir and the aisle of the south transept. Some time elapsed before the work of restoration was begun, and while the choir was out of use canons and vicars choral celebrated divine worship in an apsidal chapel. A year after the disaster Archbishop Booth of York offered an indulgence of forty days to all who would contribute to the rebuilding of the tower. Rebuilding went on from ca. 1460 for the next fifteen years, and as late as 1477 the canons were donating half their emoluments towards the repairs. The plan was to encase the crossing piers in a sheath of new masonry in the form of shafts, and to replace each of the existing semicircular arches with a new steeply pointed arch. Only half the underpinning was completed, and this accounts for the disturbing lack of symmetry when one is looking east from the nave, while at the same time it affords a glimpse of medieval work in progress. The northwest pier on the left of the picture with the arch springing from it belongs to the late twelfth-century work of Archbishop Roger's mason. The tall clustered shafts on the right are part of the new uncompleted work masking the earlier pier. The eastern arch and piers show what the master mason intended: shafts, starker and more severe than those of the Canterbury nave, dating from more than half a century earlier, mounting aloft uninterrupted by a single fillet and supporting an unusual stilted arch suggestive of the orient.

The beautiful stone pulpitum was erected soon after the rebuilding of the tower and crossing. The composition, an ingenious play upon ogival forms – a central door surmounted by an ogee which, above the crown of the richly moulded opening, holds a sculptured Majesty with angels and which is flanked to left and right by four niches. These niches are crowned by steep, crocketted, narrow ogee gables with little ogee headed niches on either side of them, repeating on a diminished scale the pattern they themselves make. All the niches, small and large, are furnished with brackets and pedestals for images. The originals have all vanished and have been replaced by modern sculptures. The whole is surmounted by a cornice adorned with shields.

There is an odd feature on the east face of the pulpitum which must be described, although of course it is not visible in the photograph. It is a projection exhibiting a finely carved small wooden hand which, when the organ is played, moves up and down, beating time. The organ which has been in position since the seventeenth century was remodelled in 1872.

The pulpit in the foreground of the photograph, marble with bronze and silver Arts and Crafts style decoration, was the work of Henry Wilson in 1913.

Opposite. RIPON
Crossing and Pulpitum from the Nave

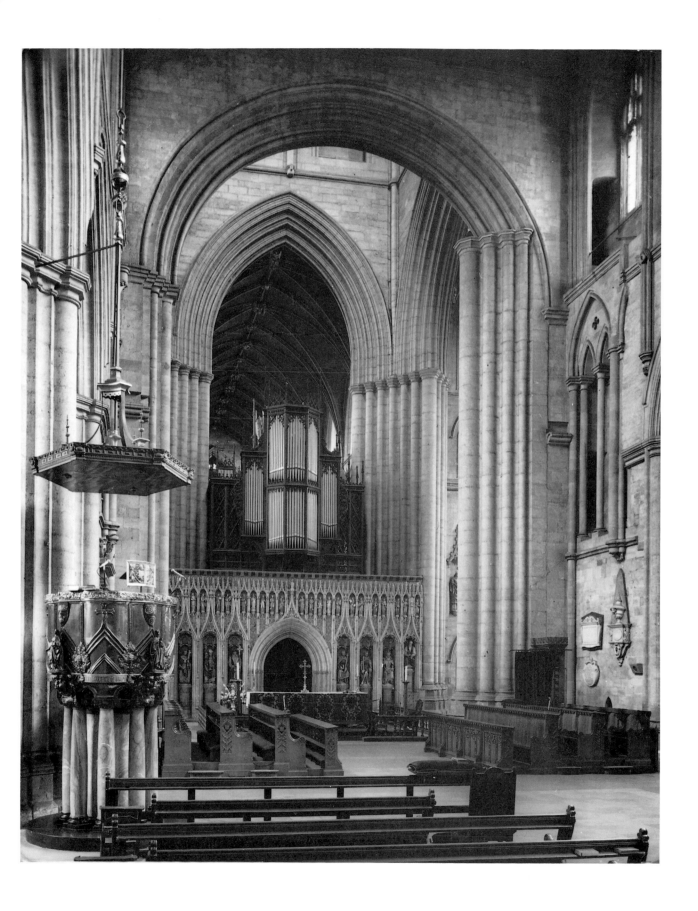

William Wynford the designer of this noble vista (though of course it was not open to the east end in the Middle Ages) had been a friend of his patron William of Wykeham for many years when he was asked to complete the remodelling of the Norman nave which Wykeham's predecessor, Bishop Edington, had inaugurated nearly thirty years earlier. Wykeham and Wynford had met at Windsor Castle when the Bishop was clerk of the works there and Wynford was master mason. A year or two later when William of Wykeham had become Provost of Wells Cathedral, Wynford was appointed consultant master mason. In 1372 Edward III granted the mason a pension for life, so he was able to please himself in his choice of work. Some years later he settled in Winchester. He is recorded as dining frequently with Wykeham, and from 1399 he was privileged to dine free every day at the prior's table. Wynford had prepared the magnificent designs for New College, Oxford, and Winchester College for the Bishop and had supervised the construction before starting work on the Cathedral nave. Bishop Edington had only made a small beginning at the west end and it is William Wynford's plan upon which the whole character of the nave depends. Wykeham died in 1404 at the age of eighty when work had been going on for ten years, but Wynford remained in charge under Cardinal Beaufort until the nave reached completion in 1414.

Like the choir at Gloucester the Winchester nave is a fantastically skilful conversion of a Norman building. Wynford has brilliantly retained the Norman vaulting shafts running uninterruptedly to the roof, and veiled the enormous piers to which they were originally attached by multiple fine mouldings all enhancing the vertical emphasis of the design. The vertical movement is however moderated by the square-framed panelling enclosing the tall arcade arches and the shallow panelled balconies that take the place of the Norman triforium. The dark, suggestive depths behind the meshes of the high-arching lierne vault impart a sense of mystery to the cool clarity of the grand elevations.

The romantic pinnacles of Scott's screen also contrast very effectively with the severity of Wynford's arcades and clerestory though the screen it replaced, a design of 1870 by William Garbett, architect to the Dean and Chapter, based on the west front, preserved the function of the medieval pulpitum of shutting off the eastern arm from the nave which Scott's screen does not. Garbett's screen took the place of Inigo Jones's fine classical pulpitum of 1637 which survives in part in the Archaeological Museum, Cambridge.

Opposite. WINCHESTER: *The Nave*

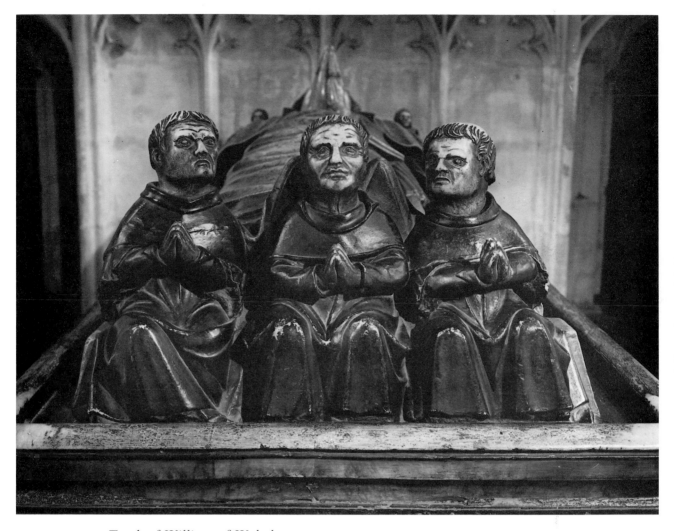

WINCHESTER: *Tomb of William of Wykeham*

The remarkable career of William of Wykeham is one of many examples in medieval history of advance through ability. Born in 1324 the son of a free peasant in the Hampshire village of Wickham, he became Chancellor of England and Bishop of Winchester by the time he was only just over forty, as well as holding many other church preferments. It was perhaps because he was conscious of his own lack of academic education that education became a passionate concern.

William of Wykeham founded two great innovatory seats of learning; New College, Oxford in 1379 and Winchester College in 1382, and his own house was always open to scholars. As a young man he had been clerk of the works for Edward III at Windsor Castle and the knowledge he acquired there was invaluable when he himself became a patron. He supervised every stage of his great building projects, the last of which was the rebuilding at his own expense of the nave of Winchester Cathedral, but, close on eighty, he died on September 28, 1404, before it was completed. The Bishop was buried in the chantry

chapel he had commissioned in 1394 and which was finished in 1403. The site Wykeham chose for it, half way down the nave on the south side, marked the spot where he had been wont to pray as a boy, and at the same time linked the monument with his architectural achievement. Only a month before he died he made arrangements for three monks to say mass three times daily at his tomb and it is upon lively caricatures of these monks that the sculptor of the effigy has set the Bishop's feet. The designer of the Chantry Chapel was William Wynford and although Wynford may well have been a sculptor as well as a master mason, the figure of Wykeham, which is of alabaster, was probably made in London. The strong, calm features appear to be taken from life but the crozier is not the one Wykeham bequeathed to New College, so the head may be a stock type. The accomplished modelling of head and hands contrasts with the feeble carving of the supporting angel which must be by another hand.

Members of the college Wykeham founded saved his tomb and chapel from mutilation at the time of the Reformation.

We are looking at a strange and complex image – a late Gothic spire set on a geometrically decorated Norman tower and a lofty chancel with huge windows and vigorously prancing buttresses rising high above a most curiously shaped chapel. There is another on the south-east side, and between the two is the St Saviour's Chapel of 1930 on the site of the former Lady Chapel.

The original wooden spire collapsed in a gale in 1362 and damaged the Norman apse clerestory. Both were rebuilt under Bishop Thomas Percy in the 1360s, the clerestory much raised and lit by tall four-light windows. In 1463 the fourteenth-century spire was struck by lightning and the wooden vault of the nave was burnt. Spires, as has been remarked, were not common in the late fifteenth century when an earthbound habit of mind prevailed, yet it was decided to rebuild. The slender tapering structure, perhaps the work of Robert Everard, with its tiers of alternating lucarnes and crocketted angles, recalls the style of fourteenth-century spires such as those of Oundle or King's Sutton, and was probably based on the design it replaced. The spire powerfully concentrates the disparate features of the whole building. It springs from the inner edges of the tower walls leaving room for a parapeted walk round the base from which scaffolding was set up during building operations. The battlements are ornamented with shields, and the crocketted spirelets at the angles are miniatures of the great central feature. The work was completed between ca. 1464 and 1472 and during that time Robert Everard vaulted the nave. The choir vault, the design of which continues that of the nave and which also replaced a timber structure, was rebuilt in ca. 1472–99 under Bishop Goldwell, a great builder. Like the spire and the nave vault it is ascribed to Robert Everard. The spreading ribs of these vaults recall those of Exeter dating from more than one and a half centuries earlier. But there is an important development: the ribs merge into a central lierne design of irregular star shapes. The design is close to the fan vault and is the precursor of the wonderful pendant vault of Oxford. It was in order to shift the weight of the roof from the walls with their large area of glass that the master mason built the bold flying buttresses which add so much to the visual impact of the cathedral.

Above. NORWICH: *Exterior from the East*

Opposite. NORWICH: *Choir Vault*

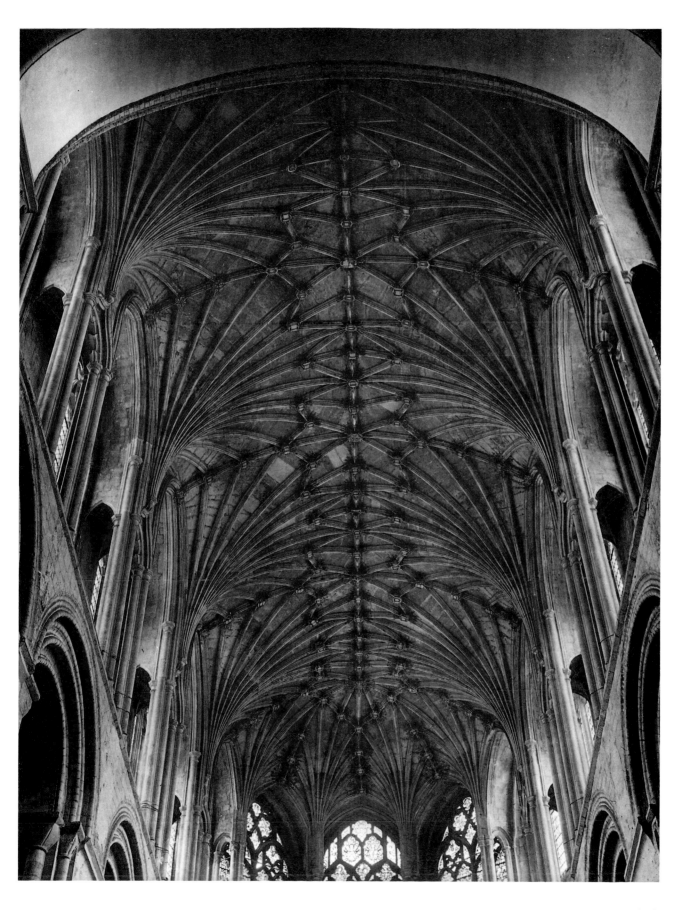

CANTERBURY: *Boss in the North-East corner of
the Cloisters*

CANTERBURY: *Cloisters, North Walk*

On the previous two pages:
CANTERBURY: *Cloisters*

The vaults of the cloister walks, right and on the previous pages, are roughly contemporary, that of Canterbury is of the time of Dom Thomas Chillenden, treasurer and from 1391 Prior, described as 'the greatest builder of a Prior that ever was in Christes Churche', while the north walk at Worcester was built in 1404–22. The architect of the Canterbury vault was Henry Yeveley's pupil, Stephen Lote, who also designed the great pulpitum and built St Michael's Chapel and the upper part of the Chapter House. The author of the Worcester vault cannot be named with certainty. Both structures are arrangements of tiercerons and liernes, sheaves of ribs fanning out towards a central octagon pattern of liernes in each bay, but the Worcester design is simpler. Both vaults anticipate Robert Everard's superb vaults at Norwich but the design is brought so much closer to the eye in the low cloister that the spectator is acutely aware of its vibrant force. The decoration of the intersections of the ribs is in both cases unusual. At Canterbury painted shields, one of which can be seen at the foot of the photograph, take the place of bosses. They represent donors and include kings, emperors, nobles and prelates. Among the few figure subjects are the portrait of a humble monk and a representation of Becket's martyrdom. He is shown at Mass between two murderers, although there were in fact four. At Worcester bosses with shields mark some of the intersections but the distinguishing feature of this vault is the continuous line of shield-bearing angels posed all along the ridge rib and interrupted only by a central image of the Virgin and Child. Some of the angels wear flowing albs, others are dressed in feathered tights, doubtless suggested by the costume of actors in the mystery cycles. The visual delight of this feature is matched by that of the striking embellishment of the window embrasures with a large-scale reticulated chain pattern. In the Canterbury cloister it is the contrast in feeling and proportion between the wall arcading with its moulded trefoiled arches and the bold ribs which attracts attention. The arcading belongs to the time (1226–36) when the refectory to the north of the walk was reconstructed.

163

The rebuilding of the cloisters of Gloucester Abbey between ca. 1351 and 1412 was as sensational as the transformation of the choir for it resulted in the first appearance of that peculiarly English invention the fan vault. This was in the east walk. Like the walls of the choir the cloister vaults are visualised as a system of panels, here adapted to the swelling conoidal shapes which are a natural development of the spreading rib clusters seen in the Wells retrochoir and the nave of Exeter. The ribs are not separately cut but together with the tracery are part of the solid block. It is possible to see the joints in the masonry in the foreground of the photograph.

The battlements on the left are the cornice of a row of little recesses or carrels, each lit by a small window, which the monks used for study.

The present Cathedral of Christchurch, also a college chapel, began as the church of an Anglo-Saxon nunnery. It became an Augustinian priory in the twelfth century, was suppressed in 1525 at the request of Wolsey, who used the church as the chapel of Cardinal College; and in 1546 it became the cathedral of the new diocese of Oxford. The spectacular lierne star vault seems to hang net-like above the Norman interior and *under* the strong arches which in reality support it. They resemble the hammerbeams of a timber roof and the pendants strengthen that impression. Built more than a century later than the Gloucester cloister, the roof was probably designed by William Orchard in ca. 1480–1500. Orchard, who is buried in the cathedral, was not only a gifted architect – he was the author of the Divinity Schools – but a mason-contractor, a new and significant figure, specialising in the production of ready-made details and ornaments.

CANTERBURY: *Bell Harry*

CANTERBURY: *Bell Harry, Interior*

By the time Bell Harry was begun the House of York had been defeated on Bosworth field, Henry VII had been crowned, the great period of cathedral building was ending and the faith which had irradiated it was waning. Offerings at the shrine of St Thomas had long been dwindling, few men now came on pilgrimage to Canterbury. Nonetheless Cardinal Archbishop John Morton and the zealous Prior William Sellinge planned a grandiose addition to the Cathedral: Bell Harry Tower. The tower is not, as might be expected, named after Henry VII but for Prior Henry Eastry, who a century and a half earlier had donated a bell to be hung in the central tower. But the tower had hardly risen above the nave roof by Prior Sellinge's time. The architect of Bell Harry was John Wastell. He had been working chiefly in East Anglia: Great St Mary's, Cambridge and the churches of Saffron Walden and Lavenham are attributed to him, and soon he was to complete Reginald Ely's work at King's College Chapel, Cambridge. It is possible that he may have come from that region and that Morton may have met him when he was Bishop of Ely.

The Archbishop made a major contribution to the cost of the tower and the frequent occurrence of his rebus on the exterior keeps his name and his munificence green. According to the Cathedral records the treasurer was paying £1,035 per annum for the construction, including £388 for 1,132 tons of Caen stone. Stone, however, was only used for the casing of the tower, for Bell Harry is an early example of the use of the most popular of Tudor building materials, brick.

The proportions of this lovely tower are so perfectly determined that from whatever angle it is viewed, whether from afar or, as in the photograph, from a distance of but a few yards, it draws the whole extended composition of Canterbury together. Unlike the fiercely aspiring towers of the early Gothic period, Bell Harry was never intended to carry a spire, and despite the vertical thrust of the sheer octagonal corner turrets, the upward movement of the building makes less of an impression than the charming detail of the ornament beneath the belfry openings and the gaiety of the little openwork lanterns.

The fans spreading over the high vault, four large ones merging into corner fans and swelling about a central roundel, seem to be spinning against an illimitable distance. It is a glorious conceit, the most imaginative of all fan vaults. Its mood perfectly matches that of the exterior.

Archbishop Morton had connections with Peterborough for while at Ely he was responsible for the building of the drain and bank running from Peterborough to Wisbech and known as Morton's Leam. So the Archbishop may have had a hand in Wastell's probable appointment as master mason when Abbot Robert Kirkton decided in 1496 to build the Peterborough retrochoir, known as the New Building, at his own expense. The close resemblance of the work to that in King's College Chapel confirms the attribution of the retrochoir to Wastell. The contrast between this late Gothic east end and the Norman nave is even more dramatic than that between the Perpendicular choir and the Norman nave at Gloucester. Nothing could be more expressive of the vast distance separating the late medieval world on the threshold of secularisation and the twelfth century with its massive dependence on the supernatural than the juxtaposition of this opulent, urbane interior of comfortable domestic proportions and the austere Norman nave, awesome symbol of the majesty of the spiritual world.

Opposite. PETERBOROUGH: *Retrochoir*

On the two previous pages: CANTERBURY: *Bell Harry Tower and Interior*

CANTERBURY
*Trinity Chapel, Angel
on the Tester of
Henry IV's tomb*

The interesting fashion for great wooden testers to be suspended over tombs developed during the fourteenth century and must have originated in the wooden covers that crowned the shrines of saints. The underside of Henry IV's tester is painted with the arms of England and Navarre on an ermine ground. But the photographer has concentrated on the only poetic detail of the sumptuous but rather heavy composition, the sensitive carving along the sides of the canopy of shield-bearing angels. They are ascribed to the royal master-carpenter William Toutmond. The idea of using angels to hold the shields of arms, which were so important in an increasingly worldly society, dates from about the same time as the monument, 1413.

170

Perhaps the most elaborate of all alabaster effigies, these sculptures are more remarkable for brilliance of execution than for the sensibility which informs the likeness of Edward II (p. 131). They are careful portraits and every minute detail of the jewelled crowns, the rich clasps of the mantles and the embroidered robes has been skilfully rendered in the readily worked material. The queen's hair is confined in the fashionable crespine or jewelled net and bunched over the ears. Magnificent in effect though these images are that they were probably shop work and from resemblances to other monuments of that date such as that of the Earl and Countess of Arundel (ca. 1420) at Arundel, which is known to have been made by Thomas Prentys and Robert Sutton of Chellaston, it seems likely that these royal effigies were the work of the same firm.

171

BRISTOL: *Effigy of Abbot Newbery*

Above. SALISBURY: *Dog from the tomb of Robert, Lord Hungerford*

The fashionable materials for funeral effigies in the fifteenth century were alabaster and Purbeck marble. Lord Hungerford's tomb chest is of Purbeck marble while his armoured figure and that of his dog, dating from ca. 1460, are carved in alabaster. They were made in the Nottingham workshops. The texture of the detail which caught the photographer's eye has been made more interesting by mutilation and the passage of time, which fortunately have in no way diminished the sculptor's masterly rendering of the pent-up energy of the watchful hound. The monument was moved to its present position in the nave when Wyatt demolished the Hungerford Chantry in 1789.

Bristol masons had long been conspicuous for their resistance to the influence of the Purbeck marblers and the alabaster workshops. The tombs of the knights of the Berkeley family in the cathedral testify to their fine tradition of stone carving. The effigy of Abbot Newbery (d. 1473), made more than a century and a half later, shows that Bristol craftsmen had lost none of their skill and their mastery of fine, pristine detail. The sculpture is of local oolite.

WORCESTER: *Retrochoir, Prince Arthur's Chantry*

WINCHESTER: *Retrochoir, Cardinal Beaufort's Chantry*

As the Middle Ages drew to a close so the burial arrangements of the higher clergy and the aristocracy became ever more elaborate. Concern with worldly policies and worldly ambitions enhanced the importance of the commemorative function of the tomb, and funerary monuments and chantry chapels of great and growing splendour are among the most arresting additions to cathedral churches during the last half of the fifteenth and early sixteenth centuries. The small scale of chantry chapels gave master masons wonderful opportunities for experiment and limited though the number shown here must be, they bear witness to the variety and idiosyncrasy of these little buildings.

Familiarity never quite subdues the enjoyable shock of coming upon the front of Bishop Alcock's chantry at the end of the north choir aisle at Ely. It could be a Gothick folly but for the skill and precision of the carving. A date stone in the north-west corner of the chapel gives the year of its construction, 1488, so it was begun more than a decade before the Bishop's death in 1501. The photograph celebrates the most inventive and exciting feature of the chapel, the north wall, which the architect has designed as a screen in front of a window. The device highlights the whole bejewelled casket effect of the structure, which persists despite much damage and the removal of all the figure sculpture during the Reformation.

The mood of Prince Arthur's Chantry Chapel is quite different. This is a basically severe and rectilinear building, the essential horizontality of which is accented by the broad band of Tudor ornament, the rose, the portcullis and the royal arms. One charming detail gives life and individuality to the closely controlled little structure: the use of cusped arches in reverse to act as the transoms of the tall narrow openings. We are looking at the chapel from the retrochoir, where it is one storey lower than on the chancel side. The tombs seen through the openings do not include that of the Prince who lies on the upper level. These are the effigies of Bishop Giffard (d. 1302) and a lady of his family. Prince Arthur died at Ludlow in 1502 when he was only fifteen. His father Henry VII, who had already commissioned a magnificent memorial on his own behalf at Westminster, was anxious that his son should be suitably commemorated and met the cost of the Chantry tomb at Worcester, though work was not started until two years after the funeral when, according to an eye witness quoted by John Leland in *Collectanea*, the Prince was laid to rest 'at the South End of the High Altar' on 'the foulest old wyndye and rainey Daye' (April 25) and 'he had a hard Heart who wept not'. The Chantry Chapel was spared at the time of the Reformation because the young Prince was a Tudor.

Cardinal Henry Beaufort, a statesman prelate remembered for his condemnation of Joan of Arc, died in 1447. His proud chapel is as disciplined as Prince Arthur's but more adventurous. Attenuated shafts and the narrowest of panels rise with increasing momentum to merge in a crescendo of tall narrow openings and severe canopies, the upward movement checked only by the low balustrade in front of the central opening and by the horizontal emphasis of the ornamental panels on either side of it. The high arched opening displaying the tomb and the interior of the chapel is an unusual feature. The Cardinal's hatted effigy is a seventeenth-century copy replacing the original which was destroyed by the puritanical Bishop Horne (1560–80).

The exquisite coffer-like little building beyond Cardinal Beaufort's chantry with its rich cresting and pretty open panelling in the form of ornate ogee arches within four-centred arches, is Bishop Fox's chantry. In the low niche lies an horrendously realistic rendering of the bishop's corpse. He died in 1528, but his chapel, built during his lifetime, is still Gothic in detail, although the proportions and horizontal emphasis are of the Renaissance. Inside is a tiny recess to which the bishop used to retire for meditation in old age.

Manchester became a cathedral in 1847. Before that it was a parish church, as it had been in the Middle Ages until in 1421 Henry V granted a licence to the rector Thomas de la Warre to refound St Mary's as a collegiate establishment with a warden, eight priests, four clerks and six choristers. The college was dissolved in 1547, re-established under Queen Mary and finally suppressed by Parliament in 1636. Humphrey Chetham, a merchant of Manchester acquired the college buildings and founded the famous school named after him, while the church became parochial.

It was the third warden of Thomas de la Warre's college, Ralph Langley, who in 1465–80 rebuilt the choir of the church, the part least affected by later restoration and reconstruction. The photograph yields a glimpse of the rich pattern of Tudor ornament – rosettes, shields and cusping – which fills the arcade spandrels and which preceded the appearance of this device in John Wastell's East Anglian churches of Great St Mary's, Cambridge, Lavenham and Saffron Walden. But it is the extraordinary choir stalls which are the subject of the picture. More than a century later than the famous stalls at Chester – for they date from 1505–9 – they are of the same canopied, three-dimensional type, and an even more dazzling example of the woodcarver's virtuosity. Like the Chester stalls they consist of two tiers of canopies, the upper ones like miniature chapels with traceried windows and crowning pinnacles, the lower like fretted oriels. But the detail of the lower tier at Manchester is so loaded with intricate nervously carved ornament and so web-like in its delicacy that the structure is no longer sharply defined. This brilliant display of technical dexterity is an emphatically horizontal design, for the pinnacles are relatively insignificant and the heavy line of the cornice and tester overhanging the stalls dominates the composition. A change has come over the spirit of faith and high endeavour which engendered the soaring pinnacles and strong verticals of the Chester stalls.

Opposite. MANCHESTER: *Choir stalls*

The bookcases and desks of the Chained Library were made in 1611, as the style indicates, but the contents of the shelves are medieval, and some of them relate particularly to the last years of the Middle Ages, for they belonged to Bishop Booth (1516–35) and reveal his extraordinary interest, shared by most bishops, deans and residentiary canons of his generation, in legal and constitutional questions. The internal late medieval history of all cathedrals is a record of attempts to settle questions affecting their constitution and property, and of prolonged and very often acrimonious disputes and litigations. All the sources of civil law, with the voluminous commentaries of jurists, will be found on the Hereford shelves. Bishop Booth's manuscript volume of Gratian's *Decretals*, a collection of medieval canon laws, written in France in the fourteenth century, is among the special treasures of the Cathedral Library.

There was a library at Hereford before the Norman Conquest, and the oldest book in the collection is a copy in Latin of the Four Gospels dating from the late eighth century and probably given to the cathedral by Bishop Aethelstan. Among 227 manuscript works in the Chained Library are four Gospels of the eleventh century and as many as 92 of the twelfth century. An interesting thirteenth-century manuscript is the *Hereford Breviary*, written in about 1270 and the only known copy with music; and among 28 fifteenth-century manuscripts is the Wyclif Bible. The Library, which has moved from place to place over the centuries, is now in the upper transept and upper cloister rooms.

In the early Middle Ages the books of cathedral and monastic libraries, and there were no others, were kept in boxes. Chained libraries were a creation of the later Middle Ages; they were designed to make books available to a larger number of readers and contained standard works of reference which were in frequent demand.

V
A New Order and a New Cathedral

SOME fifty years after the suppression of monastic Durham and the establishment of a secular chapter an old man who in his youth is thought to have been clerk of the feretory of St Cuthbert and keeper of the priory register, writing when the great magnificence of the church and the solemn and impressive ceremonies of the Middle Ages were no more than a memory, described the daily life and ritual and the splendid furnishings of the cathedral on the eve of the Dissolution.

The writer had seen the shrine of St Cuthbert despoiled, the costly plate carried away, the many altars dismantled and shattered, their retables savagely mutilated and embroidered vestments cut up and put to profane uses. He had seen the fanatical Calvinist Dean Whittingham desecrating the tombs of priors, breaking up the brasses in the floor of the cathedral while his wife, a daughter of Calvin, brought 'the Holy Water stones of fyne marble very artificially made and graven' into her kitchen where they were used to 'stepe ther beefe and salt fysh'. To the author of *The Rites of Durham* it seemed as though the glory had departed from the cathedral forever. For the iconoclastic fury was the outward sign of the disintegration of the whole medieval concept of the cathedral as the image of heaven and of the idea of a universal human society which was identified with the Church and part of a divinely ordered cosmos in time and in eternity.

But meanwhile, owing to the peculiar circumstances which gave impetus to the Reformation in England, the break with the past was less drastic in its effects than it was in Holland,

France, Germany and Scotland. The Reformation in England was unique in that it was political and not religious in origin; and the church established in consequence of it was unique in its synthesis of the old and the new. The man who lamented over the passing of monastic Durham was dead long, long before Wren's cathedral of St Paul rose from the ashes of the medieval building. Could he have seen it he might have recognised it for what it is, a sublime symbol of rebirth and continuity.

After the suppression of the monasteries the cathedral churches which had previously been monastic, eight in number – Canterbury, Rochester, Winchester, Ely, Norwich, Worcester, Durham and Carlisle – were refounded, a dean and prebendaries taking the place of the prior and convent in each of them. The title of prebendary was used rather than that of canon, and the prebends were no longer given place names but were referred to simply as prebends of the first, second or third stalls, and so on. The change took place in a haphazard way often with intermediate stages. At Winchester and Ely the monasteries became 'new colleges', each with its guardian, seniors, commons and priests. Then after little more than a year both were converted to cathedral establishments of the usual pattern. Cranmer had hoped to replace the monastery at Canterbury by a college on the lines of those of Oxford and Cambridge, but was overruled, and instead the King's School was created with fifty scholars, a headmaster and an usher. A small college for six priests was founded which still survives.

Six former abbey churches escaped destruction and became the cathedrals of newly founded sees. They were Westminster, Gloucester, Peterborough, Chester, Oxford and Bristol and each had an ex-monk as its dean. Westminster, however, only lasted for ten years as a bishopric; and three years after the church of Osney Abbey had been refounded as the cathedral of Oxford, Henry VIII moved the bishop's throne to Christchurch. The deserted Osney, one of the most splendid of all cathedral buildings, stood until the Civil War, when it was utterly demolished. Another great cathedral, Coventry, was destroyed during the Reformation. It will be remembered that from the early thirteenth century this was the joint cathedral with Lichfield for the bishop of Coventry and Lichfield. It stood in the same churchyard as the present cathedral, then the parish church of St Michael, together

Opposite. ST PAUL'S CATHEDRAL, LONDON
from the East, 1949

with the parish church of Holy Trinity. All three buildings were among the most magnificent sanctuaries in England. Crowding together with their lofty spires, they must have presented an amazing sight.

The remaining cathedral churches, though assured of a continuing existence, did not survive unharmed. Bristol and Southwark lost their naves, the beautiful Lady Chapel at Norwich was destroyed, and almost every one of the hundreds of figures in the dazzling array of sculpture in the Lady Chapel at Ely was decapitated. The intricate carving of Bishop West's Chantry Chapel in the same cathedral was mutilated and chiselled away. In every cathedral the scenes of destruction which desecrated Durham were re-enacted – we read of shrines, images and altars broken and carried away at Worcester where Bishop Horne, a Puritan and philistine, pulled down the chapter house and part of the cloisters. At Lichfield brasses were defaced and shrines and altars pillaged. Plate, copes and Eucharist vestments were seized at Canterbury and the shrine of St Thomas was plundered after Cranmer had presided over the trial of the saint and declared him a traitor. The shrine is said to have yielded some twenty-six cartloads of gold, jewels and treasures which were all taken up to London to enrich the king.

Such terrible destruction of works of art was, however, accompanied by the minimum of personal violence. Despite the fact that the whole staff of cathedral clergy was much reduced, the number of vicars choral often being cut to as few as one or two, many of the inmates of former monasteries lived on, even if in different quarters, in their old homes when their churches were refounded as secular cathedrals. Six of the Canterbury prebendaries had been monks; more than twenty monks became prebendaries of Norwich; at Winchester all but four stayed on, and at Durham twenty-six out of fifty-four monks became canons of the new foundation. At Peterborough six prebendaries and seven minor canons had been members of the old community; at Ely eleven of the monks were appointed to the new cathedral chapter; at Chester the first dean was the late prior Thomas Clarke, and at Carlisle the dean, four prebendaries and eight minor canons had been monks. So, although some 'superfluous persons late religious' were 'despatched and pensioned', the change from monastic church to secular cathedral took place with surprisingly little dislocation and the actual organisation of the chapter was altered only in so far as that the distinction between the small number of residentiary canons and the greater chapter was much more marked.

A sense of continuity was deliberately encouraged by the new liturgy. In 1547 Henry VIII appointed a Committee of Convocation to provide a liturgy in the English language and to simplify the medieval services. There were thirteen divines on the committee which met at Chertsey and Windsor, but the temperate prose and poetry of the Prayer Book they produced was essentially the fruit of Cranmer's liturgical genius, and it is as remarkable a synthesis of the old and the new as Wren's masterpiece. Cranmer based his work on the medieval liturgies and especially on the Use of Sarum. He made an office of Mattins by fusing the old service of Mattins, Lauds and Prime; and he made an office of Evensong from the former offices of Vespers and Compline. The beauty of his language survived the revision of 1559 under Elizabeth I, the minor changes of 1604 and the further amendments after the Restoration, to be hallowed by the devotion of centuries.

The Psalms were divided into roughly sixty equal parts assigned to the morning and evening of each day of the month, so that the entire Psalter would be chanted in order each month. The ancient Gregorian chant was preserved in the singing of the Psalms, and provision was made for the anthem. John Merbecke, organist of St George's Chapel, Windsor, adapted the traditional plainsong to suit the accentuation of the English tongue, and the inspired translation was that of Coverdale. Meanwhile, an English version of the Bible based on the translations of William Tyndale and Miles Coverdale was placed in every cathedral and parish church. By the time Elizabeth came to the throne the Bible and Prayer Book had become the intellectual and spiritual foundation of the new national and yet traditional cathedral order which was so strikingly different from the dark Jesuit or Calvinist establishments on the Continent at that time; and the vigour, richness and poetry of the translations had already begun to exert their influence on the English imagination.

The misery and violence of Mary Tudor's reign actually strengthened the authority of the church she sought to suppress. She removed the English Bible from both cathedral and parish churches, restored the Latin mass, and ejected some 2,000 clergy because they had married. Between 1555 and 1558 nearly three hundred people were burnt as heretics, thus providing English Protestantism with its own martyrology. Among the victims were five bishops: Ferrar of St David's, John Hooper of Gloucester, Ridley, Latimer and Cranmer. Their heroic deaths were identified with virtue, courage and a loyal English resistance to a half-foreign government.

The importance of the Elizabethan settlement, coming as it did after this profoundly disturbing interlude, was that it aimed at reinforcing the compromise between the new and the traditional which was implicit in Cranmer's Prayer Book, and creating a church which, though Protestant in doctrine, was Catholic in order. This compromise remained the basis of the Anglican church and survived all the destruction and controversy of the period between the queen's death and the Restoration. The continuing link between the church of the medieval centuries and the reformed church was recognised by divines like Richard Hooker, who had so much in common with St Thomas Aquinas; and John Donne (*see* p. 194) who between 1621 and 1631 preached some of the greatest and most profound sermons of all the Christian centuries from the pulpit of Old St Paul's, was aware of it. 'You know,' he wrote to a friend, 'I never fettered nor imprisoned the word Religion, not ... immuring it in a Rome, or a Wittenburg or a Geneva; they are all virtual beams of one Sun.'

Old and new are fused in the cathedral music which is one of the great glories of the post-Reformation period in England. 'If I travel in your company,' wrote George Herbert of music, 'You know the way to Heaven's door.' And twice a week he rode from his country parish to hear the cathedral music at Salisbury. The composers themselves often reflect the spirit of compromise in their own lives. John Merbecke, who has just been mentioned, and who composed the first setting of the Anglican Prayer Book for use in cathedrals, was a Catholic who had been arrested for heresy soon after the Reformation; William Byrd, to whose genius every cathedral church still pays homage, was also an adherent of the old faith and was several times prosecuted for recusancy. Yet he was for six years organist of Lincoln Cathedral, then from 1569 organist of the Chapel Royal jointly with his master Tallis, and he composed five different settings for the Anglican service, sixty-one anthems and several settings of the Psalms. John Redford, a playwright as well as a composer, was a Catholic vicar choral at St Paul's Cathedral, but became Master of the Choristers there a few years after the Reformation. He wrote a setting for *Rejoice in the Lord alway* which has remained in the cathedral repertory to this day.

The spirit of compromise was as manifest in the way in which cathedrals were adapted to the new service as it was in the liturgy itself. Medieval cathedrals, dedicated as they were to the perpetual celebration of divine worship and the perpetual intercession for the dead by a body of clergy set apart for that purpose, were never intended for large congregations and were not suited to a communal service. But no attempt was made in the Elizabethan settlement to alter the medieval plan: the choir or part of the nave might be used for public worship and though the great rood was removed, the screens and the traditional division of the cathedral into separate compartments were retained. The altar, however, renamed the Table, was moved to the crossing and there might, as at Lincoln, be a litany desk in the nave large enough to take two minor canons. But under William Laud the altar was returned to its original position in the sanctuary and fenced in with rails to protect it from the irreverant deportment of some communicants. Laud also replaced the organs, much of the stained glass and the crucifixes which had been destroyed. His high-church principles and conservatism were not of course immediately absorbed into Anglican worship. Dr Miles Smith, Bishop of Gloucester, father of Elizabeth Williams, whose likeness appears in these pages (p. 192), and writer of the noble preface to the Authorised Version of the Bible, walked out of the cathedral when Laud, then Dean, moved the Table to the east end, and is said never to have set foot in the building again.

The Authorised Version is the greatest legacy of the first century of Reformation. The work was done at a time when the English language, reflecting all the dynamic, creative energy and the excitement and expansiveness of the age, was of unsurpassed richness and beauty. The power and majesty, the poetry and vivid imagery of the English Bible entered the hearts and minds of later generations, and for long it redeemed the loss of that all embracing celestial vision of the Middle Ages. But there was no ecclesiastical architectural achievement to equal it in the period before the Civil War. The one major project was the restoration of St Paul's which Laud undertook when he was Bishop of London. The great church had been wholly neglected since 1561 when its spire had been destroyed in a fire. The nave was used as a public meeting place, a shopping centre and a fashionable promenade. Laud appealed to the nation, raised £100,000, and put Inigo Jones in charge of the work. The first English master to be in complete command of the classicial idiom, which increasingly corresponded to the secular character of the age, Inigo Jones never thought of carrying out the restoration in any style which was not up to date. He replaced the walls, gave them classical windows and substituted pilasters for the medieval buttresses. He masked the angles between aisles and clerestory with huge volutes on the west front and set across it a gigantic and magnificent portico with columns fifty feet tall supporting a mighty cornice and balustrade. It was Charles I who defrayed the considerable expense of this portico.

Apart from this restoration the structural work in the damaged cathedrals was limited to furnishings and minor alterations. At Winchester, for instance, a wooden vault was erected in the central tower in 1634 and decorated with carved bosses and with medallion portraits of Charles I and Henrietta Maria, and in 1637 the medieval pulpitum was reconstructed in the classical style to an imposing design by Inigo Jones. Medieval pulpitums had been decorated with statues of kings and two fine bronze figures of James I and Charles I by Le Sueur adorned Inigo Jones's composition. They can still be seen in the cathedral at the west end. A great new organ was made for Worcester by Thomas Dallam in 1613 and set up on the choir screen which was altered and enlarged to accommodate it; and another splendid organ was set up in Bristol Cathedral. But the main new visual experience afforded by cathedrals at this time was provided by the monuments. They are the most moving and eloquent witnesses to the religious drift of the period. However actively the medieval past lived on in the reformed cathedral service, however closely the Protestant doctrine was associated with a Catholic order, a revolution had taken place, and the new front of St Paul's, like a pagan temple, and the classical pilasters, obelisks and urns of the Winchester pulpitum proclaimed it. The subjects of these late-sixteenth and early-seventeenth-century monuments had experienced a deeply disturbing interference with the ritual element in their lives; an English liturgy had taken the place of the Latin rites, they had seen change and desecration in the great cathedral churches which for centuries had been the living symbols of divine immutability, they had seen roods torn down and altars and pulpits shifted about at the dictate of conflicting dogmas, and they had become part of a fragmented society which in a divided Christendom could no longer be identified with the Church. No wonder that the chief architectural expression of their boundless vitality was not ecclesiastic, but domestic. Their extraordinary houses even more than their great literature and music reveal the secular emphasis of their time and their self-awareness. Their funerary images, combining native vigour with idiosyncratic, naive interpretations of the new classical, horizontal style, celebrate their importance in this world rather than their hope of salvation in the next. They appear in the fullness of life, and at the same time, because that life is extinguished, these effigies most poignantly convey the sense of its transitoriness. Elizabeth Williams of Gloucester leans on her elbow gazing out at a world she was reluctant to leave; Matthew Godwin in Exeter Cathedral, a golden-haired musician cut off at the age of seventeen, addresses his prayers to an organ against a background of viols, lutes and trumpets, defying his untimely death and the immolation of his talent; Dean Boys sits forever in his familiar bookroom at Canterbury; John Donne, though dressed for the grave, is no corpse, but stands and lives as he did when he posed for his likeness in his shroud.

The shock of the upheaval which is reflected in these figures and in the many hundreds of their contemporaries, staring at us from cathedral aisles and from the chancels of parish churches, had barely begun to be absorbed when the Civil War and the Commonwealth wrought more havoc in cathedrals than anything which had yet been witnessed. Spurred on by a fanatical hatred of things of beauty which is as incomprehensible as it is distressing, the Roundheads used cathedrals as barracks, stables and fortresses. Three of the most severely harmed of their victims were Lichfield, Peterborough and Durham. At Lichfield, where the Royalists had fortified the close, Cromwell's men battered down the central spire, demolished all the monuments, broke up the stalls, shattered the windows, tore up the pavement, burned all the cathedral records and stabled their horses in the nave, and to crown their barbarity they derided the holy sacrament of baptism by bringing a calf to the font. At Peterborough the splendid cloisters, with some of the finest glass in Europe and the great reredos which had three spires soaring almost to the vault, were wholly demolished. At Durham Scottish soldiers made a bonfire of the stalls in the chancel itself and horribly desecrated the entire interior. The new organ at Bristol was smashed and indeed organs everywhere were vandalised: Dallam's organ at Worcester was among them and vanished with the cathedral glass. Gloucester had a narrow escape for Cromwell planned its total destruction and was only thwarted by the courageous resistance of the mayor and townspeople. Chichester and Winchester suffered little harm except for defaced monuments and smashed windows, and York was spared by the intervention of Fairfax, a native of the county. Similarly Cromwell preserved Ely, though insisting on the abolishment of the choir service, 'so unedifying and offensive', and confining Bishop Matthew Wren to the Tower. At Canterbury Parliamentary troops stormed into the cathedral, pulled down the organ, tore up the communion rails, dragged the Table into the middle of the chancel, hacked out the figure of Christ from a tapestry with their knives, fired on another image of Christ, and systematically destroyed ornaments and some of the windows. The glorious window of the north-west transept glazed by William Neve in ca. 1478 with huge figures of Our Lady and St Thomas was destroyed by a Puritan preacher, Richard Culmer, who had been educated at the King's School. He was one of the six preachers given complete control of the cathedral by Cromwell. At one time three hundred horses were kept in the nave. St Paul's too became a 'Horse-Quarter for Soldiers' and their animals were neighing in the stalls. Inigo Jones's great portico was mutilated, the columns broken and the sculptures pulled down.

The Commonwealth was the bleakest period in the history of cathedrals. Unless, as at Canterbury, Exeter and St Pauls, a small area was fitted up as a preaching house, they were closed; archbishops, bishops, deans and chapters were abolished and their lands confiscated, while houses in the precincts were let to laymen. High Anglicans were regarded as disloyal to their country and an ordinance of 1643 replaced the Book of Common Prayer with the Directory of Public Worship. So there were no ordained officers to maintain the cathedral fabric or the liturgical life which, though altered in form, had endured for more than a thousand years.

With the restoration of the monarchy in 1660 the Prayer Book was once more heard in cathedral worship, and the work of repairing the buildings, in some cases ruinous, was begun. New lead, then scarce and costly, was acquired for roofs, new plate and service books were bought, new fittings designed and constructed. At Lichfield, where the Chapter House and vestry were the only places where a service could be held, the energetic Bishop John Hacket refurnished the choir and rebuilt the central spire and the great west window with contributions largely from his own purse, though Charles II donated one hundred trees and the Duke of York (later James II) paid for new tracery in the west window (replaced by Scott's tracery in 1869, *see* p. 110). Bishop Hacket also enclosed the mutilated altar screen with a painted wood structure in the classical style which is thought to have been the work of Wren. It was later removed by Wyatt. Minor repairs only were carried out at Peterborough which had to wait until the nineteenth century for much-needed restoration. Notable renovations were undertaken at Durham. Bishop John Cosin (1660–71), who had been a staunch supporter of Laud and had fled to France when the Civil War started, was conspicuous for his scholarly appreciation of medieval architecture though he never sought to reproduce it: he used Gothic elements in combination with motifs of his own period to create a style which symbolised that fusion of the traditional and the new which was the essence of Anglican worship. The high Gothic canopies and Gothic tracery of the remarkable furniture with which Cosin replaced the burnt and broken stalls of the ravaged cathedral consort with fat garlands and cherub heads, and in his oak parclose screens he again juxtaposed medieval and Renaissance details. In the most striking of the objects made for him, the elaborate font cover, more than forty feet high, Gothic tracery and Gothic crocketted gables rise in tier upon tier from an octagonal base of fluted classical columns and an acanthus frieze which perfectly harmonises with the simple baluster font of 1663. The craftsman who was responsible for all this work was a local carpenter, John Clement.

The synthesis achieved by Cosin was embodied with supreme sophistication and genius and on a monumental scale in the glorious architectural achievement which marked the end of so many troubled decades of reform, iconoclasm, dissent and civil war – St Paul's Cathedral. Repairs to Old St Paul's were resumed after 1660, only to be brought to a halt by the Great Fire six years later. The situation cannot but recall that of Canterbury five hundred years earlier. Christopher Wren, like William of Sens, considered mere restoration impracticable. 'What Time and Weather had left entire in the old and Art in the new repair'd parts of the great Pile of St Pauls's, the late Calamities of the Fire had so weakened and defac'd that it now appears like some Antique Ruine of 2000 years continuance; and to repair it sufficiently will be like the mending of the Argonavis, scarce anything will at last be left of the old.' The respective merits of restoration and rebuilding continued to be debated as they had been at Canterbury till at last in July 1668 a Royal Warrant was issued, permitting the erection of a new cathedral. Donors contributed £130,000, but, uniquely in the history of cathedral building, the cost was largely met by taxation, by a tax levied on coal and on wine.

It is worth recalling in an age when architecture is a closed profession and no artist, however great a genius, can hope to practice without 'qualifications' resulting from the passing of an examination, that Wren, the dominating architectural personality in England after Inigo Jones's death, was not an architect by training. He was a scientist, a founder member of the Royal Society, who at the age of only twenty-four was appointed Professor of Astronomy at Oxford. The background could not have been more propitious for Wren's great masterpiece. His professional sense of the importance of scientific accuracy, of clarity and proportion, determined his approach to his art, an approach which had recognisable affinities with the highly organised, synthesising attitude of medieval scholasticism. Wren spoke on several occasions of his enthusiasm for geometry. 'Firmness, Commodity and Delight, Beauty and Strength,' he says, 'depend upon the geometrical Reasons of Opticks and Staticks.' 'Beauty is from Geometry' and the test of a work of art is always 'geometrical beauty'. We are reminded of the Gothic vision of the Almighty as a mathematician holding a pair of dividers.

Some four months before the Fire broke out Wren had been asked to prepare a design for completing the restoration of Old St Paul's. The drawings he made for the work show a dome over the crossing intended to complement Inigo Jones's portico and wall casing which Wren greatly admired. The dome is crowned by a lantern and a prodigiously elongated pineapple of bizarre aspect. If the Fire had not thwarted the execution of this eccentric design St Paul's could never have figured in cathedral history with such

ST PAUL'S: *North-West Tower*

visual and symbolic significance. But the architect's concern in this plan for soaring height as opposed to the horizontality of Jones's portico already hints at the great synthesis he was eventually to achieve.

Wren's father was rector of East Knowle in Wiltshire and his uncle Matthew was successively Dean of Windsor, Bishop of Hereford, of Norwich and of Ely; both were friends of Laud, so the architect of St Paul's was closely associated with the Anglican Church and had been familiar from childhood with great works of medieval architecture. Before he came to design St Paul's Wren had also had experience of restoring historical monuments. He had directed repairs at the Bodleian, Oxford, and had completed Tom Tower 'in the Gothick manner'; and in 1669, before he had submitted his first plan for the new cathedral, Wren made a detailed survey of Salisbury at the request of his friend Bishop Seth Ward. His report shows his keen appreciation of the beauty of the structure and particularly commends the spire and the architect's ingenious use of ironwork. The bishop lost no time in carrying out the repairs urged by Wren, and perhaps it was Wren who suggested that the choir should be paved with black and white marble, for this was done, at Ward's expense, while the repairs were going on.

For Wren, with all his understanding of tradition, was wholly committed to the classical idiom; and it was his dream to see a dome as great as that of Michelangelo's at St Peter's rise above the London skyline. His first extraordinary design had a dome at the west end and a nave with external arcades and galleries; but this was discarded in favour of a centrally planned cathedral, the Great Model for which survives and can be seen in the cathedral library. Splendid as it is, with its commanding central drum and dome and noble pedimented portico, it is essentially the masterly result of a close study of the drawings Michelangelo made for St Peter's and of the domed churches in Paris where Wren had gone at the outbreak of the plague in 1665; and it lacks the quality which so distinguishes the final building, the reconciliation of 'the Gothick to a better Manner of Architecture', as Wren put it and (though this is not the accepted view) we must be grateful that the commissioners, the Dean and Chapter did not favour the Great Model. For the church which materialised is more original as a work of architecture and singularly accords with the character of the Anglican service. Wren's interpretation of the classical mode, which he did indeed consider 'a better Manner of Architecture' than Gothic, is not in the heavy Roman manner of Inigo Jones's portico but, though using Vitruvian forms with the utmost mastery and sophistication, is a synthesis of the vertical and the horizontal. For St Paul's is a Baroque building, and of all the Roman-inspired styles, the Baroque, which though classical in its symmetry, proportions and ornament moves and aspires like Gothic, is the most expressive of traditional Christian worship.

Although Wren wrote an important letter in favour of the new type of parish church of the period known as an auditory or room church, and was himself the author of the finest examples, his conception of the cathedral purpose and plan was that of the Middle Ages: St Paul's consists of a nave, conspicuously long transepts and a long chancel, originally shut off by a substantial oak pulpitum surmounted by an organ, where the clergy might perform the offices of prayer and intercession independently of the congregation. Like a medieval cathedral the nave has a clerestory and is flanked by lower aisles, and flying buttresses counteract the thrust of the vaults, though these are all hidden by a two-storeyed outer screen wall. And though the style is classical the rhythm is not. The two-storeyed central portico, with six pairs of columns on the ground floor and only four pairs above, merges into the bays which form the bases of the flanking towers, a design reminiscent of Wells, though more subtle. And these towers with their complex play upon diagonal, convex and concave forms, their strange volutes, their urns and ogee caps and above all their bold chiaroscuro, lead upwards with a thrilling flame-like motion which most movingly contrasts with the calm repose of the hovering dome. The interior, again, is full of movement. The individual parts, the huge piers, the colossal niches, are as overpoweringly massive as the giant Norman arcades at St Albans or Durham, but just as they set up an irresistible rhythm so Wren's placing of niches and windows, panel vaults and saucer domes and especially his treatment of the domed space and its mammoth arches create a sense of undulating, aspiring and dynamic motion. Wren's interpretation of the classical mode speaks of that same fervour of devotion as the Gothic cathedrals; his masterpiece, a building raised to the glory of God, is their peer.

The arresting photograph with which this section opens, taken after the air raids of the Second World War had reduced the surroundings of the cathedral to rubble, enables us to see Wren's great church as it was before greed and rampant commercialism had closed in upon it to destroy the architect's conception of St Paul's as the central monument of a noble city planned to enhance its splendour. It also enables us to appreciate the miracle of the preservation of the cathedral on that night in 1940 and the renewed opportunity it offered for fulfilling Wren's vision of the architectural and spiritual role of his creation.

Launcelot Salkeld, the last prior of the house of Augustinian Canons which had surrendered on January 9, 1549, was a king's man and became the first dean of the cathedral which was refounded in 1541. The monks at Carlisle were fortunate, for not only the dean but four prebendaries and eight canons had been members of the old community. Salkeld's screen to the north aisle was made between 1542 and 1547. The motifs show no trace of Gothic but, like the moulded brick lights in the windows of Layer Marney Tower, the Renaissance arabesques of the openings still suggest cusped ogee forms. The medallions enclosing profile human heads, the chimeras, dolphins and leafy scrolls which make up the ornament, the proportions and mouldings of the panelling are all familiar Renaissance themes. In the centre of the brattishing are the royal arms encircled by the Garter. The royal arms began to appear prominently in churches under Henry VIII and when, according to the Royal Injunction of 1559 shrines, pictures and images which had given rise to 'idolatrous practices' were removed from cathedrals, the royal arms were among the few decorations officially permitted. The screen bears the initials of the donor L.S. and D.K. for *Decanus Karleolensis.*

The photograph shows something of the character of the chancel which survived the onslaught of the Scots between 1645 and 1652 when the greater part of the nave was destroyed. The arcade was rebuilt after a fire of 1292 and the capitals, carved with the labours of the months, small figures amid knobbly leaves, are among the most attractive examples of Decorated sculpture.

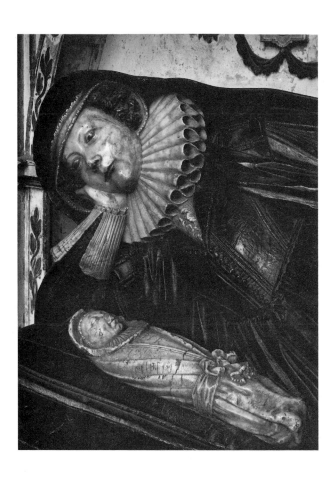

GLOUCESTER: *Detail from the monument to Elizabeth Williams in the Lady Chapel*

The great changes that had come with the passing of the Middle Ages and the emergence of a society ruled by secular interests are nowhere more vividly illustrated than in the character of the monuments commemorating not only ecclesiastics, royalty and the nobility, but merchants and country squires and their families, which now became conspicuous features of both parish churches and cathedrals, vying for attention with the chantry chapels of the fifteenth century. These figures do not always lie stretched on their backs in calm resignation, nor are their hands always clasped in prayer: they turn on their cushioned tomb slabs, they kneel, sit and take up familiar attitudes, proudly proclaiming their zest for life in the face of death. A merely realistic effigy was no longer acceptable, the strong sense of individuality insisted on a portrait. Agreements commonly specify 'exact similitude' or a 'resemblance as he was in life'. Elizabeth Williams, alert, bugle-eyed, wearing her most fashionable dress and hat, leans on her elbow gazing down at her infant. The wife of W.J. Williams and the daughter of Bishop Miles Smith, she died in childbirth in 1622. Her sister Margery Clent died only a year later and kneels near her. The sculptor of both effigies was Samuel Baldwin of Stroud. The arresting commemoration of the Hales family, dating from the end of the sixteenth century, is an early example of the hanging wall monument. It is an extraordinary three-decker structure of classical form, with three-dimensional figures posed against narrative reliefs. At the top Sir James Hales, who led the naval expedition sent to Spain as a reprisal in the year after the Armada, is being buried at sea from an Elizabethan ship of the line. He died of an epidemic which decimated the crew in that disastrous enterprise. His wife Alice kneels at a classical prayer desk in the middle of the monument just below the scene of the committal. Their son Chenies (d. 1596) kneels at the foot of the composition dressed in a smart doublet and hose, and another family tragedy, the suicide of Sir James Hales senior in the river Stour, is recorded in a painting.

The new realism of post-Reformation funereal sculpture was accompanied by a Shakespearean insistence on mortality: skulls, cross-bones, hour glasses and spades frequently adorn Elizabethan and Jacobean tombs. John Donne, Dean of St Paul's, sat in his own shroud for his own monument, exquisitely carved by Nicholas Stone (1631). This is the first of a series of standing, shrouded effigies. Nicholas Stone gives some details of the commission in his notebook, now in the Soane Museum: 'I made a tomb for doctor Donne, and sett it up in St Paul's, London, for the which I was payed by doctor Mountford the sum of 120£. I took 60£ in plate in part of payment.' The sculpture was the only monument of Old St Paul's to escape uninjured from the Great Fire.

Nicholas Stone made this monument in 1626, the year of Orlando Gibbons's sudden death of apoplexy at the age of forty-two at Canterbury, where he was composing music for Charles I's reception of Henrietta Maria. As the sculptor's notebook records, the monument was commissioned by the composer's widow and cost £38.

Of white marble, dramatically set within a black marble niche surmounted by a heavy segmental pediment, the portrait bust on its pedestal introduced a new theme in funerary sculpture. Gibbons composed more than forty anthems for the new liturgy, many of which are still part of the cathedral repertory.

The archbishop, who died in 1628, is represented in the traditional recumbent pose with hands folded in prayer. The sculptor of this finely carved portrait is unknown, although Nicholas Stone had executed a group of monuments in the Minster and at Beverley some years earlier, and this piece is stylistically related to his work. One of the interests of the effigy is that it shows details of episcopal dress after the Reformation. The archbishop wears the black chimere, full white lawn embroidered sleeves, scarf, ruff and black skull cap. The ruff, which began as a secular innovation, soon became liturgical and grew larger and larger until by the middle of the seventeenth century it had become the 'millstone ruff'.

196

Dean Boys's monument, like that of Sir James Hales (p. 193) immortalises the scene of his death, but with an even stronger sense of realism. The Dean died suddenly at his table in his library in 1625 and the sculptor has reconstructed the whole scene in marble. The Dean sits in front of book-lined walls in cassock, ruff and gown, leaning upon his elbow, his head turned away from an open book on a sphinx-supported rest, to look towards the altar.

Opposite. WAKEFIELD: *Screen, Chancel and Retrochoir*

The Maddison monument is a conspicuous object in an interior which, although adapted to cathedral worship more than a century ago, is still that of a large parish church. The composition, flanked by classical columns and surmounted by a segmental pediment, coats of arms and scrolls, takes the form of a tableau with three-dimensional figures at prayer in a room furnished with fashionable shell niches. The master and mistress of the house kneel on either side of a centrally placed prayer desk; behind each of them, facing the transept, kneels a male relative, while below the scene, like an orchestra in a theatre pit, kneel their sixteen children. The adults died in 1611, 1624, 1634 and 1653 and the monument itself dates from ca. 1635. The liveliness of the effigies immediately catches the eye, but it is the curious shape of the composition which insists on attention: it juts forward like the prow of a ship and is supported on a bracket like a large Ionic capital adorned with giant foliage, a typical example of the exuberant, idiosyncratic use of classical imagery in this creative period.

The Wakefield screen, which is of the same date as the Maddison monument, is another, yet more robust fantasy on the classical theme. The spirited carving, the thin, tapering supporters and baluster-like pillars of inverted obelisk shape and the eccentric capitals suggested by the Ionic mode are wonderfully free, imaginative interpretations of motifs taken from Flemish pattern books of the time.

The Laudian period, though chiefly associated with dissension over the position of the altar, was one of screen building, though the parish church screen, which this then was, served not, as in cathedrals and as in pre-Reformation days, to set apart the clergy from the laity but to provide separate places for different services, each attended by both people and priest. Wakefield was then the centre of the Yorkshire clothing trade and so there was money to spend on refurbishing the large parish church of All Saints. The screen has affinities with those of St John's, Leeds, and St Andrew's, Slaidburn.

Here Lockyer lies interr'd enough his name
Speakes one hath fewcompetitors in fame
A Name soe Great, soe Generalle may scorne
Inscriptions wch doe vulgar tombs adorne
A diminution tis to write in verse
His eulogies, wch most mens mouths rehearse.
His virtues & his PILLS are soe well known
That envy can't confine them vnder stone,
But they'll surviue his dust and not expire
Till all things else at th'vniversall fire.
This verse is lost, his PILL Embalmes him safe
To future times, with out an Epitaph:

Reputed Octo. 1711

Opposite. CANTERBURY: *Monument to Colonel William Prude in St Michael's Chapel*

Above. SOUTHWARK: *Monument to Thomas Lockyer in the North Transept*

The crude, simple version of 1672 of the Ionic order which confronts us in Thomas Lockyer's monument contrasts with the bold, highly individual rendering of the same classical mode in the memorial to Colonel William Prude, made forty years earlier. Here the exaggerated detail and odd proportions, the term-like figures in Renaissance military dress growing out of the flanking pilasters and the allegorical sculptures standing on the capitals frame the kneeling colonel with a bold theatrical flourish. Yet the suppliant, armoured image makes less of an impact than the inert, half-recumbent effigy of Thomas Lockyer. The optimistic angel head has no power over the fearful vision of mortality conjured up by those haggard lineaments and that strange, uneasy serpentine shape. They establish the memory of the quack doctor more surely than the pills celebrated in his epitaph.

Colonel William Prude died at the siege of Maestricht in 1632, and is one of a number of post-Reformation soldiers buried in this chapel.

ST PAUL'S CATHEDRAL, LONDON: *West Front*

202

ST PAUL'S CATHEDRAL: *South-West Corner*

While they do not and cannot show St Paul's in the setting Wren planned for his cathedral, the photograph of the west front taken from Ludgate Hill and the romantic photograph of the south-west corner taken on a stormy late afternoon in March do convey a sense of the architect's vision of a great church dominating the City. The classical idiom, though used with such mastery, and in so personal a manner, suggests a complete break with the past; but Wren's design is actually a synthesis of new and traditional forms. It is this which gives St Paul's its significance both in the architectural history of the English cathedral and as an expression of Anglican worship which incorporated so much of the past and was then still animated by divine unreason.

St Paul's, as the photographs proclaim, conforms to a traditional cathedral plan with a twin-towered west front and a central dominating feature over the crossing; and even though this feature is a dome instead of a tower, the method Wren used to poise it over the huge central space was, as has often been noted, inspired by Gothic precedent at Ely where his uncle was bishop. The immense dome, unusually tall in proportion to the building it crowns, aspires rather than rests, and its vertical movement would have been still more obvious had the architect's original intention of surmounting it with a tiered steeple been carried out. As for the towers, they echo the theme of the enchanting lantern perched on top of the dome, their tapering verticality and upward direction enhanced by the rich variety of their different stages and by abrupt changes from convex to concave forms. Movement again informs the noble transept with its pediment, gesticulating statues and swelling semicircular porch like the facade of a Baroque Italian church.

As with medieval cathedrals, the building started from the east end; so we are looking at work which belongs to the later stages of the undertaking. The transept dates from 1681, the west front from 1684, the towers and dome from as late as 1702. The dramatic relief in the west front pediment showing the conversion of St Paul and the lively figures of the apostles and evangelists on top of the pediment were the work of Francis Bird. Bird also designed the pineapples on the summits of the towers and the ball and

cross of the dome lantern. The flaming urns were carved by Jonathan Maine (fl. 1680–1709).

The upward surge of the dome is more strongly felt within than without the cathedral, contrasting as it so spectacularly does with the processional movement of the nave. The photograph emphasises this vertical thrust and brings out the connection between the dome and the Ely Octagon and lantern. The sudden sensation of space and brightness and infinite soaring experienced at Ely is felt as keenly at St Paul's. Not only does the dome rise from a tall drum but it is pierced by a circular opening through which another dome appears to float aloft, though this is an illusion: the structure is in reality a brick cone which supports the lantern and helps to uphold the outer dome seen poised above what remains of the older City. The internal effect is intensified by the architect's inspired play upon the geometric motifs of arc, circle, rectangle, square and diagonal.

The photograph enables us to appreciate the remarkable way in which Wren, through his personal enthusiastic surveyance of the craftsmen he employed, harmonised work by diverse hands. The pilaster capital was the work of Jonathan Maine (he was paid £5 for it) and he also carved the frieze, 346 ft of stone ornament which rises above the gallery. The keystones of the arches were carved by Caius Gabriel Cibber. The illusionist frescoes by Sir James Thornhill in the dome were not Wren's choice: he had specified 'mosiack work as at St Peter's'. The decoration of the diagonal apse *is* mosaic but by the Victorian artist William Richmond.

The dome was completed thirty-five years after Wren had been charged with the task of building a new St Paul's. The topmost stone was laid by the architect's son in the presence of his father, who had been hauled to the top of the scaffolding in a basket.

The photograph, taken on a bright October morning with sun streaming through the clear glass of the windows (clear as Wren intended it to be: the stained glass inserted in Victorian times was by good fortune shattered by blast during the Second World War) gives the transept the dramatic chiaroscuro and warmth for which the architect planned. The picture also emphasises the contrast between the immense solidity of the forms and the spatial dynamics of the huge coffered arch, suggestive of a tunnel vault and necessary for the support of the central dome, the diagonally placed pier and the clerestory window arch leaning forward to touch the saucer dome. Flaxman's monument to Admiral Howe, life-size figures raised on a lofty pedestal, gives a sense of the overwhelming scale of the building.

ST PAUL'S: *Looking South-West from the Choir*

The camera is so placed as to sharpen our awareness of the vast proportions of the central feature of the design and of the audacity of Wren's conception: the diameter of the domed space equals the width of nave and aisles. At the same time the point of view makes clear the link between Wren's building and the Gothic past. The photograph should be compared with that of Ely (p. 123), for though the language of St Paul's is classical, its plan is medieval and the structure of the nave is based on medieval practice. The thrusts of the vault are concentrated at the corners of each bay and are met by flying buttresses behind screen walls.

The organ originally stood on the oak pulpitum, an essential feature of Wren's design which was swept away by Victorian ecclesiologists in 1858. The organ was made by Schmidt in 1694, and its glorious case adorned with cherubs and angels can fortunately still be enjoyed in its present position.

This screen in the east bay of the north chancel arcade is made up of the original gates to the chancel which have been replaced by a low communion rail. For Wren had intended his sanctuary to be screened as it was in a medieval cathedral. The gates were moved when the pulpitum was destroyed. They are distinguished by medallions of the evangelists which, such is the magical art of the ironsmith, seem to materialise out of the scrolls and leafy fronds enclosing them.

The photograph reveals the individuality of the wrought forms and the superb artistry of the vibrant and elaborate pilasters and panels. A few years before he completed the gate Jean Tijou had published *A New Booke of Drawings, containing Several Sorts of Ironwork*. None of the engraved designs is the equal in richness and originality of the work Tijou accomplished under Wren's direction.

208

One of the great delights of St Paul's is the beauty of the fabric and the exquisite quality of the stone carving. The material is Portland stone, almost marble-white since the removal of the soot which used to exaggerate the chiaroscuro of the design. It came from the quarry by the sea. The chief mason when the front was going up was Edward Strong, one of a family of Burford masons and contractors who supplied some of the stone for the interior. For the rubble core of the masonry Wren used stone from Old St Paul's. The decorative stone carvings were the work of Edward Pearce, Jonathan Maine and Grinling Gibbons. The imagery, as ravishingly precise as that of the early fourteenth century but totally different in character, celebrates life and immortality in the form of opulent flower festoons and Renaissance-derived cherub heads in feathered frills.

Above. ST PAUL'S: *Detail of the cornice of the Choir stalls*

Opposite. ST PAUL'S: *South Choir aisle showing outer face of stalls*

Grinling Gibbons was at the height of his powers when in 1696 and 1697 he was working on the choir stalls at St Paul's. The detail shows both the miraculous delicacy of his art and the command of form which enabled him to invest so unlikely a subject as a cherub head with monumental grandeur. For 60 cherub heads he was paid £66. This was part of Gibbons's account for £1,561. 4s. 6d. for carving completed by 1697. The pendant flowers and oak leaves, when seen at such close quarters, disclose something of the way in which the artist achieved his effect of naturalism: each flower is kept rather flat with a crisp outline, but they are in different planes and thus animated by strong light and shade; and there is just enough modelling to give a feeling of growth. While the forceful wing-like scrolls and cherub heads and the moulding above them express a familiarity with the classical idiom for which we look in vain in the Wakefield screen

(p. 199), the flowers are as peculiarly English as the leaves of Southwell (p. 112). The same contrast gives a movingly individual quality to Gibbons's splendidly formal columns and naturalistic flower wreaths at the back of the choir stalls. The wrought-iron grilles which complement Gibbons's work were made by Jean Tijou.

Gibbons was the first to use lime wood for carving. The minuteness of his work demanded a tougher and smoother grained wood than oak and his intricate relief carving was done in lime applied to oak. The artist also liked the contrast in colour between the pallor of the lime and the warm brown of the oak. In Wren's day it was usual to stain oak with a reddish colouring matter and to varnish it. Much of the oak for St Paul's was donated by the Duke of Newcastle from his estates and brought to London by sea.

VI
In the Light of Reason

THE plump worldly cherub (*opposite*) clasping a flaming torch and raising a chubby hand in salutation of the departing soul of Judge Reynolds (d. 1738) suitably introduces a period of metaphysical optimism. He is one of two attendants on the Judge, whose marble likeness wearing robe and wig sits under a pediment against the west wall inside the Cathedral of Bury St Edmunds. Frozen tableaux of this kind, imposing architectural compositions like the Mildmay memorial at Chelmsford (p. 227), classical female mourners drooping over urns like Rysbrack's monument to Lord Wyndham at Salisbury, gentlemen attired in Roman dress like John Bacon the Elder's Dr Johnson standing uneasily and rather ridiculously with bare legs and bare chest in St Paul's, elegant nightgowned ladies smoothly carved in the finest grained and chilliest white marble, among whom Mrs Digby of Worcester (p. 229) is typical, and sentimental child effigies like that of little Ernest Udney at Chichester (p. 228), all part of the rapidly growing stone population of cathedrals in the Hanoverian age, powerfully evoke the spirit of the time, and remind us of the gulf dividing it from the medieval view of man and the universe. For though the liturgy preserved firm links with the past, the architectural innovations and the theological background of the eighteenth century were inimical to it.

Wren was a scientist yet held fast to his religious faith, and his great creation reflects a mind and an age in which the worlds of scientific experiment, of Bible history and belief, of classical art and learning and of Christian morality were distinct but not divided. Sir Thomas Browne

BURY ST EDMUNDS: *Detail from the monument to Judge Reynolds*

had written that science could offer no threat to religion, for God 'received small honour from those Vulgar Heads that rudely stare about and with a gross rusticity admire His Works'. He prefers those 'whose judicious inquiry into His Acts and deliberate research into His Creation return the Duty of a devout and learned admiration'. It is the Janus view, the thrilling fusion of disparates, which makes the reading of *Urn Burial* a perennial delight, and, on a far grander scale, imparts such emotional power to Wren's hybrid cathedral. The full effect of the scientific discoveries which had followed on the Reformation, of the work of Kepler, Boyle and Newton, was only beginning to be felt during the last quarter of the seventeenth century, when St Paul's was going up, and though science had unveiled the design, law and order which regulated the universe, though it had banished ignorance, the 'mathematicks of the City of Heaven' remained mystical, and a work of the highest genius like St Pauls as well as a humble unsophisticated monument like Dr Lockyer's (p. 201) could still have something in common both with the strange imagery of a poet like Herbert and with the spirit of the Gothic centuries.

But by the time the great cathedral was completed Newton's discoveries and Locke's philosophical writings, especially *The Reasonableness of Christianity*, which, expressed in prose as lucid and harmonious as the language of classical architecture, epitomises the basic attitude of the age, had changed the intellectual outlook. The steady light of reason illumined a world in which Nature's laws had become the only acceptable foundation of faith. Explanations based on Revelation and the supernatural, upon which religion had rested in the Middle Ages, could no longer satisfy, and the universe came more and more to be regarded as a Great Machine ordered by a Divine mechanic:

> The spacious firmament on high
> With all the blue aethereal sky
> And spangled heavens, a shining frame
> Their great Original proclaim.

Episcopal blessing had been given to the exaltation of reason by Thomas Spratt, Bishop of Rochester and author of a book on the Royal Society (founded under the patronage of Charles II) in which he declared that miracles were not to be expected in the modern world where 'the course of things goes quietly along its own channel of natural causes and effects'. And Archbishop Tillotson, whose sermons, extolling charity and ethical values, but never ardent, remained influential long after his death in 1691, had said that 'all the duties of Christian religion which respect God are no other but what natural light prompts men to'.

The outlook encouraged worldliness, and it was not through services rendered to the Church that men were raised to the episcopate, but for services given to political parties or to lay patrons. Bishops were no longer servants of the king as they had been in the Middle Ages; instead, their secular duty was to attend the sessions of Parliament, to vote for the Minister who had appointed them. At the same time the eighteenth-century Church was renowned for scholarship and culture: at least three bishops, Joseph Butler, Berkeley and Warburton, were distinguished philosophers and scholars.

In the seventeenth century the divorce of religion and everyday life, of the natural and the supernatural, which was an inevitable consequence of the Reformation, was still not wholly accomplished. Church ales were still celebrated under Archbishop Laud and the church might still be used for some civic purposes. But in the Hanoverian age it was a place for worship only, a place to be visited only on Sunday. The building itself was as far as possible arranged for congregational liturgical worship in which altar, reading desk and pulpit could be seen by all the worshippers. This meant that when a new church was built it tended to take the form of an oblong room in which screens were open or non-existent. As some eighteenth-century parish churches have since become cathedrals, and appear in these pages, it is necessary to refer to their purpose, though this is, of course, quite different from the principal function of the cathedral. In the eighteenth century as in all other ages, except during the Interregnum, the cathedral clergy went on offering up their daily choral praise and prayers of intercession regardless of the presence or absence of a congregation. But in this time of religious torpor choirs were sometimes ill-trained, the behaviour of the choristers was often irreverent, canons were non-residential, there were few ritual processions, and choir books and vestments were shabby. Community services in cathedrals usually took place in the choir, which was screened off for warmth, for of course there was then no form of heating in the vast buildings. At Hereford the choir was disfigured by

painted yellowish-grey galleries set up over the stalls for the use of the public. Sometimes, as at Ely, Exeter, Chichester and Wells, a pulpit and seats were provided in the nave for the hearing of the sermon.

No new cathedrals were built in the age of reason, no new sees were created, and the challenge posed by the developing towns in the Midlands and the North was largely ignored. At Bristol, where the nave had been lost at the time of the Dissolution, no attempt was made to rebuild and the cathedral was left without a western limb until the nineteenth century. The Georgians were not sympathetic to the mystery, symbolism and irregularity of Gothic architecture, except as elements of the Picturesque, and many of the restorations and re-arrangements they did carry out have been deplored by both Victorian and modern historians as vandalism. James Essex was responsible for one of the most serious depredations of the period, the destruction of the twelfth-century pulpitum at Ely, which had miraculously survived the Reformation and the Civil War. Wyatt showed scant feeling for the Galilee porch of the same cathedral when he arranged for Mr Bernasconi to repair it by substituting tracery for the original tympanum and obscuring a remarkable view of the interior from the chamber above it by inserting tracery and mullions into a formerly open arch. When summoned by the Dean and Chapter of Lichfield in 1788 to carry out 'a thorough and substantial repair' Wyatt threw the choir and Lady Chapel into one by removing the medieval altar screen which, mutilated in the Civil War, had been covered with a Baroque altarpiece by Bishop Hacket. Wyatt built a large traceried screen in the crossing arch, topped by a handsome organ, though this was later demolished by Scott. This late-eighteenth-century work showed indifference to the majesty and meaning of the medieval cathedral, but at least the building was restored 'for convenient use'; thirty years earlier that indifference had resulted in an act of purposeless destruction: the library which Deans Heywode and Yotton had built in the fifteenth century to the north-west of the north transept was torn down, though the books were preserved and transferred to the treasury.

At Hereford after the fall of the west tower in 1786 Wyatt rebuilt the front without the tower and, with little regard for the original design, removed the spire from the central tower (for spires were alien to the taste of the time) and restored and altered the nave in his own style (*see* Introduction p. 8). The splendour of Norman Durham triumphs over all later alterations and restorations but the cathedral suffered a good deal in the century after Bishop Cosin had repaired the damage wrought during the Civil War. Under George Nicholson, architect to the Dean and Chapter from 1773, the medieval tracery was removed from the cloisters, the whole of the north side of the cathedral was scraped, and new carvings and pinnacles were added, while the two-storeyed north porch was demolished and rebuilt as a one-storeyed structure. In 1795, on November 20, the great Norman chapter house was razed to the ground by Nicholson's successor, Morphet. Wyatt had reported its ruinous condition but had not recommended its destruction. It must have been the decision of the Dean and Chapter. Wyatt was, however, the author of the rose window in the east wall of the Chapel of the Nine Altars. Though it concentrates attention on the wall its spidery design consorts ill with the vigour of the shafted lancets and arcading below it. At Salisbury Wyatt pulled down the free-standing bell tower, destroyed two small porches, one on the south side of the retrochoir and the other at the end of the north transept, and instead of restoring the neglected Hungerford and Beachamp chantry chapels removed them. The dispossessed monuments from the chapels were brought into the body of the cathedral and set between the nave pillars in two long orderly rows. No care was taken to place the effigies on the right slabs.

It was not lack of understanding of medieval building construction and unawareness of Gothic architecture and sculpture which led to procedures such as these. James Essex's design of 1769 for the stone reredos of the Angel Choir at Lincoln reveals the most sensitive appreciation of the architectural character of this beautiful room. He had the idea of copying the canopy of the monument of Bishop William de Luda (d. 1299) in Ely Cathedral, a tall central arch flanked by two smaller ones, all cusped and with leaves in the spandrels. A gable above the tall arch contains a trefoil shape enclosing a seated figure. The reredos, made by a mason called Pink, who has signed his work, is not only in harmony with its setting, it convinces. Essex also largely reconstructed the Octagon at Ely, and although he altered it by removing the upper flying buttresses, and by replacing the battlements with needle-like pinnacles, his work was done with a fellow

architect's grasp of the medieval mason's unique achievement. Another admirable eighteenth-century renovation, the surprising work of a champion of the Greek Revival, was William Wilkins's restoration of the exquisite fourteenth-century chapel of Prior Crawden at Ely, which shows complete command of medieval forms and techniques. Wilkins's work at Ely was described in the *Journal* of the Society of Antiquaries, which had been founded as early as 1717, and had encouraged scholarly interest in the medieval past. A few enthusiasts like Horace Walpole (*see* p. 226), John Milner, antiquarian and author of a *History of Winchester*, and Valentine Grey, the Worcester historian, advanced the work of the Society. At the same time the remarkable flowering of English topographical art fostered an appreciation of the pictorial effects of Gothic architecture. John Buckler alone made over 13,000 drawings of cathedrals, including many details which have since provided an invaluable record for restorers and historians.

No, it was not through ignorance that William Kent designed a three-bayed classical pulpitum in 1742 for Bishop Martin Benson at Gloucester, and adorned it with fanciful Gothick trimmings; and it was not through ignorance that he longed to transform the great Norman pillars of the nave into Palladian columns by fluting them, or that James Gibbs decided on fashionable mahogany for the pulpit in the north-east transept of Lincoln and provided it with classical balusters, that the same architect furnished the rooms under the west tower of Lincoln with stone panelling and classical doorways, that Lord Burlington paved the nave of York with marble geometry, that Bishop Philip Bisse of Hereford hid the Norman pillars and arches of the choir behind lath and plaster covered with oak panelling, and turned the altarpiece into a 'Grecian screen', and that it was a general practice at this time to whitewash cathedral interiors. The reason for it all was the complete confidence of the age in the attitude of mind which had brought about the triumph of the classical orders. There would be far more evidence of this eighteenth-century spirit in cathedrals if so much refurnishing of the period had not been swept away by Victorian restorers.

Perhaps the most enduring contribution of these Georgian decades to the cathedral image is to be seen in the domestic building of the close. The horizontal mode inspired some of the most perfectly designed country houses and some of the most elegant urban squares and terraces ever

LINCOLN: *Houses in the Close*

to be created, and cathedral closes, some of which have already been described, were transformed. The row of stone Georgian houses at Durham, varied by charming irregularities in size and treatment, all along the south side of the Green, comes at once to mind. It is difficult to imagine Ely without the contrast of the two fine Georgian houses on the north side of Palace Green and the Georgian houses in St Mary's Street; the atmosphere of College Green, Gloucester is determined by the Palladian accent of its houses, and the serenity and intimacy of Lichfield owes much to the beautiful early-eighteenth-century Deanery and the Georgian facades of the Close. And the predominating memory of Salisbury is of the great cathedral rising from the centre of a calm green oasis surrounded largely by classically fronted houses of dignified proportions.

The smooth sward to the north of the cathedral was an ill-kept, boggy graveyard until, almost at the end of the eighteenth century, Wyatt turfed it. As pictorial as the wonderfully contrived setting of the ruins of Fountains Abbey, it makes the cathedral the focal point of a grand Picturesque composition, which a few years later was appreciated as such by Constable. It was of course in the interests of his splendid design that Wyatt destroyed the bell tower. It would have interrupted the striking view of the cathedral from the north. Wyatt would have landscaped Durham too had not the Society of Antiquaries frustrated him. We must be grateful for its intervention for the architect wanted to demolish the Galilee Chapel to make way for a romantic carriage drive round the west end of the cathedral on the edge of the cliff above the Wear.

The cult of the Picturesque was one aspect of the Romantic Movement which as much as the growing scholarly interest in medieval architecture was to lead to the great outburst of Victorian church building in the Gothic style. The background to the change from the horizontal to the vertical mode was dominated by the disintegration of the rational view. The impassioned preaching of the Wesleys and Whitefield undermined it; and although Bishop Butler was hostile to Methodism and is famous for his rebuke of Wesley ('Sir, the pretending to extraordinary revelation and gifts of the Holy Ghost is a horrid thing – a very horrid thing') his monumental and influential work, *The Analogy of Religion, Natural and Revealed, to the Constitution and Course of Nature* (1736), played a major part in the repudiation of reason. With disquieting clarity Butler showed that simple logic could not resolve the mystery and irrationality of life. Like Dr Johnson he looked about him with a sombre melancholy and shattered the easy eighteenth-century confidence in natural law.

It might be thought that Butler's awareness of the inadequacy of reason might find an echo in the art which more than any other reveals truths and plumbs depths of feeling beyond the reach of words, but much of the church music of the period is as devoid of mystery as the interior of Derby Cathedral. William Croft's setting of the Burial Service, rather unexpectedly still in use, is the musical equivalent of the bland, torch-bearing and weeping cherubs of contemporary funeral monuments; and through William Boyce and his master Maurice Greene, both choristers of St Paul's, made a notable collection of early cathedral music, their own devotional anthems have none of the fervour and poignancy of the work of Tallis and William Byrd, and none of the invigorating and uplifting assurance of Purcell's setting of the psalms and anthems and of his great *Te Deum* and *Jubilate*, and they lack the dramatic, urgent momentum of John Blow's services, of his inspired motet *Salvator Mundi* and of the anthem he wrote for the opening of St Paul's. Thomas Attwood was a pupil of Mozart but he was deaf to the author of the tragic *Dies Irae* of the *Requiem*: his service settings and anthems are elegant, graceful, neat and well balanced but with none of Mozart's emotional intensity.

All the same this was the age of Handel's *Messiah*, one of the most sublime and profound affirmations of faith through revelation, and it was in the eighteenth century that cathedrals and their daily choral services began to be the centres of events which renewed their importance in the weekday and not just the Sunday lives of the people. The Three Choirs Festival was founded in 1724 with the purpose of alleviating the poverty of widows and orphans of the clergy of the dioceses of Worcester, Hereford and Gloucester. But, centred on the choirs and organists of these three cities, the Festival established a remarkable tradition of commissioning contemporary music as well as of performing cathedral music of the past which has flourished and spread to other cathedrals. Diocesan choral festivals were to become popular throughout the country in the Victorian period, and contributed to the awakening from the eighteenth-century spiritual torpor which so profoundly affected both theology and architecture.

PORTSMOUTH: *Cupola and Central Tower*

The photograph (taken in 1950) of the tower and cupola rising above a great mound of disordered hawsers and tackle reminds us of the close connection of the church and the Dockyard. It was built to serve the needs of the community at the mouth of the harbour and the tower, both in the Middle Ages and after the Reformation was used as a naval watching tower. Founded as a chapel of the church of St Mary of Portsea Island in the twelfth century, then from 1320, as a parish church, St Thomas's became a cathedral in 1927. The former parish church has been enlarged and extended westwards since then but with a lack of zest and conviction at variance with the character of a traditional cathedral. So these two photographs concentrate on Portsmouth's original aspect as a parish and Dockyard church. Both the tower and nave (now the choir) were damaged in the Civil War. Rebuilt during the last years of the seventeenth century and the first decade of the eighteenth, they already speak the language of the age of reason. But the Gothic past is not forgotten. The tower, which since the building of the new nave in the 1930s is central but which

in 1693 was at the west end of the old nave, acknowledges its medieval predecessor by a suggestion of angle battlements in the raised corners of the plain parapet. The nave arcades, though so classical in feeling, present in their simply moulded arches a delightful variation on the pure sweep of the broad blank enclosing arches of the late-twelfth-century choir, one of the two bays of which we can see. The tower is surmounted by a charming domed and octagonal wooden cupola upon which stands a second miniature cupola supporting a slender spirelet, a golden ball and a gilded weathervane in the form of a barque. The cupola was designed to take a peal of eight bells and was a familiar landmark in the city until the high rise developments of our own century started to close in upon it. The weathervane was blown down a few years after the photograph was taken and a replica was put in its place.

The tall octagonal bases of the nave piers mark the height of the original pews. The coved ceiling above the dentilled cornice is pierced by homely dormer windows and dormers also light the aisles. The west gallery is not as it was built in the eighteenth century, though panels from the galleries of 1706 and 1750 which then extended along the aisles, have been re-used in the present structure. The west gallery was the singing loft and contained and still contains the organ with its exquisite case of 1718, the work of Abraham Jordan, Junior. It now faces the new nave. The exuberant carving attached to the first bay pier is the Royal Arms of William and Mary made by Lewis Allen, Master Carver of the Dockyard in 1694.

Opposite. PORTSMOUTH: *Old Choir and Nave*

218

Above. DERBY: *The Nave*   *Opposite.* BIRMINGHAM: *The Nave*

These two interiors, both inspired by knowledge of classical architecture acquired in Italy, present an exciting contrast in interpretation. James Gibbs's light, low, elegant room at Derby wholly reflects the cool rationalism of the period. It is immediately apprehended as a single oblong space, the calm of which is unruffled by the variety of diagonal vistas cleverly created by the inward leaning of the arcade arches.

In Thomas Archer's Birmingham church the traditional distinction between nave and aisles is effectively preserved. The immensely tall arcade arches with their huge keystones and the giant pilasters on either side of the tower arch impart an aspiring motion to the stately nave, though this is firmly held in check by the frieze of rich plasterwork. But the full impact of this Baroque composition is ruined by the dark band of oak-panelled galleries. The columns of both interiors are raised on pedestals so that the box pews with which the naves were originally furnished should not hide the bases.

Both the parish church of St Philip, Birmingham, begun in 1709 and completed in 1725, and the parish church of All Saints, Derby, originally a collegiate church, then a Free Chapel, rebuilt in 1723–5, were raised to cathedral status in the present century.

221

That the Memory of an honest & well deserving Man
may be transmitted to Posterity;
This Monument was Designed & Erected by

Opposite. ELY: *Cloister,*
Humphrey Smith's monument

On the right. LEICESTER
Detail of slate memorial
slab

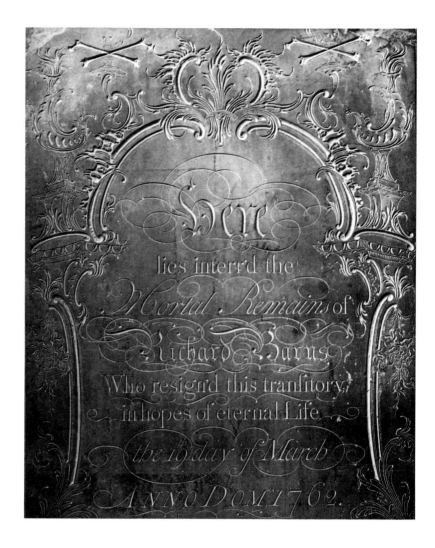

The slab, one of a number, commemorates the amazingly skilful local slate-engraving craft which was centred at Swithland and which flourished in the eighteenth and early nineteenth centuries. Leicestershire gravestone engravings of this period rival the most dazzling efforts of calligraphers and recall contemporary engraved trade cards and frontispieces. On Richard Barns's memorial the first word of the inscription has been taken from its context and turned into an elaborate central heading; below it lettering of every variety breaks into a riot of interlacing, looping and twirling patterns. Writing masters referred to such decorations as 'strikings'. The engraver, whose work closely resembles that of one James Sparrow who signed several slabs, and may indeed be by him, must have studied the manuals of writing masters such as George Bickham whose compendium of contemporary work was published in 1743. The lettering is set,

like a frontispiece, in a whimsical framework in the fashionable Chinese-Rococo taste, loosely controlled by Classic order.

The memorial to Humphrey Smith of 1745 was carved by Charles Stanley, a pupil of Scheemaker. It was not made from life but was taken from a portrait after the subject's death. It is typical of the excellent portrait busts of the period which were often, as here, set in a medallion ornamented with emblematic plant forms and putti. Marble had taken the place of native freestone and alabaster for funeral sculpture by the end of the seventeenth century, and the white marble of the bust, medallion and elegant leaning putto stand out against the grey marble of the background obelisk, symbol of Eternity. Stanley's subject wears contemporary casual dress: he has discarded his wig for a cap, and relaxes in a loose house coat, the popular banyan.

223

Opposite. DERBY: *detail of the Screen*

Above. MANCHESTER: *detail of the Communion Rail*

The great distinguishing feature of Derby's graceful interior is its wonderful wrought-iron chancel screen. It brings all to life and instantly draws the eye. It was the work of a local craftsman, Robert Bakewell, who died in 1752. One of a number of brilliant provincial ironsmiths, his work is as rich as anything from the hand of Tijou, yet little is known of him, and his skill was so little appreciated that the gates he made for the west end of All Saints churchyard were pulled down by Victorian restorers and auctioned. His workshop stood in Oak's Yard, off St Peter's Street, Derby, and he acquired it with payment he received from another glorious work, the Arbour at Melbourne.

For the screen he received £338. 10s. The tenor of the age is emphatically announced by the presence of the spirited and finely detailed Royal Arms in the central position, which in the Middle Ages would have been occupied by the Rood. From the time of the Reformation the Royal Arms were set up in all churches to remind worshippers that they were members of an earthly as well as a heavenly kingdom.

The communion rail at Manchester, dating 1750–1, the work of an unknown artist, reveals an entirely different personality, and affords an insight into the astonishing variety of talent of the period. The design, based on naturalistic tendrils, plant forms, classical motifs and urn shapes, is witty and utterly enchanting.

In the early years of the Reformation the altar was unprotected and for the Holy Communion service people knelt round it in a disorderly group. Matthew Wren was among those who pointed out the disadvantages of this, and Laudian churchmen adopted the idea of railing the altar.

The photograph records one of those unexpected visual encounters common in cathedrals which have stood for as long as York Minster. Medieval alabaster keeps company with classical imagery and Italian marble. The flat effigy of a little prince, William Hatfield, who died in 1344, aged 8 dimmed by attrition and vandalism (for Horace Walpole who was responsible for its restoration found it 'thrown aside into a hole') but never a likeness, lies close to the strongly personal memorial to Admiral Henry Medley, who died four hundred years later in 1747. His vivid portrait bust (not visible from this angle) is flanked by naval trophies and his sarcophagus exhibits the relief of a naval battle in which he distinguished himself. Angels, denizens of Heaven, support the little prince's head; pagan putti extinguish torches, symbols of death, and lament the Admiral's demise. The sculptor of the Medley monument was the popular Sir Henry Cheere who, like Stanley (p. 223), trained under Scheemaker in his studio in Vine Street, Piccadilly. Cheere was paid £262. 10s. for the work.

The North Chapel of this former parish church of St Mary, raised to cathedral rank in 1913, was the burial place of the Mildmay family from the time of Elizabeth I. The monument to Benjamin, Earl Fitzwalter, who died in 1756 shows a type of memorial which became popular during the last half of the eighteenth century: an urn takes the place of the effigy, often, as here, set in an alcove flanked by classical columns. The scale of the huge urn in the monument, the broken pediment and the nervous carving of the ornament above the alcove bring the composition to life. But this graceful and sophisticated architectural piece with its pretty attendant cherubs, one of whom reverses a torch, is wholly without the power to move.

227

Mʳˢ SARAH UDNY, his afflicted Grand mother
erected this Monument as
a public Teſtimony of her Affection
for an amiable and moſt endearing Child.

Above. CHICHESTER: *detail from the monument to Ernest Augustus Udney under the South-West Tower*

Opposite. WORCESTER: *monument to Mrs Charlotte Digby in the Retrochoir*

The robust realism of early-eighteenth-century portrait effigies and the later theatricality of the overlarge urn and broken pediment were followed by a reaction in favour of antique models stimulated by the writings of Winckelmann. The photograph divorces Henry Westmacott's sentimental, poppy-drowsed figure of little Ernest Udney (d. 1808) from its noble surroundings, so it can be relished as a comic period piece. It lacks the sharp definition of Stanley's bust of Humphrey Smith and marks the decline of a great tradition. Chantrey's effigy of Charlotte Digby, on the other hand, idealised and passionless though it is, ranks high among the visual pleasures of Worcester. The monument is exquisitely composed and carved and perhaps because the building was so heavily restored in the nineteenth century there seems nothing incongruous about this white figure of 1825 resting on her sofa on a high sarcophagus in a medieval cathedral.

228

TRURO CATHEDRAL

230

VII
Cathedrals in an Industrial Society

DURING the centuries which have already been briefly reviewed cathedrals like all old buildings were changing and growing, taking and keeping something of every generation. But only rarely was any attempt made to emulate the style of earlier work, and then, as with William Wynford's towers at Wells, it was an aesthetically necessary and ingenious adaptation rather than an imitation. New work was carried out in the mode which expressed the spirit and habit of mind of the age, and which made use of new technical skills. It was not through lack of understanding of medieval architecture that when Essex restored the Octagon at Ely he introduced Gothick openings into the lantern or that the Dean and Chapter of Lichfield chose the recently invented and fashionable Roman cement for the restoration of the west front or that Inigo Jones designed a classical pulpitum for Winchester. These choices were all determined by an instinctive acceptance of the idiom of the day. So it is astonishing to find a cathedral begun in 1879, a picture of which can be seen on the opposite page, looking for all the world like an Early English building. Yet the spires, short though they are, and the smooth masonry do not seem part of the Cornish setting, and the trim silhouette, by comparison with that of medieval Salisbury or of Lichfield, another three-spired cathedral, seems a little unconvincing. And once inside the building the presence of the north aisle of the parish church of St Mary, which Truro Cathedral replaced, a typical Cornish late Gothic interior of homely atmosphere, with wagon roof, granite piers, whitewashed walls and large traceried Perpendicular windows glowing with bits of old glass, exposes the cold and scholarly perfection of the architecture in which it is encased.

We know with what deep devotion the Victorian designer, John Loughborough Pearson, embarked on his great task; we do not for a moment doubt his integrity and his strong sense of responsibility, yet the result of all his endeavour is a brilliant exercise in historicism, a toned-down Gothic that is without the power to move. Can this reflect the temper of a society so altered from that of the Middle Ages, so increasingly materialistic and industrialised? Should not this Neo-Gothic pile have been a work of engineering, a cathedral of glass and cast-iron like Paxton's great exhibition hall? There were many and complicated reasons why in this Victorian age of astonishing conflict and dichotomy no style other than Gothic could have seemed right for Truro. At the time of the first Reform Bill the Church was in a state of crisis. The bishops and cathedral clergy who adhered to the High Tory party of the day and for the most part had obtained preferment not through service to the Church but through aristocratic connections or family favour, were under attack from the hosts of Nonconformists and free-thinking Radicals, united in their hatred of ecclesiastical privilege. Lampoons and gross caricatures of plump, red-faced bishops and prebendaries filled the press and when, after the Spiritual Peers had voted in the House of Lords against the Reform Bill, the mob stoned their coaches and set fire to their palaces, Dr Arnold of Rugby declared that 'the Church as it is now, no human power can save'. The state of many cathedral buildings, often neglected during the Age of Reason, reflected the spiritual stagnation of the Establishment. The great west transept of Ely, for instance had been boarded up since the seventeenth century and Essex had described it as 'in worse conditions than any part of the church'. As late as the 1840s it was still delapidated, cluttered with lumber, carpenters' materials and tools and used as a workshop. At Lichfield, according to Canon Lonsdale's *Recollections*, the nave had become a promenade for nursemaids and was totally devoid of furniture, while the whole interior was covered with a 'dead, yellowish whitewash'; the central tower of Peterborough was in danger of collapse; the interior of Hereford was full of broken pavements, the monuments were defaced, the great Norman pillars were coated with whitewash and the unkempt Minster yard was the scene of noisy games. At St Albans only the chancel and part of the north transept were in use. Scott described Chester as 'so horribly and lamentably decayed as to reduce it to a mere wreck like a mouldering sandstone cliff'. Worcester, another sandstone cathedral, was in as parlous a state, and the effects of time and weather on the friable fabric had been accelerated by what was known as 'scaling' (rubbing down the stone). The tower and spire of Salisbury were unstable, and only eight of the statues that once crowded the west front were still in place, while in the cloisters columns were missing and tracery shattered. The west front and tower of Rochester were unsafe; the nave of Bristol had never been completed; the reredos at Winchester had lost some of its canopies and all its statues and Waynflete's chantry was still as Cromwell's troops had left it except for the recent use of putty to repair the battered effigy.

Meanwhile English society and traditional ways of life were convulsed by revolutionary change. In the first half of the nineteenth century the population of the country had risen from 8·5 to 17 million; and by the end of Victoria's reign it had exploded to 32·5 million. Most of the growth took place in northern and midland towns where the irresistible tide of industry had advanced most rapidly. Agricultural labourers were leaving the land to become factory workers and slum dwellers. Huge cities with sprawling suburbs were transforming the face of England. And although most of the old cathedral towns were as yet physically untouched by the frightening new developments, diocesan administration, which had hardly altered between the sixteenth and eighteenth centuries, had to take account of the upheaval. At the same time the intellectual climate was fraught with doubt and uncertainty. While new churches and chapels were springing up in the spreading towns and were crowded as seldom before, and a continual outpouring of theological pamphlets, tracts and sermons seemed to bear witness to an age of faith, piety went hand in hand with an overriding preoccupation with prosperity, commerce, property and material wellbeing and was challenged by the unbelief of many of the most distinguished and influential teachers, philosophers and writers of the day. Carlyle, Matthew Arnold, George Eliot, John Stuart Mill, George Meredith and Froude all renounced the Christian creed. Literary and historical criticism of the Bible, the establishment in the 1830s of the geological succession of rocks and fossils by Sir Charles Lyall and Dean Buckland and the publication in 1841 of *Vestiges of the Natural History of Creation* by Robert Chambers of *Chambers Encyclopaedia* (though he remained anonymous at first) had shaken the authority of traditional Christianity. After the publication in 1859 of Darwin's *Origin of Species* it was impossible for an intelligent man to pay more than lip service to the orthodox view of Genesis as historical fact and the Bible as a divinely guaranteed repository of knowledge of God and the world.

Science not only 'shattered the idol of an infallible book' as Richard Church, Dean of St Paul's, who welcomed Darwin's discoveries, said, but, in a more practical manifestation, it confronted the architect with an awkward dilemma. The Institute of Civil Engineers had come into being as early as 1818 and had received its Royal Charter in 1828. Though there was at first no sense of rivalry between the architect and the engineer, the economic advantage of factory-made buildings ensured the eventual triumph of the engineer in the architectural field, and soon relegated the architect in his true role of artist to a minor position. A well-known and early instance of the new relationship was the partnership of Brunel and Matthew Digby Wyatt at Paddington. 'I am going to build a station after my own fancy,' Brunel wrote to Wyatt, 'It almost of necessity becomes an engineering work, but to be honest, even if it were not, it is a branch of architecture of which I am fond, and of course, believe myself fully competent for.' Wyatt was left to design only the ornamental details. Victorian industrial buildings are widely held to be the most significant aesthetic expressions of the period. This is questionable, but they are certainly the most appropriate, direct and honest manifestations of an industrial society, and their makers were supreme in the new materials of iron and glass. The architect's response to the threat of the engineer was to go on conceiving of his projects in terms of stone and brick. His extraordinary choice of the Gothic style was dictated by reactions to the shock to orthodoxy and by the devastating visual and environmental effects of industry, materialism and the expanding population.

The threat to the Church as an institution was averted. Fear of calamity created a sense of urgency, and the bishops, prompted by C. J. Blomfield, Bishop of London, established a Cathedral Commission in 1852 to carry out reforms which would make cathedrals the true centres of diocesan life. Chapters were drastically reduced: every cathedral had a dean and a small number of resident canons, usually four. The nonresident was practically eliminated. The resident's regular attendance at the daily services was obligatory. Prebends were suppressed and fixed annual stipends were paid; and while the picturesque names of the prebends were retained, their endowments, with very few exceptions, were applied to other uses. The stalls were appropriated to honorary canons appointed by the bishop, usually from among the parochial clergy of the diocese. These honorary canons were excluded from participation in the business of the chapter. The scandals of sinecures and nepotism were removed and definite duties involving work connected with the cathedral schools and with theological colleges were linked to preferments. Vicars choral and minor canons were no longer deputies for absent members of the chapter but became small bodies of clergy responsible for the cathedral music. Diocesan boundaries were shifted: Gloucester and Bristol were combined, though Bristol regained independence in 1897. Essex was transferred to Rochester. New dioceses were created in answer to the growth of population: Ripon became a cathedral in 1836, Manchester was raised to cathedral status in 1848, and in 1877 the dioceses of St Albans and Truro were formed; Liverpool followed in 1880, Newcastle in 1882, Southwell in 1884, and Wakefield in 1888.

These practical arrangements would have done little to revive the spiritual power of the Church without the work of the Oxford Movement. Known as 'Tractarian' from its writings, *Tracts for the Times*, published between 1833 and 1841, the movement was inaugurated by John Keble with an assize sermon entitled *National Apostasy* which he preached in St Mary's, Oxford, on July 14, 1833. A High Church association, which, unlike Wesley's mission to the poor and destitute, addressed itself to educated and fastidious minds, it restored the idea of the Church as a sacred mystery and introduced rites and ceremonials which under the latitudinarian liberalism of the eighteenth century had been allowed to lapse: altar lights, vestments, wafer bread, the mixed chalice, making the sign of the cross, genuflexions, the surpliced choir, fixed stone altars, crucifixes and statues, cults of the Virgin and the saints and the adoration of the eucharistic sacraments. Ritualism was felt to be the symbol and safeguard of deep doctrinal convictions: the Tractarians concentrated on tradition and reasserted the importance of the Apostolic succession of the bishops. Newman, who was one of the galvanising personalities of the movement, startled the bishops, who would of necessity play the chief role in restoring a sense of the divine origin, mission and authority of the Church, by telling them that they could not wish 'for a more blessed termination of their course than the spoiling of their goods and martyrdom'. But despite his unwelcome evocation of the prospect of martyrdom Newman touched old truths into new life and gave new meaning to an institution which had seemed moribund.

One result of the emphasis the Tractarians placed on Eucharistic worship was the encouragement of greater musical elaboration of the cathedral service. Mass settings by continental composers, among whom Gounod was prominent and influential, were adapted to English Prayer Book texts and the daily choral praise in cathedrals for the glory of God was enriched by an outpouring of anthems and services by a series of gifted, emotional and romantic composers. Sterndale Bennett, Joseph Barnsby, Stainer, Walmisley and Parry do not rank with the great nineteenth-century composers, yet, peculiarly English and as eloquent of their period and its upheavals as Street, Pearson, Scott, Blomfield and Bodley, they are interesting by comparison with those architects because they did not imitate models from the distant past but developed the idiom of their immediate predecessors. Cathedral choirs of today are still drawing upon the vitality of this great Victorian outburst of church music. Among its fruits was the immense growth in popularity of choral festivals. From 1865, when Lichfield organised the first diocesan choral festival, these celebrations became annual events in most cathedral towns.

The association of the spiritual revival of the Church with the Gothic style was largely due to the efforts of A. W. N. Pugin and the Cambridge Camden Society (later the Ecclesiological Society). Pugin, a Catholic convert, had travelled widely and made detailed and careful drawings of medieval monuments. He was an enthusiastic artist but his grasp of the Gothic style was above all erudite. When in 1836 he published his brilliant pamphlet *Contrasts, or a Parallel between the noble edifices of the fourteenth and fifteenth centuries, and similar buildings of the present day, showing the present decay of Taste*, the impact was immediate and revolutionary. This ardent plea for a return to the exalted and eminently Christian style of the Middle Ages, reinforced by comparisons between the insubstantial and pagan character of Georgian and Regency architecture and the variety and solidity of Gothic gave

BLACKBURN: *The Nave*

support to the arguments of the Tractarians with which it was contemporary, and a second edition of 1841 sold in huge numbers. Gothic was established as the only style fit to bear witness to the Faith.

The first evidence of the association of Gothic with the religious revival, and of the intense earnestness with which the remains of the Middle Ages began to be studied, was the abandonment of the light-hearted approach which so delights us at Shobden, and which led Wyatt, despite his thorough grasp of medieval building construction, to render its noble forms in counterfeit plaster at Lichfield and Hereford. The nave of Blackburn (though only made a cathedral in the present century) yields a glimpse of the style on the eve of the change from fantasy to scholarly revival. Originally designed by John Palmer in 1820–6, it was rebuilt after a fire of 1831 in consultation with Rickman, author of the names by which we distinguish the different phases of Gothic architecture. The tierceron star vault though medieval in form is still of plaster and the niches on either side of the entrance arch, adorned with a cable

motif, widely spaced crockets and meek, pretty angel corbels, are of their period. But already we feel a breath of that deadly pedantry which chills us in so many Victorian church interiors.

Blackburn was in course of construction when in 1839 John Mason Neale and Benjamin Webb, then undergraduates at Trinity, founded the Ecclesiological Society to 'promote the study of Ecclesiastical Architecture and the restoration of mutilated architectural remains'. They admired Rickman as a pioneer. Ecclesiology was a new word described as a 'science which may treat of the proper construction and operations of the Church, or Communion, or Society of Christians'. In fact the Society was concerned with all the details of medieval church architecture and church furniture and embraced liturgiology, church music and organs. From 1841 until 1868 its ideas and doctrines were spread through its magazine, *The Ecclesiologist*, and branches of the Society appeared in nearly every cathedral town. It was the Ecclesiologists who established the superiority of fourteenth-century Gothic ('Middle Pointed', as they called it) over the styles of all other periods. It was the Society that originated the extraordinary idea that only a churchman could be a good architect, and that a church architect should design nothing but churches. Architects, however, could not escape the utilitarian attitudes and assumptions of their age and though cathedral builders and restorers were members of the Society, though the pupils in George Edmund Street's office began the day with Gregorian chants and celebrated every Christian festival, though Pearson offered up prayers before starting a church design, and Scott wrote of being 'morally awakened' by the views of the Cambridge Camden Society, recoiling from the 'abject degeneration' of his early work, they were all highly successful examples of the new Victorian concept of the architect as a professional business man, secure and respected in the social hierarchy. Not one of them devoted himself to church building alone; all of them were profitably engaged on secular projects.

The change in the social position of the architect is one of the most interesting and significant developments of the Victorian period. It can only be touched upon very briefly here as one of the many obstacles frustrating the realisation of the dream of recalling the unity and the all embracing faith of the Middle Ages. The building trade itself was firmly in the hands of a man, whose earlier tentative appearance has already been noted but who now dominated the scene – the contractor, whose only interest in any building, even a cathedral, was financial. Purely a business man, he employed workmen in all the necessary trades, competing for great undertakings with other contractors operating in the same way. The patron of earlier ages had now become the *client* even if that meant a bishop or a dean and chapter. Although the system of articled pupilage remained the accepted method of training until towards the end of the nineteenth century when, with the institution of degrees in architecture, the profession became closed to all who could not pass an examination, the medieval workshop where craftsmen carried out the master mason's plans and designs under his supervision and on the site, had become a drawing office remote from the scene of activity. The worst effects of the system were to be seen in the mean terraces built for factory workers, for which the Victorian coined a new word – housing. Great churches at the other end of the scale still commanded, as they had always done, the foremost talents and skills, but now it was the manufacturer who brought the artist's designs to fruition. Among the major manufacturers involved in the fashioning of ecclesiastical furnishings and fittings were John Hardman and Co., stained glass and metal workers of Birmingham, who together with Potter of London made Scott's new choir screen for Ely; Clayton and Bell, stained-glass workers and ornamental painters, who are represented in nearly every cathedral; John Keith & Son, makers of church plate; the Lugwardine Tile Works, manufacturers of tiles based on medieval examples, some of which can be seen in Exeter Cathedral; Farmer and Brindley, manufacturers of statues who produced ten female saints designed by C. E. Kempe for the Lady Chapel at Lichfield; and the Skidmore Art Manufacturers Company of Coventry, who made the screens Scott designed for Hereford, Lichfield and Salisbury. Ratee and Kett of Cambridge, builders and woodworkers who made statuettes of abbots and bishops for the sub-stalls at Ely, were responsible for carving the new organ of 1851 in the triforium on the north side of the choir at Ely, and are still working at the Fen cathedral.

Designs for important buildings were now generally chosen by a committee from competition entries. In the case of Truro the Diocesan Cathedral Committee under the chairmanship of the Earl of Mount Edgecumbe appointed a subcommittee who invited St Aubyn, Bodley & Garner, Burges, Pearson, Pullan and Scott to submit designs. Bodley's and Pearson's drawings were both recommended to the General Committee, who voted for Pearson's design. At Liverpool in 1886 three architects were invited to compete – William Emerson, Bodley & Garner and James Brooke. The site was adjacent to St George's Hall. Ewan Christian was asked to advise the judges and came to the conclusion that none of the designs was satisfactory; so in 1901 architects were again invited to send in drawings, this time for the splendid site on St James's Mount. We know the result: Norman Shaw and Bodley, who were the judges, chose the design of the young Giles Gilbert Scott from 103 sets of drawings, thirty-three of which had been prepared expressly for the cathedral. Although the cathedral bodies appear to have played the minimum part in the appointment of architects for these major projects, the buildings might never have materialised without the determination and enthusiasm of the bishops. Dr Edward White Benson, the first Bishop of Truro, afterwards Archbishop of Canterbury, refused to countenance the use of the parish church of St Mary as a cathedral. And at Liverpool, where the parish church of St Peter was to have been elevated to cathedral status, the second bishop, Dr Chavasse, insisted on a cathedral building which should stand upon St James's Mount, that uplifted, rocky mass, 155 feet above the Mersey. The Cathedral Building Fund, which the Bishop inaugurated had reached £325,000 before the work was begun.

By the time the counterfeit Early English of Truro had come into being the influence of the Ecclesiologists on style had waned. The tyrannical insistance of the Society on Middle Pointed Gothic which in 1841 had led the members to vote for the total demolition of Peterborough and its replacement by a cathedral of the 'best' period (a proposal which fortunately never came to fruition) had been questioned by Scott as early as 1850. In his essay *Plea for the Faithful Restoration of our Ancient Churches* he advocated other forms of Gothic than the sacred Middle Pointed and seemed to encourage a conservative form of restoration. 'Individual caprice should be *wholly excluded* from restoration', he wrote, and 'As a general rule it is highly desirable to preserve those vestiges of the growth and history of the building which are indicated by the various styles and irregularities of its parts.... It is often preferable to retain reminiscences of the age of Elizabeth, or James, or the martyred Charles, rather than sweep away, as is now the fashion, everything which dates later than the Reformation.' Of course he did not follow his own precepts and in their passion for Gothic, Victorian restorers were often more destructive than either Thomas or Oliver Cromwell, as they so earnestly strove to 'improve' on their great models. Not one of the older cathedrals, not even St Paul's, escaped the effects of the Revival. Bodley & Garner erected a monstrous marble reredos in St Paul's in 1888 and two years later William Richmond decorated the chancel with mosaics quite alien to the mood of Wren's great creation. Before that William Burges, who detested Wren's work as what he called 'abominations', would have altered the entire interior had not his proposals, approved and accepted by Dean Church and the chapter, been defeated by public outcry.

The few instances of decay and neglect already cited testify to the urgency of the need for cathedral restoration, and the serious antiquarian approach of the Victorians ensured that some of it was highly successful. Scott's rebuilding of the tower at Chichester (p. 240) is a close and satisfying replica of the original; and the little-known J. R. Holden's rebuilding of the tower at Manchester (p. 249) is another example of inspired and convincing restoration. At York where in 1829 and again in 1840 fire had destroyed the wooden vaults of both choir and nave Sir Robert Smirke and his brother Sidney reconstructed the medieval design with commendable fidelity. After much controversy the idea, sanctioned by the dean but not the chapter, of rebuilding the tower of Peterborough with a Decorated upper stage above a Norman lower storey was roundly rejected by the Archbishop of Canterbury (Dr Benson, formerly Bishop of Truro) in favour of a faithful restoration of the existing feature. The front was also repaired with the minimum alteration and with the skilful re-use of the original stones. Scott saved the Gothic spire of Salisbury by reinforcing his knowledge of medieval construction with the resources of his own day: he introduced a complicated and ingenious system of diagonal bands connected with the buttresses at the base of the tower.

Street's nave at Bristol (p. 242) is a new building rather than a restoration, as it rose on the foundations of the nave begun by Abbot Newland (1481–1515) and swept away after the Dissolution. Street based his work on the striking invention of the fourteenth-century mason who built the chancel and it is not only technically admirable but really does recapture something of the spirit of the medieval composition. Another brilliant Victorian addition to a medieval church is W. D. Caröe's retrochoir at Wakefield (p. 248) where a new chancel and transept were needed to transform the former parish church into a cathedral. Caröe's work was done after the turn of the century, and the medieval idiom is used with refreshing freedom. Perpendicular, the style of the original chancel, is used to develop Gothic beyond the stage it had reached at the end of the fifteenth century. The long and attenuated shafts and excessively narrow aisles exaggerate medieval practice with dramatic effect.

The restoration of the ravaged and depleted reredos at Winchester shows both the strength and the weakness of the Revivalist approach. The architect was J. R. Sedding, a pupil of Street, who in addition to an extensive practice produced a great many designs for silversmith's work, embroideries and wallpapers. He matched the surviving canopies punctiliously but then proceeded to fill the niches with statues. Though they conform to the medieval iconography, and though Sedding himself drew the designs directly onto the stone, the gestures, stances and facial expressions of these figures could not be more remote in feeling from medieval sculpture. Sentimental and with the curious smooth finish imparted by the new mechanical aids to carving, they highlight the dubiousness of the whole attempted return to the art of the Middle Ages. The statues were made by Boulton of Cheltenham, Nicholls of London and Gaflowski of London. A relief by Farmer and Brindley took the place of *The Raising of Lazarus* by Benjamin West above the altar.

The removal of the painting is an instance of an alteration which was not essential, a frequent occurrence, for Victorian restorers liked to indulge their fancies and seldom restricted their activities to the repair of decay and collapse. Salvin's replacement of the ancient stalls at Wells with repulsive carved stone seating is another example. Scott's removal of Wyatt's work on the lantern at Ely in order to restore the original medieval design is too well and accurately done to cause offence, but it was not necessary and could be said to destroy a contribution which added its own period flavour to the great cathedral compendium of creative effort. Wyatt's restorations and refurnishings were never to the

WINCHESTER: *The Reredos*

taste of the Revivalists and many of them were swept away together with most Georgian repairs and additions which were regarded as 'pagan'. No one could object to the removal of eighteenth-century whitewash even though at Wells Benjamin Ferrey removed the wall tablets too. But the opening up of vistas and the destruction of screens so that the sanctuary should become the focal point of worship was destructive of the whole medieval concept of the cathedral, which, as has been said more than once, was not designed for congregational worship.

It is interesting that this unmedieval opening of the cathedral interior only became practical because of the new possibilities of the age. With the invention of central heating the whole vast building could be thrown open for the first time in its history. Earlier in the present century a winter visitor to Ely could be sure of seeing a group of old Fen men warming themselves by one of the huge circular iron stoves, each surmounted by a crown labelled V.R., which discreetly interrupted as they still do the severe perfection of the architectural progress to the chancel. At Chester, Worcester, Salisbury, Ely, Hereford and Lichfield openwork screens took the place of more substantial structures, all of them the work of Sir Gilbert Scott. He never did anything as insensitive as Lord Grimthorpe's rebuilding of St Albans (p. 245) but together with Hussey and Blomfield he left Chester aggressively Victorian rather than medieval, giving free rein to his own taste to the extent of erecting a great polygonal apse at the end of the south aisle topped by a spire-like octagonal roof. It would be absurd were it not so heavy and hard-surfaced. At Worcester Scott took over from the cathedral architect Perkins who had already been responsible for replacing the west window of 1789 with a Middle Pointed traceried opening and for renewing the west door and the east window. Scott imparted an altogether Victorian character to the surface of the external masonry, and he completely transformed the whole of the choir. All that is now so daunting in its aspect – the vaults, painted by Hardman, the shiny floor tiles, the screen, the loss of the charming tester from the choir pulpit, the stained glass, the bishop's throne and the obtrusive reredos – was introduced by Scott. The factitious nature of most of this furnishing is all the more obvious and painful because its setting is one of the most perfect and most mature of lancet compositions.

At Ely Scott substituted his own screen for that of Wyatt and also lengthened the choir by two bays westward, placed the organ in the triforium projecting over the choir stalls, altered the position of the choir stalls and boarded up the nave ceiling which until then had been open to the rafters. The painted design which Scott based on the ceiling decoration of St Michael, Hildesheim, was sensitively executed by an amateur, Mr Le Strange of Hunstanton Hall.

At Salisbury, as at Ely, Scott reversed Wyatt's work, installed a metal screen, a new reredos and bishop's throne and moved the altar westwards. Scott's renovations at Durham were on the whole disastrous; they included the erection of an ugly and incongruous screen with polished granite columns impudently confronting the grave, archaic monoliths of the nave and a ponderous pulpit in the inappropriate Italian Cosmati style. It is hard to believe that the screen at Lichfield is the design of the same man. For this wonderfully light metal structure is an original creation, deriving nothing but its form from the Middle Ages and transcending all the limitations and prejudices of the Revival. With its graceful decorative figures by Birnie Philip and delicate leaf-sprouting scrolls it is more akin to the work produced by Morris, Marshall and Faulkner & Co. than anything medieval. Another piece of Victorian cathedral furnishing that is arrestingly creative and memorable is the lectern at Gloucester. Of brass, set with crystals, made by Hart & Son to the design of Bentley, it is an imaginative and dynamic version of the eagle-lectern theme. A central shaft rises in three ornamental stages supported by six powerful eagle claws clutching balls and surmounted by a savage eagle trampling upon a dragon. Of all Victorian cathedral furniture, however, it is usually that which has nothing whatever to do with the Middle Ages that arouses the most enthusiastic response. There was no medieval prototype for the gasoliers which until well into the present century enlivened the interiors of Ely and Salisbury and they were superb expressions of their own time. Probably designed by Scott and made by Skidmore, they were of gilded iron, decorated with panels of pierced foliage and with three supports twining about a central stem before branching out through a big corona. The delightful William de Morgan tiles round the humdrum recumbent effigy of Bishop Selwyn at Lichfield and the Art Nouveau relief panel of the Resurrection by Alfred Gilbert below Harry Hems's trumpery statues on the reredos at St Albans are among examples which come at once to mind. Victorian monuments too are most successful when they do not ape the medieval tradition of a prone figure on a tomb chest under a Gothic canopy. Lt Colonel Frederick Macheson's memorial at Canterbury (1856) has a Gothic surround but the composition consisting of a female drooping over an urn accompanied by a realistic Indian and a spirited English soldier has the air of some Victorian popular art and only needs colour to become a gigantic Staffordshire figure. And when Victorian funerary sculpture takes the form of a simple unpretentious portrait like that of the sculptor Theed's son at the foot of Humphrey Chetham's monument at Manchester, it opens a new chapter in the history of English sepulchral art.

There were signs towards the end of the nineteenth century of a sense of deep disillusion with the whole idea of the Revival. To Ruskin the results of Victorian restoration seemed 'more tragic than utter ruin', and in the later edition of *The Stones of Venice* he suggests that for 'the great mouldering wall of rugged sculpture and confused arcades' of the English cathedral he so wonderfully describes we should read 'the beautiful parapet by Mr Scott with a gross of kings sent down from Kensington'. Drawings made in an architect's town office and the execution of artists' designs by manufacturers could never revive 'that spirit which is given only by the eye and hand of the workman'. William Morris, once one of the most fervent advocates of the Gothic style as a transforming influence in an industrial society,

was so appalled by the effects of the Revival on so many great medieval monuments that in 1877 he initiated the formation of the Society for the Protection of Ancient Buildings with the object of limiting restoration to the scholarly maintenance of the fabric. The bold attempt to recreate the architecture of a past age when the world was united in Christian belief, when angels turned and upheld the spheres about the motionless earth, itself the great centre of the universe, was bound to fail in the fragmented, commercialised Victorian world. There is a lack of life, a lack of all medieval humanity, closeness to nature and sense of awe, a staid and mechanical chilliness even in so masterly a simulation of Early Gothic as Truro.

Liverpool, the last and most ambitious ecclesiastical monument of the Revival, was, like Caröe's retrochoir at Wakefield, breaking new ground in Gothic composition just at the time when the Revival was losing credibility. Truly noble, eclectically imaginative, fusing elements from late Gothic Spanish and French churches with new devices such as the daring concept of the double transepts linked by giant porches, and the surprising idea of a great arch and balcony separating the nave from the west transept, and planned on a scale exceeding that of any older cathedral, it was an anachronism even when it was begun. By the time it was completed, late in our own century, the heroic Victorian Gothic crusade had long since come to an end and become part of history.

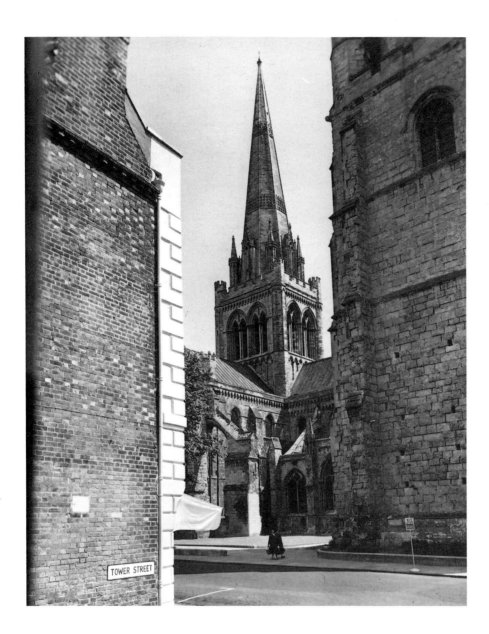

TOWER STREET

The two structures are of the same date, both begun in 1861 and completed by 1867. Both are based on close study of medieval forms, but while one imitates a fifteenth-century design the other derives from Early English examples. One is so brilliantly successful that the distant view of it prepares the visitor for all the medieval felicities and sublimities awaiting him inside the cathedral it dominates; the other, heavy and insensitive, pedantically correct, shows Victorian historicism at its most forbidding. It is already of cathedral size although the parish church of St Martin, Leicester did not become a cathedral until 1927. The architect was Raphael Brandon, known for a popular book on parish churches.

The medieval central tower of Chichester fell in 1862. The collapse was partly caused by the removal of the pulpitum by the chapter so that in accordance with views of the time the choir should be thrown open to the nave. The Perpendicular pulpitum, then described as 'a stone screen of little merit' was stored in the detached bell tower, which can be seen in the foreground of the photograph, until 1960 when it was replaced. Set between the two western piers of the tower, the pulpitum had helped to support them. When it was removed it was found that portions of the piers had been cut away to accommodate it. Built of stone-faced rubble as was the Norman practice, it was surprising that they had supported the tower and the additional weight of the fifteenth-century spire for so long. Great efforts

were made to save the spire, but despite the casing of the piers in iron hoops, the walls of the tower went on bulging, while crushed mortar poured from alarming cracks. The night of Wednesday, February 20, 1861, was one of violent storm; workmen toiled all through it, increasing the number of supports, but shortly after midday on the 21st the spire inclined spectacularly on the south-west and collapsed into the church.

The tower was restored and the spire rebuilt by Sir George Gilbert Scott largely from the old stones. The work is supremely well done, meticulously following the original design and preserving the charming medieval conceit of echoing the shape of the great tower and steeple in the little spired pinnacles clustered at its base.

Scott describes his work at Chichester in his *Personal and Professional Recollections*: 'I shared my fees with Slater, the former architect. My son Gilbert supervised the removal of the debris and every detail of the work, fixing the weathercock with his own hands.... I added 5 or 6 feet to the tower, restoring it to its former height (altered probably in the fourteenth century). Each pier was laid on a square block of masonry, surrounded by stepped buttresses and numerous footings, all built of Purbeck stone and laid on a mass of cement concrete.' The cost of the rebuilding was £53,000. The townspeople blamed Slater for the disaster. Scott's assistant related that the boys in the street would point to him crying, 'That's him as let the spire down, that big'un.'

In his *Plea for the Faithful Restoration of our Ancient Churches* published in 1850 Sir George Gilbert Scott describes three modes of restoration: the Conservative, Destructive and Eclectic. The Destructive architects 'plead the example of the medieval architects, who disdainful of the past and discontented with present attainments, were ever earnestly pressing after new developments of their art, and sometimes destroyed to make room for them, the beautiful works of their predecessors.' The Conservative restorer, on the other hand, would reproduce the exact detail of every piece of ancient work still existing at the time of the restoration, while the Eclectic would in some cases restore and in others remodel. The restoration of St Albans is the most aggressive example of the second category and affords the strongest contrast to the scholarly work of Street at Bristol.

After St Albans was surrendered in 1539 the monastic buildings, except for the gatehouse, were torn down and the townspeople acquired the church for £400 and made it parochial. By the time it was raised to cathedral status three hundred years later, in 1871, the parishioners were only using part of the north transept, the Lady Chapel had become a grammar school, a public way ran through the chancel, and the west front was ruinous. Scott drew up plans for the restoration of the noble building, but lack of funds held up the work. It was then that the most ruthless, autocratic yet generous man in the history of St Albans intervened to carry out the work at his own expense and to his own design. He is reputed to have spent £130,000 on the Abbey. He was Edmund Beckett Denison, later first Lord Grimthorpe, an amateur architect, amateur horologist, the maker of Big Ben, and amateur theologian of pronounced views. He detested Puseyites and all deans and chapters,

and referred to statues as idols, although the figure of St Matthew in the west porch of the cathedral is a portrait of himself. He thrust upon the great church a completely new, coarse and mechanical west front and north and south transepts, raised the roof ridge, thus disturbing the proportions of the fine Norman brick tower, replaced buttresses, turrets and windows throughout, and rebuilt the clerestory over the south aisle, which was shedding stones and in danger of collapse, in his own grim version of Early English. The original detail was Perpendicular, not Early English.

Some of George Edmund Street's contemporaries called him a 'robustious male', but beside Lord Grimthorpe he seems sensitive and imaginative. Like Grimthorpe, however, he considered that 'the northern art of the thirteenth century is infinitely more pure, more vigorous and more true than the work of later times'. It was therefore all the more admirable that despite his predilections he conscientiously adapted his nave at Bristol (begun in 1868) to the style of the chancel which was not Early English and was the work of an idiosyncratic genius with whom Street could not have wholly sympathised. His alteration of details in the vaulting is significant: Street retains the aisle bridges but blunts the force of the medieval architect's design by changing the rib arrangement. Yet though it lacks the sharp excitement of the fourteenth century the nave is a very fine achievement.

The west front and towers, unfinished at the time of Street's death, were completed by Pearson. Street's preference for the thirteenth century is more apparent here than within, yet he has related the towers to the Perpendicular crossing tower (later altered by Scott) in the proportions of his tall storeys and in his buttress designs: they terminate at the base of the top storey and are not continued by the pinnacles. The angle figures beneath the pinnacle are an enrichment of Street's own invention and contribute to the interest of a structure which, while without the flash of genius, seems full of pattern and variety beside Grimthorpe's monotonous and formidable front.

BRISTOL *from the North-West*

244

ST ALBANS *from the South-West*

This and the two interiors which follow show different aspects of Victorian scholarship, technical mastery and sensibility. In rebuilding the nave of Southwark, and replacing a neo-Gothic structure of 1838, Sir Arthur Blomfield's intention in 1890 was to match the style of the thirteenth-century chancel. The chancel, although smoothed and refaced by restorers, must always have been rather austere, with no adornment but simple mouldings throughout the elevation. Blomfield's model may thus partly account for the coldness of his nave. But by comparison with the medieval work his careful rebuilding seems mechanical and passionless.

The Victorian work at Wakefield and Manchester, though carried out by less well-known architects, makes an altogether more exciting impact. And the photographer has responded to it. J. R. Holden rebuilt the tower of Manchester in 1862–8 and his splendid fan vaulting and the panelling seen through the high tower arch captures the feeling of Perpendicular forms while conveying a sense of individuality. While the vaulting is reminiscent of Wastell's work it is not a copy of it. In the same way the long thin shafts and intricate stone lierne vault of the retrochoir at Wakefield are the design of a man who, after looking at the vaults of Canterbury, Winchester and Norwich was fired to invent a new variation on the lierne and branching-rib theme. He was probably W. D. Caröe, the assistant of F. L. Pearson, the son of the architect of Truro Cathedral. The retrochoir together with the chancel and a transept were completed as late as 1904, to give a cathedral air to the former parish church. The elaborately detailed stained glass seen in the photograph is one of the last works of Charles Eamer Kempe (d. 1907) who had worked with the Morris circle but by this time had founded his own firm.

Opposite. SOUTHWARK: *the Nave from the Chancel*

On the following pages are illustrated the Retrochoir at WAKEFIELD *and a view through the Tower Arch at* MANCHESTER

WAKEFIELD: *Retrochoir*

MANCHESTER: *View through the Tower Arch*

On the left. TRURO: *the Nave from the Crossing*

Opposite. TRURO: *the North Nave Arcade*

The new diocese of Truro was created in 1876 and two years later John Loughborough Pearson, who together with Bodley, Burges, Scott and Street among others had submitted photographs and drawings of work already done to the cathedral committee under the chairmanship of the Earl of Mount Edgecumbe, was asked to design a new cathedral. It was still unfinished at the time of the architect's death in 1898 and the nave and towers were completed by his son Frank. Pearson's frame of mind is revealed by a story told by A. J. Mason, and repeated more than once, that before turning his mind to the task the architect took Communion in the medieval parish church of St Mary which his own building was to replace. He was among those who believed that good buildings could only be built by good men. It all depends on what is meant by good. Truro Cathedral is the product of faith, devotion and great talent, and the photographs show that

the austere interior is not without nobility. The care lavished on the construction is revealed by the deliberate irregularities in the stonework, clearly seen in the photograph of the arcade because emphasised by Pearson's use of dark mortar. There is some affinity with Salisbury in the severity and precision of the forms, the lack of sculptured detail and the method of vaulting without a ridge rib. But the comparison only serves to bring out the originality of the Salisbury elevation, the drama of contrasting materials and above all the luminosity of the interior. Pearson's elevation, while eschewing the squat proportions of the Salisbury triforium, keeping the arcade comparatively low and emphasising the vertical thrust of the design by sending up shafts through all three storeys to the vault, is of more aesthetically correct proportions, yet the effect is curiously monotonous. Medieval in form, Truro is wholly Victorian in spirit.

On the left. LIVERPOOL CATHEDRAL *on a misty day*

The photographs were taken in 1970 when the cathedral was still unfinished. Signs of work in progress heighten the drama of the shadowy tower image rising in incredibly unreal immensity behind the foreground tower of parish church proportions. The mist obscures the detail but not the romantic character of the magnificent tower, its leaning angle turrets and the rich decorative effect of the pinnacled and arcaded octagonal upper storey.

The diocese of Liverpool was created in 1880 in response to the growth of population and industry, and authority was granted for the building of a new cathedral. But no progress was made until 1901 when Bishop Chavasse decided on the superb site commanding the city and the river, launched an appeal for funds, and invited architects to submit designs. The assessors were G. F. Bodley and Norman Shaw. Giles Gilbert Scott, then only twenty-two years of age, was chosen from more than one hundred candidates among

whom were Mackintosh (who would have built a very different cathedral) and Lethaby. Scott worked on his great project until his death in 1960, improving on his original design as the work progressed, replacing twin towers by the inspired and colossal central tower, setting it between east and west double transepts, connected by giant portals, and shortening the nave to match the choir. Scott's work was carried on by Frederick Thomas, a member of his firm, and brought to completion in 1978.

The vast size of the red sandstone cathedral is as overwhelming within as without. The photograph captures some of the original spatial effects of Scott's design, and shows the strangest and most innovatory feature of the interior, the arch and balcony with two long staircases leading up to it, which divides the nave from the west transepts, and the great intimidatingly lofty space beneath the tower.

Above. LIVERPOOL: *a view through the arch of the Nave Balcony*

The clock face, commissioned by Dean Addleshaw in 1883 and designed by G. F. Bodley, reflects the influence of William Morris and also the artist's special concern for what in his essay *On some Principles and Characteristics of ancient Architecture* he called 'refinement'. Even a black-and-white photograph conveys something of the 'the refinement of decorative colour, where gradations are gentle and colours are delicately contrasted' which was so important to Bodley. The muted tones of the clock face enhance the strong pattern of the medieval jacks and their sharp shadows, and the three-dimensional richness of the thirteenth-century pier capitals. The device of the Sacred Monogram within a ring of fire at the top of the clock face appears in the same form on the hood of an embroidered cope he designed for St Paul's Church, Knightsbridge.

It is surprising to recall that the man who created the delicate clock face at York was the pupil of the designer of this strongly accented font cover. He was Sir George Gilbert Scott who was working at Bury in ca. 1869. He was also responsible for the hammerbeam roof. Both the roof and the spired font cover, richly crocketted and beset with finials, show appreciation of East Anglian traditions, but the font cover looks coarse and mechanical beside such a thicket of progidiously inventive, quivering and finely tapering decoration as crowns the font at Ufford in the same county, and Scott's stolid roof angels quite fail to measure up to such gloriously pinioned and soaring creatures as those which adorn the roof of nearby St Mary's.

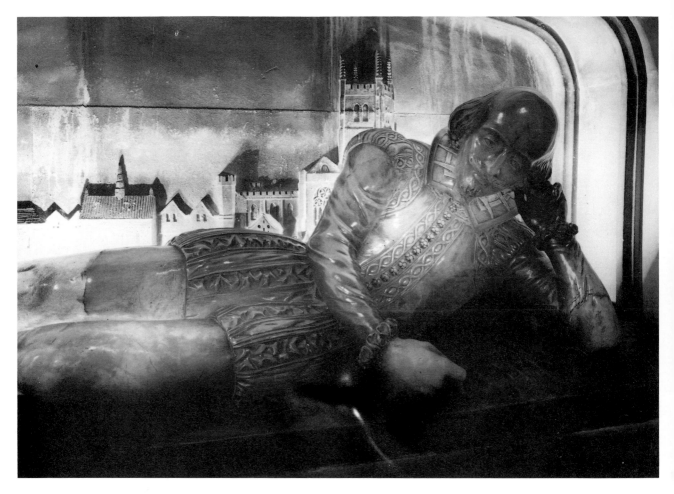

Above. SOUTHWARK: *The Shakespeare Memorial in the South aisle*

Opposite. MANCHESTER: *detail from the monument to Sir Humphrey Chetham, in the North aisle*

Humphrey Chetham, a Manchester textile manufacturer and merchant, bought the domestic buildings of the collegiate foundation, the church of which is now the cathedral, in 1643 for £400 and established a school for forty boys. The photograph shows a scholar of Chetham's Hospital sitting at the foot of Chetham's monument of 1853. The sitter was the son of the artist William Theed. The attractive marble figure, combining naturalism with a fine sense of composition and technical mastery is a typical product of a period when the image of the family loomed large, and children shown in postures of domestic intimacy, study or relaxation assumed a new importance in art.

The nerveless alabaster Shakespeare memorial by A. V. MacCarthy (unveiled as late as 1912, though it is essentially Victorian) highlights the quality of Theed's sculpture. But the effects of light behind the Southwark townscape give the camera-recorded image a strangeness which suggests the extraordinary influence and haunting presence of Shakespeare in Victorian literature and art. The photograph is like an illustration of Hugo's description of Shakespeare as the last of the Gothic cathedrals, a cathedral in his bulging compendiousness, his massive inclusion of the whole of existence.

COVENTRY: *Nave, Chancel and Lady Chapel*

VIII
In a Secular Age

THE last chapter told of a Church in crisis and an heroic attempt to surmount the danger by reviving the rich ceremonial and architectural traditions of the past. In our own increasingly secular century efforts to bolster a declining faith have concentrated on moving with the times and on the hope of widening the appeal of services by trivialising the language heard in Anglical cathedrals from 1662 until the 1960s. Parliament rejected a suggested revision of the Prayer Book in 1928. But now new versions of the Bible such as *The New English Bible* of 1961 and *The Good News Bible* of 1976 and three alternative Prayer Book services are the sources for the *Alternative Service Book* (in which God is addressed as *you* and 'And with Thy Spirit' reads 'And also with you', while the modern obsession with 'community' has resulted in the substitution of 'We believe . . .' for 'I believe . . .' at the beginning of the Creed) which has become the approved alternative to the Book of Common Prayer. Although The Authorised Version and the Book of Common Prayer can still be heard in some cathedrals, a precious fount of symbolic and allusive awareness was wilfully destroyed when the beautiful articulateness of these inspired works was vulgarised. Instead of bringing fresh life to the liturgy it has devalued the Word, the Johannine beginning.

The visual accompaniments of the Alternative Service Book are the glass front doors, the post-card, book and souvenir shops, the cafeterias, coffee areas, sinks and toilets which are now part of most cathedrals, even Durham and Canterbury, the ugly pile-up of cars and coaches in cathedral precincts and the destruction of the fabric by a deadlier agent than either time or weather – pollution which more than anything else reflects the fanatical preoccupation of the age with the pursuit of profit and material wealth.

This is the background against which the history and meaning of cathedrals in the present century must be seen.

Although the population has doubled since Queen Victoria's death no new dioceses have been created since 1927 and of the 16,000 parish churches of England more than two thousand have been made redundant. The first quarter of the century still basked in the sunset glow of Victorian Revival enthusiasm. Southwark and Birmingham were made cathedrals in 1905, the dioceses of Sheffield and Bury St Edmunds were formed, and Essex was transferred from Rochester to Chelmsford on the eve of the Great War in 1914, the significant date that in our imaginations marks the end of a world more confident, more devout, more civil and humane than any we have known since. In 1918 came Coventry, in 1919 Bradford, and in 1926 and 1927 Blackburn and Leicester, the latest English diocese. Guildford, which Henry VIII had nominated as a bishopric but which had never become one, was made a See in 1927. Except for the latter all were adapted from purely parochial to their present use. Coventry was rebuilt as a cathedral after the destruction of the parish church cathedral of St Michael by German bombs on the night of November 14, 1940.

The constitution of modern cathedrals varies according to their financial resources. In some cathedrals residentiary canons are always present, residence meaning regular attendance at the daily services, although precentor, chancellor, subdean and archdeacon may have their home in the close. In other cathedrals absence from the church is permitted, particularly when canonries are attached to professorships at universities as at Ely, Oxford and Durham and residence is only possible during university vacations. Sometimes, as at Leicester, a supplementary body of lay canons has been appointed to introduce 'an element of business acumen into the deliberations of the chapter'.

The exposure of ancient cathedral masonry to the effects of toxic waste and the thunder of heavy traffic has of course accelerated the need for repair. Acid rain has caused more deterioration of the friable fabrics of Hereford and Worcester than at any other period. Worcester at the moment of writing is reported to be in so dangerous a state that the public may not be able to enter the building by the 1990s. Traffic vibration caused such serious delapidation to the west tower of York Minster during the 70s that loose masonry was falling into the road. After years of restoration work the nave, roof and Lady Chapel of Ely are still under repair, while the spire of Salisbury is again in course of being reinforced, and the exquisite bands of ornament on the tapering steeple have been partially effaced by pollution. In 1986 the west front of Wells emerged from a clutter of scaffolding after years of restoration. Much of the sculpture had been reduced by pollution to amorphous lumps of disintegrating stone. The work has been done with extraordinary skill and with an informed concern for the medieval structure which would have pleased William Morris and which everywhere distinguishes modern restoration from Victorian rebuilding. Yet standing in front of it and comparing it with the image, made in 1956, shown in this book (p. 69), which itself differs from the front as it appeared before the Victorian restoration of 1872–3, it must be acknowledged that however brilliant and scholarly the renovation it looks like a facsimile of the work it seeks to revive. Something vital has inevitably departed, for the coherence of an ancient thing must be in direct harmony with its time. The same reaction is prompted by the far more spectacular and almost miraculous renovation of the south transept of York Minster which went up in flames on July 9, 1984 when it was struck by a thunderbolt. The rebuilding of the transept, especially the restoration of the leaded panels of the stained glass of the rose window, which had been cracked and splintered into many thousands of fragments, is a most remarkable triumph of modern scholarship and a lasting tribute to the continuing life of the traditional crafts of stone masonry, joinery, woodcarving and glass painting. Yet it remains essentially a twentieth-century replica, the spirit of which is manifest in the choice of television 'Blue Peter' subjects for some of the roof bosses.

One of the most important contributions of the present age to cathedral preservation is the use of modern techniques and materials for reinforcement. Earlier in the century both the transepts and the eastern part of Winchester began to subside and to show alarming fissures. The medieval builders had raised the great structure on the insecure foundation of tree trunks laid like a gigantic raft on the bed of peaty marsh underlying the site. The engineers who came to the rescue, Messrs Thompson & Co of Peterborough, underpinned the masonry with masses of concrete going right down to the gravel beneath the peat, working in some fourteen feet of water. At Glou-

cester in 1953 when Seiriol Evans, an authority on the care of ancient buildings, was Dean, a major scheme for the renovation of the deteriorating roofs of the nave, choir, north transept and cloisters incorporated the entirely successful and unprecedented use of pre-stressed and lightweight concrete to carry the re-cast lead of the roof coverings. But the most triumphant vindication of modern methods of reinforcement is the amazing survival of St Paul's in the heavy bombardment of the City during World War II.

The cathedral was hit by two high explosive bombs which crashed through the roofs, one penetrating to the crypt, the other destroying the high altar and damaging Bodley & Garner's reredos of 1888. The great building could scarcely have withstood the shock of the blast had it not been massively strengthened in the pre-war years. Liquid cement had been pumped into the piers to replace the original unreliable rubble cores, and great steel chain supports had been placed round the base of the dome. The technical achievement has not been accompanied by a corresponding concern for the visual importance of Wren's masterpiece. We can indeed be grateful that the intrusive and incongruous reredos was not restored and that a proposal to remove Bird's statues of the Apostles and Evangelists from the west and transept fronts to make room for modern sculptures was rejected, but a glance at the photograph of St Paul's (p. 182), as it stood amid the weed-grown ruins of the City in 1949, and then at the Cathedral in its present setting illumines more sharply than any words could do the character of our age. A wonderful opportunity of allowing the glorious building to dominate all around it was sacrificed to commercial advantage and office blocks of crushing banality crowded about Wren's great work. Another last chance to remedy the vandalism came with the news in 1987 that the land adjacent to the cathedral was to be redeveloped. At the time of writing the familiar conflict of interests between concern for the cathedral, the rapacity of developers and the arrogance of the architectural firms involved dims all hope of the creation of space round St Paul's and the opening up of distant views of its hovering dome.

Although the Revival can be said to have ended with the decision to build Liverpool in the guise of a medieval cathedral, the association of Christian with Gothic, even if it was no longer always English Gothic, persisted, encouraged by the fact that the construction of Truro and Liverpool was

ST PAUL'S, LONDON, 1964, *seen from the
Barbican. Contrast this view with that on p. 182.*

going on according to the original plans through much of the century. Truro was completed with its cloister in 1967, while the monumental conception of Liverpool with its splendid Lady Chapel and octagonal chapter house was only fully realised by 1978. When Sir Charles Nicholson designed a new east end for Chelmsford in 1923 it was thus inevitably based on Gothic example, and Blomfield's east window of 1878 was re-used. Nicholson's bishop's throne with its high canopy is an emasculated though attractive exercise in the Gothic idiom. The same architect designed a similar throne for Sheffield where he prepared a plan for the enlargement of the former parish church. The project proved too costly and a new scheme submitted by G. G. Pace also failed to materialise for the same reason. The present completed enlargement (p. 268), though it has nothing in common with Nicholson's correct Gothic, still draws on Gothic imagery if only to debase it. In the same way Pace's bell tower of 1975 at Chester, by translating a medieval timber invention into concrete and brick destroys the essential harmony of structure and material. In shape it is the type of belfry seen at Pembridge in Herefordshire and is related to the stave churches of Norway, a composition of vertical and truncated pyramidal stages topped by a pyramidal roof. The new chapter house at St Albans, a large building which is not only the administrative hub of the cathedral but provides for a youth centre, a refectory and a shop, is more successfully related to the great church: as boldly assertive as Grimthorpe's west front, its brick fabric also calls attention to the uncommon use of brick for the Norman central tower. Just as the circular angle support of this structure and the little triangular openings in the window heads are reminiscent of contemporary building practice in Northern Italy so the modern chapter house, apsidal and severe, derives from Italian sources, recalling such stark exteriors as that of the Abbazia di San Giovanni in Venere at Foscacesia. The new buildings at Southwark are not medieval in form but, clustering about the cathedral like a protective wall, they boldly display materials first combined in East Anglian Gothic churches. They take the shape of a grid of limestone filled with knapped flints. But of course the flints are not laid in the traditional manner but pre-cast in moulds on a backing of concrete. The buildings house a restaurant, kitchen, music room and exhibition and shop areas.

Like the St Albans chapter house, Sir Edward

Maufe's new cathedral at Guildford is a deliberately simplified version of a medieval church, and if regarded purely as an architectural conceit, the felicitous siting and the dream-like, subtly untraditional use of space and perspective in the interior with its thin, spicular arches and deep narrow window splays, are not soon forgotten. Yet there is no sense of awe, and its absence is made more palpable by the spiritless character of the ornament which in a medieval cathedral enhances the exuberant life of the stone forms, gives them meaning and speaks of an all-embracing faith. At Guildford stylised, self-conscious glass engraving and poor sculpture (for even the pieces by Eric Gill, executed after his death, are sentimental) hinder rather than help the effect of Maufe's cool, Chirico-like vistas.

At Coventry the circumstances which led to the surprising creation of a new Anglican cathedral consecrated as late as 1962 had aroused an emotional response of a different order from the detached attitude of the inaugurators of the Guildford project. The modern cathedral rose beside the ruins of the old as a challenge to the dark forces which had violated and shattered the House of God. The nature of the disaster fanned the feeble flame of faith into momentary vigour; and the outstanding achievement of the architect, Basil Spence, was that he gave lasting concrete expression to the emotional power of the reaction by preserving the bare ruined outline and spire of the old cathedral and setting his new building at right angles to it. The inspiration is again Gothic, but Gothic translated into a modern idiom with a sense of purpose and harmonious invention found in no other twentieth-century ecclesiastical building. Rose-coloured sandstone, concrete and glass are the materials, combined with slate for the buttresses of the polygonal Chapel of Unity and for the fins of the circular Chapel of Christ the Servant. The zigzag walls of the nave reinterpret the buttressed walls of the medieval cathedral; and the interior follows the traditional plan of an aisled nave and chancel with a ribbed vault, though it is only a paraphrase of a medieval vault and is detached from the real, concrete roof. The uninterrupted vista from west to east would not of course have been found in a cathedral in the Middle Ages and was dictated by the same insistence on the importance of congregational worship which governed the parish church proportions of the nave and choir, thus blurring the essential distinction between parochial and cathedral services.

Here and there among the pretty, sentimental glass paintings and imitation Gothic sculpture and furnishings which perforce in a secular age make up the bulk of twentieth-century additions to cathedral interiors, a work of genuine feeling testifies to the survival of religious art. Epstein's bronze portrait bust of Bishop Woods (1937–53) is like an intense living presence in the north choir aisle at Lichfield, and Graham Sutherland's sketchy and impassioned rendering of Christ and Mary Magdalen at Chichester is a not unworthy neighbour of the reliefs of *The Raising of Lazarus* and *Christ in the House of Mary and Martha.*

The most exciting and distinguishing feature of the new Coventry is its furnishing. It preserves all the atmosphere of that period when the tide of American Abstract Expressionism was beginning to engulf and destroy the extraordinary neo-Romantic English response to the threats of war, extinction and postwar commercialism. In John Piper's, Geoffrey Clarke's, Lawrence Lee's and Keith New's glass the eradication of matter by form has already begun. Though the progress in the colour arrangement towards yellow might be said to convey a vaguely spiritual message, it is neither explicit nor related to the purpose of the building. Medieval glass is always didactic, and understanding of the doctrinal points sharpens awareness of the plastic articulation.

Graham Sutherland's tapestry, on the other hand, which dominates the cathedral from its position at the end of the Lady Chapel, is one of the great representational works of those remarkable postwar years. The piercing green of the background, the colossal, white-garmented figure, the thorny, anguished, ash-grey crucifixion beneath it and the puny human being between the huge feet do convey as no Victorian Gothic Revival work succeeded in doing an overwhelming feeling of the precariousness, the insignificance and tragedy of earthly existence and of the fundamental truths which transcend the literal meaning of the myths that illustrate them. Spence's choir stalls and bishop's throne which suggest clusters of spiky stars or thickets of thorns fittingly introduce the giant Christ behind them. The throne is surmounted by a bishop's mitre made by Elizabeth Frink, and the fierce bronze eagle of the lectern which has the vitality of a wild living creature and something of the soaring rapture of St John is one of the most inspired works of her earlier years.

Britten's *War Requiem* composed specially for Coventry Cathedral, and combining the liturgical text with poems by Wilfrid Owen, is the musical counterpart of these furnishings, and conveys more poignantly, more directly and more imaginatively than them all the uprush of religious feeling that gave birth to the new cathedral. Like Rubbra's great mass written for Canterbury and Walton's Chichester Service, the *Requiem* gloriously reveals and affirms the profound underlying import of words which we have too often ceased to hear. It is the flourishing musical life of cathedrals, the festivals of which they are the centres, the high standard of the continual choral worship which, together with the spires, the arches, the groined vaults, the flying buttresses, the stained-glass windows, the majestic dome, all brought into play not for the satisfaction of physical needs and not for material gain but for the more fundamental pursuit of significance, bear witness to the incalculable importance of cathedrals in a world in which human energy is applied more intensely than at any other time to the glorification of Mammon, a world which has overthrown the necessary restrictive practices of religion and has sacrificed quality to quantity in every sphere. Cathedrals are tangible reminders of a more civil, more confident past, a past sustained by faith; they stand as a powerful, consoling and inspiring bulwark against our present bewildered feeling of disarray, our regress into violence and into moral stagnation.

The diocese of Guildford was formed in 1927 when increase in the population of the diocese of Winchester forced the creation of an independent See. Like Truro and Liverpool the new cathedral was built by the winner of a competition. Sir Edward Maufe began work in 1936 when the foundation stone was laid by Dr Lang, Archbishop of Canterbury. The work started at the east end as in the Middle Ages, the chancel was consecrated in 1950, the nave in 1961. The photograph of the exterior celebrates the splendid choice of site and the harmonious relationship of the stoneless Surrey landscape and the brick building. The bricks were actually made of clay from Stag Hill and are laid with a unique bond of two stretchers to one head. The roof of reinforced concrete covered with copper was the work of an engineer, Burnard Gren. The cruciform plan, the tall, pointed windows with simplified traceried heads and the central tower are all part of a belated, sober and unadventurous Gothic Revival image. The interior of pallid limestone from Doulting in Somerset, though equally lacking in fervour, reveals a strange and original use of Gothic forms, of needle-sharp arches and narrow, dream-like perspectives, the effect of which is enhanced by the unexpected flood of light through windows which are as tall as the arcade arches. Though Guildford is planned with a long, truly cathedral-like chancel with a lady chapel projecting beyond it, the seat-filled nave and the absence of a screen point to the modern emphasis on congregational worship.

Raised to cathedral rank in 1919, the millstone grit parish church of St Peter was enlarged by Sir Edward Maufe from 1945. The new east end towards which we are looking is a disciplined sequel to the Gothic Revival and the knife-thin arches, piers without capitals and high rectangular clerestory openings show it to be the work of the architect of Guildford. The bell-shaped light fittings are also unmistakably Maufe's. He re-used the fine William Morris glass of the original chancel, with designs by Ford Madox Brown, Bürne-Jones and Rossetti, in his Lady Chapel where it can just be glimpsed in the photograph.

The Bishop's Throne, a charming if anaemic exercise in Gothic, was designed in 1937 by Sir Charles Nicholson who prepared plans in 1919 for enlarging the parish church of St Peter and St Paul which had been made a cathedral five years earlier. Nicholson's proposals proved to be financially unacceptable and the extension which runs athwart the medieval nave was eventually built by Arthur Bailey. The photograph yields a view of the lantern which is part of the new building and which is intended to suggest the Crown of Thorns.

On the right: BLACKBURN
from the South-East

Opposite. SHEFFIELD
from the South

When the parish church of St Mary, Blackburn became a cathedral in 1926 the architect, W. A. Forsythe added a Gothic east end and transepts entirely in keeping with Rickman's restoration of 1831. An intended octagonal lantern over the crossing was rejected on financial grounds and the present feature built by Lawrence King in 1961 is eloquent of its period, totally unrelated to the rest of the building and itself a calamitous conjunction of a corona and a meaningless thin spike of a spire. Fortunately the west tower, not seen in the photograph, survives to give a strong vertical accent to the building.

The photograph of Sheffield (*opposite*) shows the uneasy juxtaposition of the former parish church of St Peter and St Paul, a Perpendicular building of Derbyshire limestone, renovated in 1880 by W. Flockton and the extension built of the same stone by Arthur Bailey and consecrated in 1966. The concept of an enlargement running from south to north across the nave was G. G. Pace's. He had intended to make the old nave into a transeptal feature of a grand new nave. His project was not carried out and the cross extension is now taken up by the narthex tower, the baptistery and two chapels. This accounts for the seeming awkwardness of the design. The old tower, with its pinnacles like miniature versions of the surging, crocketted spire, draws attention to the capricious use of Gothic-derived forms such as angle turrets and stepped buttresses in the design of the narthex tower and to its arbitrary proportions.

COVENTRY: *entrance porch*
and South wall of the Nave

See also the photographs on pages 272 and 273

The disaster which led to the building of Coventry is mentioned on page 259 and is too well known to bear further description here. Basil Spence won the competition for a new cathedral held in 1951 with a design which mirrored the powerful emotion which lay behind the commission by preserving the charred ruins of the medieval cathedral, formerly a parish church of great splendour, and by setting his new building at right angles to them. The enterprise was carried forward on a wave of enthusiasm recalling the ardour and devotion of medieval builders and patrons. Donations poured in from all over the world, from Denmark and Sweden, from Hong Kong and China, from Tanganyika, from Canada, from Stalingrad and Germany and from countless benefactors in our own country.

The photograph opposite concentrates on Sir Basil's gigantic porch and the sharp rhythm of the (ritually) south wall which, because each section half points to the east, sets up a zigzag motion contrasting with the calm grid patterns of the huge panels of square and oblong windows and with the gentle swell of the enormous baptistery window. The visual effect is disturbed by Epstein's mannered bronze of St Michael hovering over a Lucifer who reclines on nothing. The circular building to the right of the nave is the Chapel of Christ the Servant. The openwork structure, rather like an attenuated pylon seen rising above the flat roof is intended to vie with the spire of the old church. Like the ridiculous fleche at Blackburn (p. 269) it shows how closely the successful creation of the wholly unfunc-tional, symbolic form of the Gothic spire was associated with the medieval habit of mind.

The proportions of the east end of Coventry, the subject of the two following photographs, are, in relation to the nave, those of a parish church rather than a cathedral, and though it is arch-itecturally Gothic in inspiration it fails to preserve the important distinction between the two build-ings. But the interior of Coventry is remarkable for a display of furnishings and fittings which, nearly all created in the heat of reaction to the special circumstances of the rebuilding, include particularly expressive examples of an interesting early postwar period.

Like Gothic choir stalls those at Coventry, designed by the architect, are provided with can-opies which take the exhilarating form of three-pointed stars, a hedge of sharp thorns or a flight of birds. It was Sir Basil too who was responsible for the ingenious idea of arranging the organ pipes so that they should enliven the vistas along the choir aisles. The photograph of the Lady Chapel enables us to experience the strangely moving effect of the full light falling from the clear glass of the tall and narrow windows which contributes so much to the overwhelming impact of Graham Sutherland's mighty tapestry of Christ in Glory filling the east end of the interior. We are looking across the massively plain High Altar of hammered concrete, past the pottery altar candlesticks by Hans Coper which are taller than a man, towards the silver-gilt crucifix by Geoffrey Clarke, an abstract interpretation of both cross and piercing thorns.

COVENTRY: *South Choir aisle*

Opposite. COVENTRY: *Lady Chapel*

SELECT BIBLIOGRAPHY

OF ORIGINAL AND SECONDARY SOURCES

Anderson, M. D. *Misericords: Medieval Life in English Woodcarving*, 1954

Andrews, F. B. *The Medieval Builder and his Methods*, 1925

Barrett, W. A. *English Church Composers*, 1882

Bentham, J. *The History and Antiquities of the Conventual and Cathedral Church of Ely from 673 to the year 1771*, 1771

Bony, J. *The English Decorated Style: Gothic Architecture Transformed, 1250–1350*, 1979

Bradshaw, H. and Wordsworth, C. *Statutes of Lincoln Cathedral*, 2 vols, 1892–7

Briggs, Martin C. *A Short History of the Building Crafts*, 1925

Briggs, Martin C. *Goths and Vandals*, 1952

Britton, J. *Cathedral Antiquities: Historical and Descriptive Accounts of English Cathedrals*, 6 vols, 1836

Buckler, John C. *Views of Cathedral Churches of England and Wales*, 42 plates, 1822

Bumpus, John *A History of English Cathedral Music*, 1908

Bumpus, T. *The Cathedrals of England and Wales*, 1921

Callus, R. A. (ed.) *Robert Grosseteste, Scholar and Bishop*, 1955

Capes, W., Parry, J. H. and Bannister A. T. (eds) *Hereford Episcopal Registers*, 16 vols, 1907–21

Chadwick, Owen *The Mind of the Oxford Movement*, 1960

Chadwick, Owen *The Reformation*, 1964

Chapman, F. R. (ed.) *Sacrist Rolls of Ely*, 2 vols, 1907

Clifton-Taylor, Alec *The Cathedrals of England*, 1978

Cobb, Gerald *English Cathedrals: The Forgotten Centuries*, 1980

Colchester, L. S. (ed.) *Wells Cathedral, a History*, 1982

Cook, G. H. *Medieval Chantries and Chantry Chapels*, 1963

Cowan, P. *Rose Windows*, 1979

Cragg, Gerald R. *Reason and Authority in the Eighteenth Century*, 1964

Creed, J. M. and Boys Smith, J. *Religious Thought in the Eighteenth Century*, 1934

Deedes, C. (ed.) *Chichester Episcopal Registers*, 1905–10

Dix, Gregory *The Shape of the Liturgy*, 1945

Dodsworth, William *A Guide to the Cathedral Church of Salisbury, with a Particular Account of the Great Improvements made therein under the Direction of James Wyatt, Esq.*, 5th ed., 1798

Douie, L. and Farmer, H. (eds) *The Life of St. Hugh of Lincoln*, 1950

Dugdale, Sir William *Monasticon Anglicanum*, 3 vols, 1655–73

Dupy, George *The Age of the Cathedrals*, 1981

Eden, C. H. *Black Tournai Fonts in England*, 1909

Edwards, K. *The English Secular Cathedrals in the Middle Ages*, 2nd ed., 1967

Farley, J. *The Misericords of Gloucester Cathedral*, 1981

Fellows, E. H. *English Cathedral Music*, 5th ed., 1969

Fitchen, W. H. *The Construction of Gothic Cathedrals*, 1961

Fletcher, Canon R. J. *A History of Bristol Cathedral from Documents in the Possession of the Dean and Chapter*, 1932

Flood, W. H. G. *Early Tudor Composers*, 1925

Fowler, J. T. (ed.) *Acts of the Chapter of the Collegiate Church of St. Wilfred, Ripon*, 1875

Fowler, J. T. (ed.) *The Rites of Durham*, 1903

Fowler, J. T. (ed.) *London Episcopal Registers*, 1911

Frere, W. H. *The Use of Sarum*, 1898–1901

Frere, W. H. and Kennedy, W. P. M. *Visitations and Injunctions of the Period of the Reformation*, Alcuin Club Collections, vols XIV–XVI, 1910

Frere, W. H. (ed.) *Winchester Episcopal Registers*, 1914

Gatens, William J. *Victorian Cathedral Music in Theory and Practice*, 1986

Gardner, A. *English Gothic Foliage Sculpture*, 1927

Gardner, A. *Wells Capitals*, 1956

Gibbons, A. (ed.) *Ely Episcopal Records*, 1891

Grimthorpe, Edmund (Beckett) Lord, *St. Albans Cathedral and its Restoration*, 1893

Grodecki, L. and Brisal, C. *Gothic Stained Glass*, 1985

Hardy, T. D. (ed.) *Durham Episcopal Registers*, 4 vols, 1873–8

Harvey, John H. *Medieval Craftsmen*, 1975

Harvey, John H. *Henry Yevele*, 1944

Harvey, John H. *Cathedrals of England and Wales*, 1974

Harwood, T. *The History and Antiquities of the City of Lichfield*, 1806

Hill, Canon Derek Ingram *Christ's Glorious Church: the Story of Canterbury Cathedral*, 1976

Hingeston-Randolph, F. C., Browne, F. C. and Reichel, O. J. (eds) *Exeter Episcopal Registers*, 10 vols, 1886–1915

Hobhouse, E. and Holmes, T. S. (eds) *Bath and Wells Episcopal Registers*, 8 vols, 1887–1916

Huizinga, J. *The Waning of the Middle Ages*, 1924, reprinted 1965

Hope, W. J. St. John and Lethaby, W. R. 'The Imagery and Sculpture on the West Front of Wells Cathedral', *Archaeologia*, LIX, 1905

Hope, W. J. St. John and Legg, J. Wickham *Inventories of Christchurch, Canterbury*, 1902

James, M. R. *The Sculptures in the Lady Chapel at Ely*, 1895

Klauser, T. *Short History of the Western Liturgy*, 1969

Knoop, D. and Jones, G. P. *The Medieval Mason*, 1933

Knowles, D. *Bare Ruined Choirs*, 1976

Leach, A. F. 'William of Wykeham', *Encyclopeadia Britannica*, 11–13th ed., 1910

Leach, A. F. *The Schools of Medieval England*, 1915

Laud, W., Archbishop of Canterbury *Works*, vol V (Statutes for Canterbury and Injunctions for other Cathedrals), 1853

Leff, G. *Medieval Thought from Augustine to Ockham*, 1958

Le Huray, P. *Music and the Reformation in England*, 1967

Lethaby, W. R. 'How Exeter Cathedral was built', *Architectural Review*, 1903

Lethaby, W. R. 'The Broderers of London and Opus Anglicanum', *Burlington Magazine*, XXIX, 1916

Locket, R. B. 'The Victorian Restoration of Worcester Cathedral', *Journal of the British Archaeological Association*, 1978

Longman, W. *History of three Cathedrals dedicated to St. Paul in London*, 1873

Macready, Sarah and Thompson, F. M. (eds) *Art and Patronage in the English Romanesque*, 1986

Martin, C. T. (ed.) *Canterbury Episcopal Registers* (Rolls series), 3 vols, 1882–5

Milman, H. H., Dean of St. Pauls *Annals of St. Paul's Cathedral*, 2nd ed., 1869

Milner, John *History of Winchester*, 1798

Morris, R. *Cathedrals and Abbeys of England and Wales*, 1979

Oliver, G. *Lives of the Bishops of Exeter and a History of the Cathedral*, 1861

Panowsky, E. *Gothic Architecture and Scholasticism*, 1951

Pevsner, Sir N. *The Buildings of England*, 1951–74

Pevsner, Sir N., Metcalf, R. et al. *The Cathedrals of England: Midland, Eastern and Northern England*, 1985

Phillimore, W. P., Davis, F. N. et al. (eds) *Lincoln Episcopal Registers*

Pitkin Pictorials (Pride of Britain series) on Cathedrals, 1950s onwards

Prior, E. S. and Gardner, A. *Medieval Figure Sculpture in England*, 1912

Proctor, F. and Frere, W. H. *A New History of the Book of Common Prayer*, 3rd ed., 1905

Pugin, A. W. N. *Contrasts; or a Parallel between the noble edifices of the fourteenth and fifteenth centuries and similar Buildings of the present day: showing the present decay of Taste*, 1836

Pugin, A. W. N. *True Principles of Christian Architecture*, 1841

Raine, J. (ed.) 'The Fabric Rolls of York Minster', *Surtees Society*, XXXV, 1858

Reynolds, H. E. *The Use of Exeter Cathedral*, 1891

Ruskin, John *Collected Works*, ed. E. T. Cook and A. Wedderburn, 1903–12

Salzman, L. F. *Building in England down to 1540*, reprint 1979

Scarisbrick, J. *The Reformation and the English People*, 1984

Scott, Sir G. G. *Lectures on Medieval Architecture*, 2 vols, 1979

Scott, Sir G. G. *Plea for the Faithful Restoration of our Ancient Churches*, 1851

Simson, Otto von *The Gothic Cathedral*, 1951

Southern, R. W. *Western Society and the Church in the Middle Ages*, 1970

Stewart, D. J. (ed.) *Liber Eliensis*, Books I–II, 1848

Stubbs, W. (ed.) *The Historical Works of Gervase of Canterbury* (Rolls series), LXXIII, 1879–80

Swaan, W. *The Gothic Cathedral*, 1968

Swainson, C. A. *The History and Construction of a Cathedral of the Old Foundation, illustrated from documents in the Registry and Muniments Room of the Cathedral of Chichester*, 1880

Thompson, A. Hamilton *The Cathedral Churches of England*, 1925

Thompson, A. Hamilton (ed.) *Documents relating to visitations of the diocese and province of York*, 1916

Thorold, Henry *Collins Guide to the Cathedrals, Abbeys and Priories of England and Wales*, 1986

Vallance, Aymer *Greater English Church Screens*, 1947

Walker, J. W. *The History of the Old Parish Church of All Saints, Wakefield, now the Cathedral Church of the Diocese of Wakefield*, 1881

Whinney, Margaret *St. Paul's Cathedral*, 1947

Willey, Basil *The Seventeenth Century Background*, 1980

Willey, Basil *The Eighteenth Century Background*, 1940

Willey, Basil *Nineteenth Century Studies*, 1956

Willis, Browne *A Survey of the Cathedrals of York, Durham, Carlisle, Chester, Manchester, Lichfield, Hereford, Worcester, Gloucester and Bristol*, 1727

Willis, Browne *A Survey of the Cathedrals of Lincoln, Ely, Oxford and Peterborough*, 1730

Willis, Robert 'The Architectural History of Canterbury Cathedral', Proceedings of the Royal Archaeological Institute, 1845

Willis, Robert 'The Architectural History of Winchester Cathedral', Proceedings of the Royal Archaeological Institute, 1846

Willis, Robert 'The Architectural History of Worcester Cathedral and Monastery', *Archaeological Journal*, 1863

Willis, Robert 'The Architectural History of York Cathedral', Proceedings of the Royal Archaeological Institute, 1848

Willis-Bund, J. W. (ed.) *Worcester Episcopal Registers*, 4 vols, 1893–1907

Wilson, R. A. (ed.) *Lincoln Episcopal Registers*, 2 vols, 1905–7

Wordsworth, Christopher *Ceremonies and Processions of the Cathedral of Salisbury*, 1901

Wordsworth, Christopher and MacLean, D. *Statutes and Customs of the Cathedral Church of the Blessed Virgin Mary of Salisbury*, 1915

Zarnecki, George *Romanesque Sculpture in Lincoln Cathedral*, 1976

Zarnecki, George *The Early Sculpture of Ely Cathedral*, 1969

INDEX

Figures in italics refer to captions.